*PRAISE FOR*

# Lost in the Reflecting Pool

"An intense, true story about how an intelligent woman is sucked into a marriage that slowly becomes abusive - not physically but emotionally and mentally. A step at a time, she loses her sense of herself and her autonomy until she begins to fight to reclaim her independence and self-worth."
 —**Marge Piercy,** *New York Times* **best-selling author, poet and memoirist**

"Pomerantz's is a majestic talent for conjuring emotion and compelling the reader with a compelling and heartbreaking story."
 —**Jacquelyn Mitchard,** *New York Times* **best-selling author,** *The Deep End of the Ocean*

"This is a memoir about a relationship that spans two decades. Pomerantz excels at description and scene-setting throughout, as in passages about the couple's early days: "The luminous glow of the flames danced from the old stone fireplace through the dimpled glass windows reflecting back the white blanket that silently encased us in our warm, private cocoon."
 —**Kirkus Review**

"Pomerantz's memoir is a well-plotted, swift-paced story full of vivid details. This gem of a book stands out from the pack. Not only does the author survive an abusive marriage, but she also survives cancer. Her characters are real and multi-dimensional."
 —**Book Life / Publisher's Weekly**

"A riveting, bold, and tender portrait of a woman surviving cancer and marital betrayal. Dr. Pomerantz exemplifies how we can find inner strength and new meaning in life even when forgiveness makes no sense."
—**Janis Abrahms Spring, Ph.D.**, author of *How Can I Forgive You?* and *After the Affair*

"The emotional journey that is *Lost in the Reflecting Pool* is a story of love and life, of courage and endurance, made all the more relevant by Dr. Pomerantz's human frailty. She, like the wildflowers in the field, despite their seeming delicacy, somehow finds a way to endure and eventually thrive. Pomerantz rises from her long-suffering not as an invulnerable superhero, undaunted and unmarred by all that has occurred, but as an ever more deeply feeling and thoughtful woman, mother and therapist and more beautiful for it."
—**Charles McCormack, MA, MSW, LCSW-C**, author of *Treating Borderline States in Marriage* and *Hatching Charlie: A Psychotherapist's Tale*

"A profoundly absorbing read from cover to cover, *Lost in the Reflecting Pool* is impressively compelling and candid in thematic accord with the raised public consciousness of how women everywhere must struggle with male abuse. A deftly written and deeply personal account. *Lost in the Reflecting Pool* is very highly recommended, especially for community and academic library Contemporary American Biography collections as well as for personal reading."
—**Midwest Reviews**

"Diane's story is, sadly, the story of far too many women who fall in love with a man and ignore the early warning signs that he might just be a bad choice as a life partner. Charles woos her with flowers and says all the right things, and when he says or does the wrong thing, she dismisses it, thinking the problem is her and not him. If ever there was a story that proves how blinding it can be to fall hopelessly in love, *Lost in the Reflecting Pool* is that story. Highly recommended reading."
—**Readers' Favorite**

"*Lost in the Reflecting Pool* follows Diane Pomerantz through a harrowing psychological nightmare in which she is nearly lost to herself and her children. Is she losing her mind? Or is her spouse? A compelling, intense, and emotionally immersive read."
   —**Judy L. Mandel, author of the *New York Times* bestseller *Replacement Child***

"A psychological thriller/memoir! Is there such a genre? Diane is a trained psychologist. She knew the signals, she saw the signs, and yet slowly, drop by calculated drop, this beautiful and talented woman gets sucked into a web of lies, gaslighting, and chaos. A page-turner to the bitter end."
   —**Jane Ubell-Meyer, founder, Bedside Reading**

"At a moment in our history when malignant narcissism in our leaders has become a national obsession, Pomerantz offers intimate insight and astute clinical observations in her memoir."
   —**John Gartner, PhD, author of *In Search of Bill Clinton: A Psychological Biography***

"In the second edition of *Lost in the Reflecting Pool*, Dr. Pomerantz puts on her clinical hat to make this book tremendously important for all women to read. The book describes her personal journey of being married to a narcissist and emotional abuser while fighting a frightening diagnosis and treatment of an aggressive cancer, but now, with empathy and clarity, she also provides readers with information on how to recognize narcissistic and emotionally abusive relationships and how to deal with them. This book is a gem and should not be missed
   —***Elyse Garlick, PhD, LCSW - Licensed Psychotherapist***

"'Relationships evolve', Pomerantz wisely tells us. 'They have a life cycle." In her gripping memoir *Lost in the Reflecting Pool*, she fearlessly shares the story of her marriage to a charismatic psychiatrist whose narcissistic behavior emerges as time goes on. Her story is one of extraordinary resilience as she faces the challenges of starting a family and fighting

a deadly disease while dealing with her critical and untrustworthy husband, who undermines her sense of worth and creates an atmosphere of fear. An exceptionally honest and engaging read!"
   —**Betty Hafner, author of** *Not Exactly Love: A Memoir*

"This is a story that will resonate with people going through a swath of life's challenges: People in difficult and abusive relationships, people facing cancer diagnosis and treatment, infertility, adoption, people grieving, and issues of loss. The author's voice is strong, wise, humble, and authentic. I couldn't put it down."
   —**Alexa Faraday, M.D., Greater Baltimore Medical Center**

"This brave and extremely well-written memoir, *Lost in the Reflecting Pool*, is a must-read for victims of a personality disordered partner, as well as those seeking a quality read. Those victimized by a narcissist will relate, never considering the same could happen to a professional, a psychologist. That's where Dr. Pomerantz proves us wrong. By skillfully and concisely sharing her story of a 20-year marriage to a narcissist, enduring infertility, adoption, and eventually cancer, I can only applaud Dr. Pomerantz for her bravery in sharing her story.
Her epilogue uniquely ties the narrative together, not with pain and blame, but with beauty and love of life. One can only learn from reading this book."
   —**MrsXNomore, author** *The Secret Life of Captain X: My Life with a Psychopath Pilot*

# LOST In the REFLECTING POOL

Surviving narcissistic emotional abuse

Award-Winning Memoir
Updated with a New Afterword

## DIANE C POMERANTZ, PH.D.

Lost in the Reflecting Pool: Surviving Narcissistic Emotional Abuse
Copyright © 2024 by Diane Pomerantz, Ph.D.

All rights reserved. No part of this publication may be reproduced, distributed, or transmitted in any form or by any means, including photocopying, recording or other electronic or mechanical methods, without the prior written permission of the author, except in the case of brief quotations embodied in reviews and certain other non-commercial uses permitted by copyright law.

Without in any way limiting the author's [and publisher's] exclusive rights under copyright, any use of this publication to "train" generative artificial intelligence (AI) technologies to generate text is expressly prohibited. The author reserves all rights to license uses of this work for generative AI training and development of machine learning language models.

Printed in the United States of America
Hardcover ISBN: 978-1-960876-73-7
Paperback ISBN: 978-1-960876-74-4
Ebook ISBN: 978-1-960876-75-1
Library of Congress Control Number: 2024917060

Muse Literary

*For my children  
with unending love*

# Author's Note

In the second edition of Lost in the Reflecting Pool, I don my psychologist's hat and invite you, the reader, to embark on a personal journey with me as though you were a fly on the wall in my therapist's office. In this therapy room, I am both client and therapist, attempting to explore and understand myself so that I can move forward and extricate myself from the emotionally abusive relationship in which I found myself. I then share, in the new *Afterword*, helpful information about identifying and then dealing with emotionally abusive/toxic relationships that could be of help to you personally.

---

This memoir was written from my own recollections, journals, and correspondence.

Memory is always personal. It is filtered through a subjective lens; in this way, memory differs from truth. All the events presented in this memoir did happen; the story is told through my lens.

Other than my name, names have been changed to protect the privacy of those involved. Exact locations have also been modified.

Writing my memoir allowed me to process and reevaluate my memories, thereby changing my perception of my internal reality. That broader understanding allowed me to move on. I hope that sharing my story and understanding of what it means, allows others to find a new way to rewrite or restructure their own life narrative.

# Prologue

I listened, hypnotized by the rain, staccato taps like a piano against the window.

On that day, as I looked out at the steel-colored sky, a crash interrupted my thoughts. I jumped and saw the lithe gray shadow leap past. *Mr. Buttons?* My gut churned.

It was July 1993, only months before my mother's death. Charles and I and our two children had just moved into the charming farmhouse on St. John's Lane. Mr. Buttons, the previous owners' gray tabby cat, often found his way back to the house. He would climb onto the roof and scratch at the window. I would call his owners, the Masons, to come get him. Elisabeth, our five-year-old, and Sammy, then two-and-a-half, loved Mr. Buttons' visits.

"Let's get him some milk and tuna fish." Elli would laugh and run down to the kitchen to retrieve whatever she could find for her new love.

Sammy would squeal, "Kitty, Kitty," stroking the cat's long gray fur and playing with his toes and tail as Mr. Buttons cuddled with him on the bed.

"I hear Mr. Buttons at the window, Mommy. Can I get his food?" Elli started down to the pantry.

"Sure." I nodded and dialed his owners.

"Elisabeth!" Charles snapped. "Do *not* feed that cat. It will only make him come here more often, and we don't want that. I don't know why your mother doesn't understand something so simple." Charles glared at me; his eyes narrowed.

My response caught in my throat, unspoken.

"He's hungry. I want to give him a snack. Don't be mean, Daddy." Elli started crying. She ran into her room and slammed her door. Having already let the cat in, Sammy lugged Mr. Buttons past us as we stood in the hallway.

"Elli, I've got him. Let me in so we can play."

I heard her door open, and Sammy say, "Don't cry, Elli, Mr. Buttons is here."

Charles stood there, silent, oblivious to and disconnected from Elli's cries and Sammy's words of comfort.

"What was that all about?" I looked at Charles with controlled calm, but my head spun, and a vise tightened around my chest. I hated when he treated the children with such disregard. I hated when he treated me that way. And it was happening more and more.

"Why don't the Masons keep better track of that damn cat?" The muscle in his cheek twitched. His cold eyes pierced through me.

Outwardly I controlled my rage; inside I pushed it further down. I turned away and called the Masons.

A few evenings later, we were both upstairs, doing paperwork, when I saw Mr. Buttons through the glass. The children were already asleep, and I automatically opened the window.

"Why the hell did you do that, Di? You know how goddamn tired I am of that stupid animal. I've had it with his irresponsible owners!"

I reflexively jumped as Charles shoved his chair, grabbed Mr. Buttons, and stomped downstairs.

I heard a door slam. I held the phone in my hand. I sat and stared. Popping sounds; rain hitting the tin roof; firecrackers in my head; puffs of gray and white; difficulty catching my breath. I put the phone down and walked unbalanced into the bedroom.

I don't know how much time had passed when I noticed Charles standing in the doorway. "It's done," he muttered.

"What's done?"

"That damn cat won't be coming back. I took care of it."

"What does that mean?"

"I told you; I took care of it. He won't be coming back." Charles turned away.

I stared at the back of his head, but my gaze was on the old sepia photo of my grandmother that hung on the wall behind him. I sat silently. The hands on the clock did not move, nor did my eyes. My lips were parched. Everything stopped.

Then, without warning, a churning storm rose in my gut. I tried to but couldn't make it into the bathroom. Sitting, soaked in the foul stench of my vomit, I wondered, *Whose reflection is that in the mirror. Is it me? Is it Charles? Are we any different from each other? If I don't speak up, if I forget, am I complicit? are we the same?* I sort of knew, but at the same time I couldn't remember anything at all.

I stood up, threw my nightclothes into the trash can, stepped into the shower, and turned the hot water on full force.

# Part One
# 1980 –1997

## *The Narcissist*

*What sweetness*
*there is*
*in the fragrance of your lovely flowers.*
*What brilliance*
*there is*
*in the gemlike clarity of your voice.*
*But,*
*I have been told,*
*that bilious venom*
*has the scent*
*of*
*lilacs and lavender.*

*—dcpomerantz*

## Chapter One

Driving through the old fieldstone gatehouse onto the grounds of the hospital, I was transported back into another era. The winding lane was fragrant with blooming rhododendrons, and the rolling, peaceful hillsides gave no clue that behind the bucolic setting were personal horrors and internal demons struggling to be tamed. As I drove farther down the road and approached a cluster of late-nineteenth-century brick buildings surrounded by lush lawns and lawn chairs, I understood the meaning behind that original endowment for this institution, which was left in 1857: "Courteous treatment and comfort of all patients . . . No one is to be confined below ground; all are to have privacy, sunlight, and fresh air."

Yes, this setting could make such a terrifying journey bearable. This was where I had come to do my postdoctoral training in inpatient, intensive, long-term psychotherapy. This hospital was one of the few places where this kind of treatment was still done. It was July 1, 1980. I was twenty-nine and excited about the opportunity. I planned to return to California after my training, although I hoped that I might meet someone with whom I could return there.

---

"BALTIMORE is a jewel," I said to my friend Donna, who sat beside me as we drove, looking at neighborhoods, trying to decide where I would live. I was staying with her and her family in Washington until I found my own place. "I never imagined there were so many interesting places. I'd only seen the worst of Baltimore before."

"It's beautiful here," she said. "I'm so glad you moved back East."

We soon found ourselves meandering along narrow roads, in a neighborhood with rolling hills and old Victorian houses.

"This is so nice. I love it," I said softly. The sunlight made dappled patterns on the windshield, and I felt myself being carried off into a dream-like state.

Donna gasped as I started to drift into the curb. "I can tell by the look on your face that this is it... but please, watch the road."

"I saw it, but you're right—this is where I want to live, and it's not too far from the hospital. Did you see the outdoor cafés and shops in the little village? It was so quaint. Let's drive around and see if we can find any rental signs."

It didn't take long—a couple of turns, up and down a few hills, majestic oaks and grand maples—and then it was there. Set back from the road, a lovingly restored, small painted lady stood serenely. On a post by the road, a sign read FOR RENT.

"Donna, write down the phone number and I'll call as soon as we get home. I have to live here." I felt as if the bay windows and wraparound porch were inviting me personally, so as to make my transition across the country easier, bringing me comfort from the sense of loss I felt about leaving my dearly loved Berkeley. Two weeks later, I moved in.

---

CHARLES and I met the next year. It was a blind date. He was thirty-eight, a psychiatrist, and was recently separated.

He called and said, "Can we get together on Thursday evening? There's a concert at Ladew Gardens."

"It sounds wonderful, but I have an audition for a play that evening that I really can't miss."

"So, you're both a psychologist and an actress?"

"Well, I'm not sure I would call myself an actress, although half of my high school class has my autograph, which says, 'Keep this. Someday it will be worth a lot of money.' I haven't done any acting in years, but someone told me about a production of *Abelard and Héloïse* by a local group. I was so excited to hear about it. Do you know the play?"

"No, other than that it's a tragic love story. I take it you want to be Héloïse?" I could hear the smile in his voice.

"Of course I do. I loved the play. Diana Rigg was wonderful as Héloïse. I have little free time, but if I can play Héloïse, I'll find a way. Why don't we get together another evening?"

"How about Friday? You can tell me if you got the part."

"That sounds great. I'm not expecting to get the part, but I can tell you all about the audition." We made our plans for Friday evening, and after I hung up, I started studying the script I had gotten from the library. But while I studied the lines, my mind kept wandering back to Charles and to our conversation. Words came so easily with him that I found myself thinking of more and more things I wanted to tell him. There was something about his voice, its timbre and resonance, that made me smile and feel powerful anticipation about actually seeing him on Friday.

Other than the stage lights, the theater was dark when I walked onto the stage for the reading. Only Abelard was there: a tall, muscular man, with sandy-colored hair that swept across his forehead. His voice was deep and resonant. Another young woman stood in the wings, waiting for her turn to become Héloïse. But when I started reading, I knew I had it. There was an intense, breathless silence as everyone listened to the words Abelard and I exchanged:

HÉLOÏSE: God knows I never sought anything in you except yourself. I wanted simply you, nothing of yours.

ABELARD: If I am remembered, it will be for this: that I was loved by Héloïse.

The next day, I got the call that I had indeed gotten the part, and I couldn't wait to tell Charles. Finally, at six thirty, the doorbell rang, and I saw him standing on my white-painted porch. He was smiling through the large front window, tall, bearded, blue eyes twinkling, wearing a silly-looking red baseball cap with three gold rams' horns. He was looking at the two big brown eyes, the long, dangling, pink tongue surrounded by a mass of white fur, and black nose pressed hard against the glass, staring up at him. My sheepdog, Winnie, was always ready to greet a guest.

I answered the door, laughing as I tried to keep Winnie from knocking him over - "This is Edward, Duke of Windsor, who answers to Winnie."

Charles laughed and didn't seem at all bothered by Winnie's enthusiasm. "Hey, guy, go get that ball." He pointed toward a ball lying under the window, and Winnie turned on all fours and went for it.

"Here, these are for you." He held out an earthenware bowl filled with blackberries. "I picked these from the bushes in my yard. My grandmother says that a man should always bring a lady a gift to make her smile when she opens the door."

For years, Charles continually surprised me with thoughtful gestures like this. Every time we went out for dinner, there was always a beautiful bouquet of flowers on our table. We always laughed because I was always surprised.

When we met on that first evening, I told him all about the audition and getting the part. I told him about having seen the production of *Abelard and Héloïse* in London and then in New York, both on opening night and, some six weeks later, on closing night. I shared all these things with enthusiasm because I liked him and felt a powerful connection to him, though I can't remember now if he asked me directly about any of them.

After chatting in my living room for a while, we drove to Harbor Place. He turned to me, his long fingers around the steering wheel, and said, "Di, I feel as if I've known you forever."

I smiled and nodded, indicating I, too, felt as if I were reconnecting with someone who had always been a part of my life. Maybe it was talking about egg creams, or the movie *The Little Fugitive,* a haunting, low-budget 1940s film about a little boy who runs away to Coney Island, or our mutual Brooklyn, New York, roots, which seemed to give us an unspoken understanding of where we had both come from. Whatever it was, the link between us showed itself from the start in private and insightful laughter that we shared only with each other.

As we got out of the car, Charles was still wearing the red cap with gold horns. *Is he actually going to wear that to dinner?* I wondered. "Oh, I think I'd better take this hat off." Charles laughed, tossing it back into the car. Relief swept over me, and we then spent our evening at the harbor, discovering that we knew many of the same people and had similar interests, likes, and dislikes.

Over dinner, I learned that before Charles had gone to medical school, he had been an architect. By the time we left the restaurant, it was late, and the waterfront was quiet. "I want to show you something," he said, as we strolled along the quiet walkways. "When I was an architect, I worked at an office in Boston. Long before Harbor Place was built, when it was only an idea, our firm was asked to render drawings of what the waterfront might look like."

We came to a reflecting pool with a marble wall, down which water fell softly. We sat down on the smooth stone of the pool, looking in. "Our firm didn't actually do the work on Harbor Place, but back then everyone in the office had to do drawings for it. My drawings were almost identical to this pool."

He told me all about his design of the pool; he had it in his drawings and promised to show them to me. Charles had so many stories to tell. He seemed to know so much.

Whether from the light of the moon or from the lamppost above us, as we looked into the water, our images merged. We both noticed it and smiled. So maybe it's understandable that I ignored a thought I had as Charles was driving me home. We had exited I-83 at Northern Parkway and were winding our way along the darkened, tree-lined streets of Mt. Washington, when I asked him, "So, what's your relationship with your parents like?"

In a somewhat detached but clearly disparaging and subtly contemptuous tone, he replied, "I really cannot tolerate being around them for too long. My mother is awful and a flake. I can't stand hearing her voice; it gives me a headache. And my father is a mean-spirited little man with no backbone at all."

I swallowed hard, wondering, *Shouldn't he have worked through those feelings about his parents by now?* But the thought passed quickly.

Later, we sat on my porch swing, glasses of wine in hand.

Stars glistened in the blackness through the tall oak trees. A growing intensity punctuated my feeling of a calm space within an old friendship. Our eyes excited, our lips roused, Charles pulled me close, and our mouths came together fully, when suddenly the screen door pushed open and Winnie bounded outside and jumped onto the porch swing between us, smashing the wine glasses, his big tongue ruining the mood.

We both laughed. Laughing at the absurdities of life seemed to be one of the things that drew Charles and me together.

## Chapter Two

I watched Charles drive off, too excited to go to bed. I made myself a cup of tea, put on a John Coltrane album, and, with his soulful sounds in the background, curled up in my favorite chair, replaying the events of the evening. Then, when I could no longer fight sleep, I climbed into bed. It seemed like I had just closed my eyes when Winnie's barking startled me awake. He jumped on the bed, with more barking and licking, and then ran to the doorway, indicating I should follow him.

"What is it, Win? You hear something, or do you just want to go out?" I forced myself from the softness of my comforter and got up.

I peered out the large glass window beside the door. "There's no one there, guy," I said, but then something lying on the porch caught my eye. Against the door frame lay a bouquet of colorful flowers. Their sweet fragrance, mixed with the early-morning air, wafted in as I opened the French door that led to the porch. A note card was attached, written in the most beautiful architectural writing:

*Di, I just wanted to let you know that I enjoyed our evening together so much. I'm hoping that there will be many more.*
*—Charles*

*He really is sweet,* I thought. As I placed the flowers in a cobalt blue glass vase, the phone rang. It was Charles.

"I thought I'd call to say good morning. I just got to the hospital."

"Good morning to you, too. I just found the flowers; they're beautiful. Thank you. It was such a nice way to wake up. I had a wonderful time last night, too."

"Well, I'm glad about that. I'm wondering if you'd like to come out to my place Friday after work. I'll make dinner. You can bring Winnie so he can run free in the fields. I'm sure he'd enjoy that."

Without hesitation, I told him that we would love to come.

We spoke on the phone for hours each evening that week. I learned more about him and his childhood. As a boy, he spent hours riding his bike and doing daredevil tricks on the dangerous hillsides of Fort Tryon Park, overlooking the Hudson River. He also was very smart.

"When I was in the first grade," he told me, "I got a full scholarship to the Little Red Schoolhouse, but my father was too cheap to pay the hundred dollars it would have cost for bus transportation."

I just listened, but it was hard not to notice that long-held resentment he still had about that missed opportunity.

He shared stories about his mother's depression and the two times when she was hospitalized, once when he was five and then again when he was seven. The first hospitalization was right after his younger brother, Mark, was born.

I told him my stories, too. The things I didn't usually talk about. My older brother, Paul, who teased me mercilessly as a kid. His emotional problems became clearer, the behaviors more intense, meaner as he became an adolescent and, like many kids of the time, he experimented with drugs. For Paul, though, it wasn't a passing phase. I laughed, as I always did when talking about painful things, and concluded, "I guess that's why I became a psychologist."

---

FRIDAY came, and Winnie and I headed out of the city to see Charles. I hadn't been that far north during my first year in

Baltimore, and I was surprised at how quickly the landscape changed. The city and soon suburbia gave way to rolling hillsides and spectacular vistas dotted with sparkling ponds and manicured horse farms. The serene views stirred thoughts of the conversations Charles and I had had during the week.

Despite his mother's depression, Charles's family life sounded quiescent compared with the discord of my adolescence. I recalled battles my brother had with my parents: his rages, screaming, kitchenware flying through the air, fruits and vegetables smashed and dripping from the walls. Amid the chaos, my parents tried their best to shield and protect me, and I'm sure as a defense, I protected myself by saying that I didn't feel that I had a damaged childhood. I had protected myself by being an observer. I learned to see without emotion, without judgment. Again, I laughed to myself as I thought, *it's a good quality to have as a therapist, but what about in my personal life?*

Charles, on the other hand, despite having experienced none of the emotional turbulence I had, sounded so disdainful of his parents, mostly his mother. With some discomfort, I registered it and then placed it on a shelf in a far corner of my mind.

As I drove, the sprawling pastures where the horses and their foals grazed, gradually turned to fields high with stands of waving corn. I soon realized I had driven to where Maryland pushed up against the Pennsylvania line. I made my way down the winding road, passing a beagle farm and a small sign marking the entrance to a vineyard.

A black kitten ran across the road, and I had to make a sudden stop. The kitten sparked a memory of one of the other things that Charles had shared as we'd spoken on the phone earlier in the week.

"I guess I was a mischievous little kid. When I was about three, I found a little black kitten. I put him down the sewer because I wanted to see if he could get out."

"What happened to him?" I asked.

"I don't know."

*Didn't he think to get some help?* I asked myself, feeling a fleeting twisting in my gut.

I rounded another bend, passed a red barn, and saw the 1890s fieldstone house that Charles had described. That unpleasant feeling in my gut gave way to excited anticipation and to readjusting my blinders as I saw Charles wave from the porch when I pulled into the drive. Winnie, also excited to see Charles, charged from the car, almost knocking him over once again.

"While it's still light, I'll show you around the farm. I'm renting it, but I feel like a landowner."

His eyes and smiling beard twinkled in the sun as he spoke in his resonant, sexy voice. He took my hand and, with Winnie close behind, led me beneath a lush grape arbor and past a hedge of blackberry bushes heavy with fruit. He pointed out the stone marker, just below the roofline of the house, dated 1898.

Charming. I loved the exterior shutters that opened and closed, unlike modern constructed shutters, and the working well just outside the front door. Charles told me that when there were power outages, neighbors came by to get water because his was the only well that wasn't power-operated. There were two large red barns, one that Charles used as a garage and the other as woodworking shop. The sweet smell of hay wafted from the loft up above. We climbed up into it and fell onto the slippery bales, laughing at Winnie, who was climbing and falling from the stacks. Then we left the barn and walked back out into the sunlight, breathing in the soft, sweet summer air. I was enthralled with it all. Charles had a story to go with everything he pointed out.

We followed Winnie over to a pond, long grasses swaying against the fields of corn behind. Lily pads floated gently on the surface, their reflections glistening through the sun's rays. Winnie dove in, and the tranquility, and lily pads, splattered, soaking us both.

We laughed.

"Di, there's this great little store down the road where they make their own ice cream. They use fruit they grow on their farm. Why don't we pick up some for dessert, and then we can come back and have dinner" He squeezed my hand.

"That sounds great. I know I've already told you how I love ice cream."

Charles and I walked to the barn, and Winnie jumped into the back of his old Peugeot. We drove the short distance to the small store in the middle of nowhere.

"Wow, I can't believe these flavors." My eyes widened as I saw the list of homemade ice creams for the day. "It's not going to be easy to decide on just one."

"So, let's get one of each," Charles suggested.

"That sounds like fun," I said, thinking that he would get a small cup of every flavor.

"Do you know what you want?" the woman behind the counter asked.

"Yes, yes! We'll have a quart of peach-raspberry, a quart of peach-cherry, a quart of blueberry-plum, a quart of strawberry peach, and a quart of cherry-plum."

I stood there with my mouth open, thinking, *Isn't that an awful lot of ice cream?*

As if reading my mind, Charles laughed. "We'll eat all of it eventually."

I smiled, and we headed back for dinner.

I remember that he made scallops with angostura bitters and asparagus, and that the dinner was delicious. "You really are a good cook. Is there anything you can't do?" I asked teasingly.

"I'm sure there is," he teased back.

The evening was far beyond expectation. Winnie and I didn't leave until Sunday, and so began our relationship, with belly laughs, long talks into the wee hours of the morning, great sex, and ice cream.

Immediate, intense comfort—that's what it was. We could talk for hours when we were together, drinking glasses of wine, sitting on the porch, watching the sunset and sometimes the sunrise. When we weren't together, we spoke on the phone. I found that between work and my new relationship, I didn't have time for the rehearsal schedule for my role as Héloïse, and so, without any deliberation, I decided to give it up. Charles in no way encouraged that— at least, I didn't think he did. But now I can see so much more clearly how willing I was to put Charles and the relationship before anything else, even before myself. *Isn't that what so many women do? – especially when they have a biological clock to consciously or unconsciously think about.* I got into canoeing and camping—his interests. Acting and psychoanalytic training *seemed* far less important.

Summer turned to fall, and winter came early that year. The snow fell steadily in December, and we spent a lot of time cross-country skiing and snuggling in front of the fireplace.

"Would you like to go to Dominique's in DC for your birthday?" Charles asked, as he stoked the fire one snowy evening.

"That would be fantastic. I've heard they have all kinds of exotic dishes. I'd love to go."

"And I love you."

It may or may not have been the first time in our relationship that that phrase was spoken, but in those words, at that moment, with the scent from the steaming mugs of mulled cider with Calvados and cinnamon wafting softly through the air, was the feeling that this was real, and this was forever. The luminous glow of the flames danced from the old stone fireplace through the dimpled glass windows, reflecting the white blanket that silently encased us in our warm, private cocoon.

---

DESPITE all of the wonderful ways in which Charles and I connected and enjoyed so many things, there were some fundamental differences between us. Charles seemed to be searching in a way that I had done when I was in my late teens and early twenties. He was taken with all of these New Age, quick-fix solutions to life's problems that seemed to be without depth. At that time, he was participating in a personal-growth training program called Lifespring, which claimed to help people get their lives to work better by casting off old beliefs and creating a new future. He was very excited about it.

"Di, you really ought to do the training. It's given me so much; I feel as if I have so much more power and control over my own life and destiny. At least do the basic training, to see what it is. I'll pay for it. That way, you can know what I got out of it."

It didn't seem as if I had anything to lose, so I registered for the training and Charles kept Winnie for the days I was away. As I drove to Virginia from Baltimore that February, the weather forecast was foreboding: a major snowstorm was headed our way. But when I arrived at the motel where I had booked a room, the snowfall hadn't yet started.

That first evening, at precisely seven o'clock, we met Andrew, our Lifespring trainer. His Italian suit and shoes and boyishly handsome good looks were clearly part of the sales package.

Although he looked perfect, we learned that Andrew's life had not always been so wonderful. He had been depressed and in a rut. Then he found Lifespring, and his life changed. Now in his mid-thirties, he was happily married, expecting his first child, and traveling across the country, spreading the good word of Lifespring to others.

Then the training began. There were lectures, there were group exercises, there were exercises with the person who sat next to you, and there was a lot of sharing. There were some things that were interesting, but for the most part I felt like an observer, most interested in how some of the participants gave up so much personal autonomy to this process. There was something about it that seemed to have the quality of a cult.

By Friday afternoon, there was no way to leave the hotel where the conference was taking place. Heavy snow was falling and continued to accumulate on Saturday and most of Sunday. I slept in the lobby. When the training ended early Sunday evening, I worried about how I was going to shovel out my car. I walked out of the meeting room into the lobby, and there stood Charles, in winter gear, holding a shovel, and smiling.

I ran into his arms. "What are you doing here?"

"I didn't know if you had a shovel, so I came and cleaned your car out so you wouldn't have to do it."

"You are too wonderful." I pressed my mouth fully against his cold, wet lips.

We stood in the lobby in that embrace for a long time. Then we found a Chinese restaurant, had dinner, including fried ice cream, and, much later, drove back to Baltimore in tandem, arriving in the early hours of the morning. It was beautiful—the echoes that come with the serene soundlessness of the world covered in white. In that moment, everything was wonderful.

The phone was ringing as we walked through the door of my house. It was two o'clock in the morning. I reached for the phone, but whoever was on the other end hung up.

"Damn it. It doesn't stop!" I had been getting these hang-up calls for months, at all times of the day and night. I thought maybe it was a patient, though I had no idea which one. It was now more than just annoying; the harassment had become frightening. I called the phone company and the police and put a tracer on my phone, and I was waiting to hear the results of the investigation.

Several weeks later, the trace on the phone calls was successful. "Dr. Pomerantz, we have been able to identify the person who has been making the calls to you." The officer on the other end of the line sounded very matter of fact as he gave me this information.

My heart raced and my throat felt parched as I wondered if I really wanted to know who it was. Finally, I asked, "Can you tell me who it is?"

"Sure, her name is . . ."

*Her* name is. I thought. I hadn't expected it to be she.

"Her name is Mara Winters. Do you know her?"

"No, I have no idea who she is. Why would she be calling me? It's clearly not a wrong number, because she's made hundreds of calls to me at all hours of the day and night."

"Well, we'll be investigating this. We'll keep you informed of what we discover, and of the court date, and anything you'll need to know."

"But who is this person?" I asked again, feeling even more confused and anxious than before. There was no satisfying answer.

When Charles came over that evening, the first thing he did, as usual, was transfer his calls from his home number to my number. Then I told him about what I had learned.

"It's Mara?" He looked incredulous. "I can't believe it."

"You know her? Who is she?" I was shocked that he knew who she was. Silence.

"I can't believe that she would be making these phone calls," Charles repeated.

"Who is Mara Winters? You still haven't told me who she is." I found my thoughts blurred and fuzzy. I could feel my heart beat faster, and I took a deep breath.

"She's someone I met around the same time we met, and I've been seeing her every once in a while. I just can't believe she would make these phone calls."

"You mean you've been dating her? Sleeping with her?" My body shook, I was so angry. "I can't believe that you're more concerned with the fact that she made the phone calls than you are about the fact that you've been deceiving me. That's much stranger and more upsetting to me." I was confused, questioning the seven months we had been together, while Charles stood there, so calm, so rational.

After hours of talking that night, Charles and I decided to take a break from seeing each other. I went along with his plan.

"Let's take a break to figure out what we each want," Charles proposed.

I thought, *You mean what* you *want . . .*

He went on, "Let's take a minimum of two weeks with no contact, a maximum of five weeks. Then we'll get together and see where things stand."

Héloïse's words resounded in my head:

*Lewd visions of the pleasures we shared take such a hold upon my unhappy soul that my thoughts are on their wantonness, instead of on prayers, but I can only sigh for what I have lost.*

"Okay, let's do that, and you can decide what you want. I know what *I* want." I know I also thought " but it has to include honesty," I'm just not sure if I said that. With each word I spoke, and those I failed to say, it was a beginning step towards things unfolding wrongly.

On the sixth day of our break, Charles called and asked if he could see me sooner. "I miss you so much. I've ended it with Mara."

I was thrilled—until we got together, almost a week later.

"So, how did it go with Mara when you spoke with her?" I asked, pouring us each a glass of wine as Charles started a fire.

"Well, I haven't actually told her yet. I just had one brief conversation with her on the phone," he said casually, not turning from the fire.

"Charles, how could you? You had almost a full week before seeing me in which you should have taken care of it, but maybe you didn't actually want to do that." The muscles of my abdomen clenched like tightening coils. Hot bolts of anger welled up inside me and burst out: "You should have done it before you even called me, or at least before you saw me!" I shouted. "I feel like you're playing games with me."

Charles turned and stood there, perplexed. "Well, I didn't want to hurt her feelings. You really should try to be more sensitive to that."

He was acting as if there was something wrong with me. My head spun. *Why in the world should I be sensitive to her feelings?* He *should be sensitive to* my *feelings; this has nothing to do with this other woman. This is crazy making.*

## Chapter Three

When I told Charles I would not see him or speak to him again until I was sure he had ended things with Mara, he ended the relationship with her within forty-eight hours. Somehow, at that time, my desire to work things out with him allowed me to believe it had been just a blip in the early part of our relationship.

Three months later, Charles went to court with me about the phone calls.

I don't know what I expected, but Mara seemed nice. She looked like she was in her early thirties. She was slim, with short, dark hair and a pretty smile.

As we stood before her, the judge, a woman of about sixty, looked from Mara to me and said, "Ladies, believe me, you will both come to realize that no man is worth it." She then looked at Mara and continued, "Ms. Winters, no more phone calls. Case dismissed."

There was an uncomfortable silence as Mara and I both smiled at her, and then, out of the corners of our eyes, we looked at each other and we smiled.

Charles seemed strangely high-spirited as we left the courthouse.

"Why don't we go have some lunch at Bonjour?" he suggested, pulling me close.

"Sure, that sounds good," I said, but in my mind, I wondered why he hadn't said anything about having seen Mara.

"So, Charles," I found myself trying to sound casual. "Was it uncomfortable for you to see Mara?"

"Why would I be uncomfortable? She's nobody to me. I heard they have some new things on the menu at Bonjour—maybe we'll experiment." He laughed as he opened the car door for me, and I slid in, ignoring the hollow feeling in my gut. It was as if this woman Mara were a nonentity, as if he hadn't known her, as if she didn't really exist, had never existed.

Around that same time, Charles and I had introduced my dear friend Allyson to his close friend Harry, and they had really hit it off. Being a foursome with our closest friends made it much easier to ignore those quirks of Charles's that I didn't want to see. I could brush off the behaviors I noticed, like his dismissal of Mara, or the characteristics I wondered about, like the times he discounted something I'd said and then the next day would say, "I have this great idea . . ." and it would be exactly what I had suggested; or the fact that he was still so angry at his mother. These things didn't happen all the time, and it wasn't as if I didn't question anything he said or did; I just thought I was accepting that this was Charles and there was so much about him that was good.

One morning in May, as Charles and I were leaving the house, my landlord stopped by.

"Hi, Ken. I haven't seen you in a while," I called to him as we were getting into the car.

"Hi. I'm glad I caught you before you left. I just wanted to drop off your new lease. Look it over, and if you have any questions, just give me a call, okay? It's pretty straightforward: no changes; rent is the same."

"Great. I'll get back to you with it. Thanks for dropping it off."

"No problem, Di."

That evening after dinner, as Charles was reading, I pulled out the lease that I had gotten from Ken.

"What's that?" Charles asked, looking up from his journal.

"Oh, it's the new lease that Ken dropped off."

"Are you going to sign it?"

"I was planning on it."

"Oh. I thought this might be a good time for you to move out to the country—for us to live together."

Things had been going well, but I hadn't been expecting this—not yet. I just sat there, smiling.

"Well, what do you think?"

I did love my place and my independence, but I also knew I loved Charles and wanted to be with him.

"I think it would be wonderful; let's have some wine to celebrate."

Charles got the wine as we laughed and tore up the unsigned lease.

In July, we packed all of my stuff into a U-Haul, and I moved out to the country to live with Charles. I loved the peaceful rhythms of our life. The early doubts seemed to be gone. I felt as if I had found someone with whom I could have both independence and intimacy.

We added to our family of sheepdogs. The person from whom I had gotten Winnie could no longer care for Winnie's mother, Ginger. She was old and overbred, but she was very sweet. We loved Winnie—how could we say no to his mother? And so, Ginger came to live with us. We still wanted Winnie to have a playmate, though, so we also got a sheepdog puppy, Benjamin Disraeli, whom we called Dizzy.

Life was good. The dogs came with us cross-country skiing across the snowy fields. We laughed as Ginger barked fervently at Winnie and Dizzy when they ran out onto the ice-covered pond, chastising them for their risky frolic. Afterward, we went home and sat with hot drinks in front of the fire, surrounded by our furry family.

As the snow began to melt in Maryland and the crocuses began to push their colorful heads upward, Charles suggested a whitewater canoe trip. "I have a friend in Maine who's an outfitter and guide. How about I call him and see if he can arrange a canoe trip down the St. John River during ice-out? The water will be moving, but it won't be too difficult for you. It'll be fun."

I could tell this was something Charles really wanted to do. "Sure, it sounds like fun," I agreed, "but I've never done any whitewater canoeing. Two weeks sounds like a long time to be on the river."

"You'll love it. The St. John is really an amazing river. In the summer the water can get so low that you can wade across it, but during ice-out, in early spring, it's another story. There can be blocks of ice thirty feet tall that crash through the trees and the river channel."

"It sounds spectacular. I just don't know if I have the skill for that kind of trip."

"I can get us through the difficult stuff; most of it won't be too hard, though. These are mostly Class II rapids, so they're easy—only a couple of Class III. Haven't you enjoyed the canoeing we've done? And I know you love whitewater rafting, so you'll love this, too. It really will be an adventure."

It was hard to not absorb Charles's enthusiasm, and I did like adventures. "Okay, I'm in."

Charles made all of the arrangements for the fourteen-day river trip. Over the next few weeks, we got our gear together, including a heated snifter to enjoy a little warm brandy in the tent after a long day on the river.

To kick off the journey, we took a leisurely drive through New England, stopping at inns along the way. We arrived in Bangor, Maine, and met Barry, the outfitter who'd drop us off at Fourth St. John Pond, where we'd put in, and then would pick us up fourteen days later.

There were four of us who would be paddling: Sean, our guide; Susan, a single woman, paddling solo; and Charles and I, paddling together. The air was chilly, the sky dishwater gray, as we started out in the back of Barry's pickup for the north woods. We drove for a couple of hours on back roads darkened by towering spruce and alders.

We arrived at Fourth St. John Pond late that afternoon. Barry, Sean, and Charles unloaded the canoes while Susan and I unpacked the rest of the gear from the truck. Then Barry took off for civilization, leaving us in the wilderness. The dense, still forest surrounded us as we set up camp and evening fell. We hadn't eaten for hours. Thankfully, Sean was a great cook—the hobo stew and cornbread he made were delicious— and Susan and I put together a pretty good apple crisp. After we ate, we sat around, telling stories.

"I have a story," Charles began. "It's supposedly true. Pretty Face was a beautiful young girl. More beautiful than all the others. She thought she was too good for all the young men in her tribe. One day a strange man arrived in the village and approached Pretty Face's wigwam, saying that he had come to marry her. Her parents objected; they didn't know this man. But Pretty Face would not listen to reason, and she agreed to marry him.

"Together, they went to the river. 'Amankamek, you should not have brought her here,' the man's mother yelled in anger at her son when they arrived at the river."

Charles's voice got deeper as he continued.

"'Amankamek? I know that name. That is the river snake.' Pretty Face remembered that this was the great snake who could change his shape and devour women. 'What a fool I've been.' She shuddered."

A cacophonous boom interrupted the story. At that moment, we felt the first splatters of rain. Thunder rumbled; heaven's clangorous clap of fury drummed and rolled in with rage. A flash stunned the cracked sky, and torrents poured down. We ran for our tents, but the zipper on ours was stuck. Charles and I were soaked, along with everything in the tent, before we could get it fixed.

Charles slept soundly that night, but as I listened to the pounding rain and roaring wind, all I could think was, *Why did I agree to do this for my vacation?* I was cold and wet, lying there in the dark, shivering and wanting to scream. It didn't seem like an adventure anymore; it was a nightmare.

Morning came. The wind still wailed, and the rain battered us mercilessly. Still, we stowed our gear in the canoe and paddled across the pond. I stared at the towering stands of trees surrounding us and felt this eminent and lofty wall of green closing in on me. There was no way out. Charles tried to speak to me, but I was silent. I felt like a trapped animal, and I knew if I spoke, I could easily attack. I was a prisoner in this mad folly until we got to the other end of the river. I looked up into the sky and imagined sending a rescue signal to some helicopter flying overhead. That was my only possibility for escape. Short of that, I was stuck.

Suddenly, with that thought, I started to laugh. It was a soaking-wet epiphany. There was absolutely nothing I could do. I could be miserable and angry for the next two weeks, or I could just accept that this was where I was. I had agreed to go on the trip, so I could make the best of it and maybe even enjoy it. It was up to me.

Until then, I hadn't been talking in more than monosyllables to Charles. "I'm sorry I've been such a prig this morning. I was indulging myself, but I'm okay now. I really do want this to be a fun adventure, even if we're wet, muddy, and cold. Even if my hair is frizzy."

It rained the first three days and nights, and I was surprised at how exhilarating it was, feeling the force of the river on my paddle, the wind and rain in my face, and the feeling of just being present in the moment.

After dinner each evening, Charles and I returned to our tent to drink warm brandy and laugh about the day's adventures.

When we awoke on day four, there was a thin coating of frost on the tent, the air was cold but dry, and the wondrous song of loons echoed through the forested hillsides. The rain had stopped, and the sun reflected brightly on the water.

We paddled all morning, stopping for lunch, and then spent the rest of the day at the next campsite, where we swam in the cold water, ate freshly caught trout, and laughed.

When Charles, Susan, and Sean decided to go for a hike, I stayed back at the campsite to wash my hair, read, and relax. They were gone for quite a while, and while I sat in our wooded campsite, I could hear coyotes howling in the distance. I wasn't afraid, but I began to think about what it would be like to have to survive in the wilderness. I began to think about feral children.

That night, as Charles and I lay together in our tent, I said, "You know, I had some interesting thoughts while you were off hiking this afternoon. There was something surreal about being all alone in the woods, hearing the coyotes in the distance."

"Were you scared?"

"No, not really. It just made me think about feral children and also about how someone can become paranoid or how baser instincts can emerge when someone is isolated and has to depend totally on their own resources." I waited for Charles to say something, but he was quiet. I kept talking.

"I could just understand, in a way that I hadn't thought about before, how a person's interpretation of what's going on around them can be dramatically influenced when survival is at stake." Charles was still quiet.

"Anyway, those thoughts took up a lot of the time you were gone." I laughed self-consciously as I finished.

He looked at me oddly, but I never gave any of it a second thought. I noticed something, but once again I failed to question. I didn't think, though, that Charles had an internal life that I knew nothing about, that his slowness to respond was designed to make sure his response was what he wanted it to be.

I really didn't need to worry about my inexperience with white water canoeing, either. Charles was a great teacher and support. In the couple of situations where my stomach was doing somersaults, his calm control and skill gave me some confidence, too. We developed an easy rhythm to our paddling.

We took out at Allagash Village after nearly 143 miles of paddling. Barry picked us up, and we drove back to Bangor. We looked as if we had been in the back woods for months when he dropped us off in the parking lot. We were covered in dirt and mud as we packed our gear back into the car.

We traveled through New England on our way back to Maryland. As we drove, Charles said, "You know; I think we did pretty well on that trip. It's not so easy to paddle tandem and get along, but we didn't have any problems."

I thought about our two weeks together. We had laughed at every problem. We had slogged through rain, paddled miles and miles, mostly laughing, and drinking brandy by candlelight at night. We had learned a lot about ourselves and each other on that trip. It turned out to be one of the best vacations we ever had.

"You're right—it was an amazing trip, and it could have been a disaster. I think it says a lot about us as 'us.'"

When we got home, after picking up the dogs at the farm where they were boarded, we crashed. We worked all week, and the next Saturday night, we went to our favorite restaurant for dinner. On our table, I spotted a bouquet of yellow flowers. After I experienced my usual response of not realizing that the flowers were for me, I noticed the note:

*Di, I want to spend the rest of my life with you. Will you marry me? I love you. C.*

I looked into Charles's eyes, smiled, and then threw my arms around him and gave him a big, salty kiss. "I'd love to be your wife, forever."

We spent the next few months crafting handmade invitations, creating a wedding canopy, and planning our at-home, outdoor wedding. For weeks beforehand, we picked mounds and mounds of grapes, blackberries, and raspberries, freezing them to be part of the wedding feast.

September arrived, along with the prediction of a hurricane. We were not sure how it would play out, if the storm would actually hit us, but then, only thirty-six hours before our wedding was to begin, the clouds rolled in. What was at first dusky gray cloud cover turned to black, ominous masses covering the entire sky above us. There was an eerie calm; then the dogs began to bark and run in circles. The trees swayed. The breeze picked up, and the first crash of thunder sounded.

The wind howled throughout the night. Pellets of rain shot at the windows like bullets. The shutters, which we had neglected to close, smashed against the fieldstone walls outside. By now, all three fluffy sheepdogs were huddled together under the bed. There was no power and no phone service. Charles and I sat by candlelight, listening to the pummeling of the storm, drinking wine, surrounded by baskets of flowers, trying to decide what we would do if the weather did not improve enough for us to host our wedding.

By morning, the rain ended. The power and phones were restored. We watched the clouds rolling out and clear patches of blue begin to shine through. The tent was up, the flowers in place, the wedding cake delivered; we had the dinner for out-of-town guests as scheduled. By Sunday morning, the day of the wedding, a cool breeze rolled gently through, pushing out any remaining clouds. A crystalline sky, green vistas, fields of corn, and blue ponds shimmered in all directions.

Our wedding was lovely—elegant in some ways, simple in others. The green-and-white tent stood in a field surrounded by grape arbors and bushes lush with ripe blackberries. The red barns and our hundred-year-old stone farmhouse stood in the background. We wrote the ceremony; we created our own ketubah, the traditional Jewish wedding agreement. I made the wedding canopy. My friend Stan, a jazz saxophonist, flew in from San Francisco to play during the ceremony.

Winnie, Dizzy, and Ginger, with big red bows around their necks, were delightful participants when, at the end of the party, we let them out of their fenced area to mingle with the guests.

---

AFTER a honeymoon in California and much laughter, we returned to our mostly harmonious life. Occasionally, something Charles said or did raised doubt in me, but that was always the case in a relationship—that was what I told myself. Nevertheless, I do remember one incident in particular, shortly after we returned from our honeymoon, in January 1985.

It was something I didn't give a lot of conscious thought to at the time, though maybe I should have paid more attention to it. I don't recall exactly what the conversation with Charles was about. It seems as if it had something to do with my having a "bad day" and Charles's not liking it. Our house was very tiny, with a narrow, winding stairway. The stairs came out into a small vestibule lined with bookshelves that I used as an office. Up one step, you entered a large space that was both a living space and Charles's office. He was sitting at his desk. I had just come in and was standing in the doorway.

"Do you think your mood is any better now than it was this morning?" he asked.

I stood there, thinking about how critical Charles sounded, how he was not concerned about why I had been feeling "down." He often had "black moods," yet he was critical of me. But the very important thought I had, the thought that was indelibly imprinted in my mind, even though it was unconscious then, was, *If I am ever really sick, he won't be able to be there for me.*

## Chapter Four

The fields that glistened with sugar-like frost began to turn a dazzling, bright green. The sunshine lingered longer in the sky, and the bees hummed as they moved from flower to flower. Charles and I began to think about finding a place to own, a place that would really belong to us. He still wanted to be in the country, and I wanted to be closer to town. He was anxious to have a place where he could have a home-based office; in fact, he wanted both of us to work from home.

We started the search for the perfect house, but none of the options that seemed fine to me satisfied him. Although he didn't articulate what he wanted, I knew he had something particular in mind. I knew he wanted the feeling of total privacy, of being away from everything—his own world, our own world.

Walking up to our house after work, I saw that all of the windows were open, and I could hear Charles's voice from inside.

"Sounds great. How soon can we see it? Any chance we can get in there tomorrow?" I realized that Charles must be on the phone with Tim, our realtor.

"This might be the one." Charles turned to me with a huge grin as he hung up. "It's a small cottage on four acres surrounded by farmland, with the possibility of buying more land if we want."

Ten minutes later, Tim called back and told Charles we could see the house the next morning.

"I have a premonition. Let's open a bottle of wine."

That night, we made love. Charles was less passive than usual; not only was he the initiator that night, but he was much more attentive to me than he typically was, and he didn't just turn over and go to sleep afterward.

In the morning, Tim picked us up and we drove along familiar winding roads, closer to town, passing horse farms where mares and their foals grazed on lush grass. We wound our way up and down the hilly countryside, passing parsley-green fields where bleating lambs frolicked. As soon as we turned off the road, we crossed a small bridge with a rippling creek below and began the quarter mile drive down the wooded lane. Charles grabbed my hand. At the end of the drive stood a small yellow cottage. Surrounding the property were cornfields bordered by majestic oak trees and rolling hills covered in golden buttercups that danced gently in the breeze. The only other visible building was a partially standing, abandoned house on the crest of a distant hill. From behind that structure, a herd of deer appeared, gingerly walking in a graceful line across the hilltop.

The two-bedroom cottage had been renovated and updated with a modern kitchen; a living room; a small, glass-enclosed sitting area; a dining room; and a lovely, large deck. There was a sizable fenced-in horse pasture with a run-in shed, and a chicken coop. The family selling the property were willing to leave their seven chickens and their daughter's beloved rooster, Mr. Doodle-Doo.

"It'll be great to have free-range chickens and fresh eggs every day, won't it, Di?"

I didn't yet know how much going and collecting the eggs each day was going to come to mean for me. "Well, I never thought about having chickens, but I love the idea of having horses," I said, as I opened the gate to the pasture and imagined my childhood wish for a horse of my own.

Touring the house was next. I looked in the bathroom and saw a shower curtain around the tub. "Oh, Charles, I'm so glad this house has a shower. I love our old claw-foot tub, but I've missed having a real shower."

As it happened, there wasn't any shower behind that shower curtain. I should have looked, but, as with so many things in my life, I tended to make assumptions, not thinking that perhaps there was no wizard, or showerhead, behind the curtain.

The shower was installed immediately upon our move into the house. Then Charles dove headfirst into plans to build an office. He rented a trailer to use as a temporary space, arranged financing, found an architect and a contractor, and within several months, a separate cottage that would become his office—and, later, our office—was built.

It was exciting, but Charles, in his rush to do all this, gave little thought to the terms of the financing. There wasn't ever a great deal of discussion or planning about financial issues.

Despite that, we forged ahead.

Within six months, I left my position at the hospital and moved my private practice to our home office. I did some teaching at a local university and continued to consult at the hospital. Life was full and we were happy. Our practices were separate, although at that time we did some work for an insurance company that required us to work together on some cases. Sometimes I would see someone who needed to be evaluated for medication, and I would call in Charles for a consultation. I remember one woman in particular whom the insurance company referred to me because she was painfully anxious. Her vulnerability was palpable; her fear and self-loathing seemed to scream for confirmation from the outside world. After a long session, it was clear to me that she projected this image of herself as a victim out into the world every day, in many ways beckoning those who bullied and took advantage of her. She pulled at her hair, causing big bald spots, which increased her self-consciousness. I told her I thought she might consider anxiety medication, in addition to psychotherapy. She agreed, and Charles joined us.

Charles's response to this woman's vulnerability astounded and disturbed me.

Tearfully, she explained to him, "I can't stop pulling on my hair. I have these huge bald spots."

"Why don't you just sit on your hands?" he said. *Was he trying to be funny?* It didn't sound that way; he seemed to be trying to kick her harder. I know my stomach became upset and that I needed to excuse myself from a portion of the interview. When I returned, Charles was handing her a prescription and then explained to me what medication he had prescribed. She and I met a bit longer to wrap things up, and then I asked, "Should we schedule an appointment for next week?"

Without making eye contact, in a barely audible voice, she replied, "Oh, yes, of course. Same time?"

"Sure, that will be fine. I'll see you then."

She did not call to cancel the appointment, but she did not appear, either. I tried to contact her several times but got no response. I remember thinking that I was glad she was healthy enough not to come back—I certainly wouldn't have—but I have never forgotten her and have always carried some professional guilt about that experience. Back then, I told myself that the way Charles treated this woman was out of character for him. Nevertheless, the aching discomfort I felt about it remained in my chest like a sheathed needle, always ready to pierce my heart.

Did I speak to Charles about it? I don't remember, but if I did, I am certain it was in some way that would have been so nonthreatening and noncritical that he might even have missed the point about how inappropriate he had been. I certainly didn't use the word *sadistic*—not then.

We stopped working with the insurance company shortly after that, and our practices became entirely separate. That made it much easier for me to push it all away. Besides, we had other things to focus on. We knew we wanted a family. We had proclaimed that in our wedding vows. It was wonderful waking up each day and going to the chicken coop to collect fresh eggs. It seemed symbolic. Nevertheless, I still wasn't pregnant.

Although I had just turned thirty, I was already experiencing symptoms that I knew were due to hormonal changes. I was vomiting often, and, although it wasn't funny, we laughed about it. I took our shared affinity for laughter as proof of how well Charles and I coped together, how "right" we were for each other.

I had stopped using birth control about six months before the wedding, and I went to a fertility specialist shortly after we returned from California. I so desperately wanted a family that I was willing to take all of the responsibility for our fertility problems. I also wanted to protect Charles's sense of adequacy because I knew, even then, that he was shaky. I loved him, and back then it did not seem to matter who was having the problem. Little did I know how invested he was in making the problem all mine.

Charles and his previous wife had tried to get pregnant without success for a long time. I knew I could get pregnant. I had had four pregnancies during my first, brief marriage, to a man named Bram, right after college. I had easily become pregnant when I wasn't even trying.

Carrying a pregnancy to term—that was another story. Pregnancies two, three, and four ended in miscarriage. The first pregnancy ended in abortion in 1973, the year abortion was legalized in the United States; that is the pregnancy I have always believed would have gone to term. My belief, or fantasy, call it what one may, has always been that had I not had that abortion, I would have given birth to a daughter on or around April 4, 1974. Her name would have been Rebecca.

It was when Bram and I moved back East from San Francisco that our differences became clear. He did not want children, and I always knew I wanted a lot of them. So, "knowing" this, when I became pregnant, we didn't really talk much about "what to do." We didn't actually have a conversation about how to handle this pregnancy. I just went over to the clinic at Bethesda Naval Hospital, where we got our medical services, and they handed me an authorization, gave me the name of a physician, and that was that.

Bram and I were together another two years. We remained friends when the marriage ended. I regretted the abortion, but, although it was sad, I never regretted the end of the marriage.

Just before we separated, I told Bram something I had not told him before.

"You know, I really wanted that baby. I didn't even know it then."

There was a heavy silence, and then he said, "You know, we could have had the baby if only you had said something."

---

WHEN I went to the doctor in the early months of my marriage to Charles and expressed my concerns about getting pregnant, I did so both because of the hormonal changes I was experiencing and because Charles's interest in sex seemed to be diminishing. I worried there would be no way I could get pregnant when we made love so infrequently, and I looked more and more to the new technologies to give me my family.

The fertility treatments were long and arduous. Nevertheless, we still laughed a lot, including when Charles had to produce a sperm specimen.

"Okay. So I have to go down into the bowels of this place to give my donation. They say it's a real cool place, everything I need. Do you want to wait up here or in the lounge down there?" Charles asked, as we walked out of the doctor's office.

"Oh, I'd much rather be closer to the action. I'll come with you," I said. I hooked my arm in his, and we made our way down to the hospital basement and wandered the dark, echoing stone hallways until we found the glass doorway to the lounge, where comfortable couches and soft lights welcomed us into what could have been a den of iniquity. I sank down into one of the lush sofas, picked up a magazine, and waited.

After a while, Charles walked into the waiting area with a big smile on his face, nodded good-bye to the receptionist, and took my arm. After we walked out through the double glass doors, he burst out laughing.

"What's so funny? What happened?"

"Well, it was a good load . . ."

"Great . . ."

"But it all landed on the floor. Don't worry, I used the three second rule and scooped it all up and put it in the container; it'll be fine."

"As long as you got it all, that's great—and if I give birth to a cockroach, it'll be a great story, and it will be all ours."

We roared with laughter for days. As it turned out, I did get pregnant that cycle, but I also miscarried. We never knew whether or not it was a cockroach, but we always laughed that we knew the reason for that particular miscarriage.

We spent three years trying to get pregnant before we considered using in vitro fertilization. My doctor hadn't believed me when I'd said I was going into early menopause. Had he believed me, and had we had done in vitro to start with, it probably wouldn't have then taken another three years for me to have a full-term pregnancy.

When I didn't seem to be responding to the fertility treatments, my doctor recommended an exploratory laparotomy to ensure there was nothing physical preventing conception. I went into surgery with two working fallopian tubes; I came out of surgery with one. For that surgery, I was in the hospital for a week. Charles visited each day. Some days he brought lunch; other days he came in the evening with dinner. After we ate, Charles would say, "Come on, let's go down to the lobby," and each day I was there, we'd make our way through the unit, down the elevator, and into the domed entryway of this renowned medical institution.

We'd walk through the heavy doors to the administration building and there he would be.

"He's so big, so powerful," I would say, as we gazed up at the ten-and-a-half-foot marble statue of Jesus. Standing there together in that space, gazing upward, always brought us a sense of healing and hope.

"Okay, are you ready?" Charles would ask, and before we walked back through the heavy doors to go up to my room, we'd each rub the statue's big toe on his right foot. That was for good luck, said hospital lore.

I had to go back a month later for a second, same-day procedure: removal of any scar tissue that might have resulted from the first surgery. Charles dropped me off at the hospital that Friday morning and went to work.

Why that didn't bother me at the time would not become clear until years later. I met the anesthesiologist, who started the IV, and into the operating room I went. I awoke sometime later, still in surgery, on the operating-room table, with a breathing tube in my throat, lights in my eyes, and excruciating chest pains. I couldn't talk because of the tube, but I flailed and tried to let them know what was wrong. Someone rubbed my neck, and I heard someone say, "Give her morphine."

I awoke in the recovery room many hours later. I was the only patient there. No doctor came to see me. Charles was not there, either. At eleven o'clock at night, an orderly pushed me outside in a wheelchair to the curb, where Charles waited in the car. We drove home; with every movement, I felt the same awful chest pain.

The nurse from the recovery room called the next day to check on me.

"I'm having terrible pains in my chest whenever I move," I told her when she asked how I was doing.

"Don't worry. It's just from the anesthesia. We had to give you a lot of morphine while you were in recovery because of all the pain you were having. It'll pass," she casually assured me.

But it didn't pass, and I was in bed all weekend, still unable to move because I felt as if a sword were being thrust through the wall of my chest over and over.

Charles seemed concerned enough that before he left for his DC office on Monday morning, he told me he wanted me to call my doctor. It was six in the morning when I phoned, and the doctor sounded as if he'd expected my call.

"I thought I'd hear from you," he said.

I didn't understand: if he had thought there might be a problem, why hadn't he called me? Now he told me to come to the hospital as soon as possible.

"Call your parents so they can take you to the hospital," Charles said, as he gave me a kiss, grabbed his things, and left for his day in DC. He didn't wait for a reply.

My parents were in New York, four hours away, yet he wanted them to come and take care of me? I placed the call, and they arrived quickly and took me to the hospital. I then saw multiple doctors, had X-rays and scans, and was admitted. As it turned out, I had been given too much anesthesia. My small stature and thin frame had not been taken into consideration. My lung had been punctured—they called it a pneumothorax, a hole the size of a dime—and my lungs and chest cavity were filled with bloody guck, called a hemo-pleural effusion. I was in the hospital for ten days and each day had frequent chest taps to drain the fluid; the needles were the longest I had ever seen, though in reality they were more frightening than painful.

In the hospital's attempt to check everything, they ordered an angiogram. In the end, it was not so bad, but beforehand I was terrified. They gave me something to sleep that night, but I awoke during the night. I knew that before I had fallen asleep there had been a cup and a water jug on the bedside table—I was certain of it. The bedside table was now empty. I felt as if I was going crazy. My heart started racing. I started to sweat. The walls were closing in. I called Charles. "You've got to come. There are strange things happening here."

He then called the nurses' station to tell them I was having a panic attack.

I begged him to be with me for the procedure. He did not come, and only said later that he had known my parents would be there.

Damn it, I needed him, but he had no clue about being there for anyone. He had no clue about love or compassion; it was as if there was *nothing* inside him. He was an empty shell. I had only a glimpse of it then, but not in the way I would come to see him later. Back then, it emerged from the depths of my consciousness only in times of anger. At those times, I shouted at him, shaking with rage, "You weren't there for me!" But, for the most part, I pushed my feelings away.

Despite Charles's lapses, I thought he was committed and loyal. I believed we were right for each other. I refused to see the subtle and not-so-subtle ways in which he assigned to me the responsibility for everything that went wrong. He felt terribly injured by my criticism of him for his lack of support. I didn't realize the degree to which he needed total adoration. His sense of inadequacy was disguised under layers of a brittle veneer. I didn't fathom how fragile he really was.

*Beware, for if you drink from the River Lethe and you forget, you will not know what it is you need to remember.*

## Chapter Five

There were babies everywhere, and I felt as if I were the only woman who didn't have one. I was obsessed. All around me were big, round, breathing bellies and nursing newborns—everything that I longed for. Everyone else on the street, in the malls, at work seemed to have succeeded where I had failed.

I couldn't turn around without feeling the longing and the loss. One evening in early May, Charles and I were sitting outside at Germano's, listening to a jazz quartet, having dinner with our old friend Jordan. As we sipped cappuccino and shared tiramisu and cannoli, we spoke about our fertility struggles.

"Have you thought about adoption?" Jordan asked.

"We've been talking about it, but we've not done anything yet," I said, glancing at Charles as I spoke.

Jordan went on, "Do you know Ani and Eliot Horn? He's an obstetrician?"

"Sure, I've known them for years. Ani introduced us," Charles said.

"Why are you asking?" I said. "We haven't seen them in a long time."

"Did you know they adopted a baby about two years ago?" Jordan said.

"Really?" My heart beat faster.

"It's such a great story." Jordan's voice became more hushed as he started to tell us what had happened.

"A young woman from a prominent Boston family was pregnant, and she was traveling by Amtrak to stay with her grandmother in Florida until the baby was born. She had already decided that she was going to give the baby up for adoption. Somewhere around Wilmington, Delaware, she went into labor, and by the time the train reached Havre de Grace, Maryland, they had to stop the train and get her to a hospital. There was a choice of hospitals the ambulance could have taken her to, but they took her to Franklin Square. The doc who was on call knew Eliot and Ani wanted to adopt a baby, and so, first thing after the delivery, he called them.

"'Do you want a baby?' he asked when Ani answered the phone. The rest is history . . . Amtrak Amy is what they called her in the hospital. I think her name is really Bella."

"Wow," Charles said. "What a great story."

I sat silently, smiling, colorful balloons floating through my mind, my eyes filling.

As we drove home that night, Charles and I began a discussion that lasted into the early-morning hours.

"I've had enough of all this fertility stuff, Charles. I just want to be a mother. Whether or not I have a successful pregnancy, let's start the process for adoption."

"You know that's okay with me." Charles pulled me close on the couch, and we nestled into an embrace.

A long-needed peacefulness came with that decision to stop the fertility treatments, to not go ahead with in-vitro fertilization, and to focus on adoption as a way to have a family.

The next morning, the pungent aroma of coffee wafted gently through the house. That invigorating odor lifted the foggy veil of sleep from my eyes and drew me to the kitchen, where Charles was making omelets, bacon, and biscuits for breakfast.

"Wow, you've been busy. Smells delicious in here. What can I do to help?" I saw that he had set the table.

"Why don't you sit and keep me company? I'm almost finished."

The sunshine streamed in through the open windows, the fresh scent of spring filled the house, and the world was a full array of color. Charles filled our plates, and suddenly I was overcome with a sensation of deep, primal gladness. I walked over to him, startling him, took the plates from his hands to the table, wrapped my arms around his neck, and pressed my lips hard and passionately on his.

"I think I'll call Eliot, start the ball rolling," Charles said, smiling, as we finished cleaning up the breakfast dishes. I sat on the couch, looking out over the green pastures, as Charles made the call. I listened to the beginning chitchat of old friends who hadn't spoken in a while, and I heard Charles invite them over the following weekend.

"We saw Jordan last night, and he told us that you've added to your family. That's quite a story. Congratulations!" Their conversation continued, and Charles told Eliot about our decision to pursue adoption. I could tell, too, that he would be happy to put out the word to his OB colleagues to be on the lookout for any Amtrak babies that might come through.

Then I heard Charles say, "Really? That's fantastic! When is she due? We'll have lots to talk about when you guys come over next week. Tell Ani congratulations, and we'll see you Saturday."

When Charles hung up, he had a big grin on his face. "Guess what? Ani is pregnant. She did IVF, and it worked."

I couldn't help it—I dissolved into tears. It was 1986, and I didn't know anyone who had been successful with IVF. My resolve not to do it seemed so easy, yet this news simply washed it away. I still wanted a pregnancy. I wanted all the things that would take away any feelings I had of being different, of not fitting in.

"I'm happy for them; that's not why I'm crying, Charles." I rushed into the comfort of his arms. By the end of the afternoon, we had decided that we would go ahead with our plans to pursue adoption and we would also attempt IVF.

In May 1986, we began the adoption process. As with everything I have ever been determined to do, I threw myself into this quest. I read all there was to read about adoption, particularly private adoption. As a child psychologist, I already knew quite a bit. I found an attorney who handled private adoptions. I found a support group in Washington, and every other Sunday Charles and I drove to DC and met with six other couples to talk about our progress and problems with the process. We put in a separate phone line, and we advertised from Maine to the Mississippi in small-town newspapers.

The calls began soon after that, and our support group was a haven. The members provided some reality testing for the weird and crazy phone calls that we received.

In June, there were two responses from young women in Louisiana, and we decided to meet them. We flew to Shreveport, rented a car, and made the drive to a trailer park on the outskirts of town. There we met Maddie, a lovely twenty-four-year-old woman, petite, with dark, curly hair, who looked very much like me. She was divorced and had two young sons. Maddie had just ended a relationship with the father of the child she was carrying. She knew she couldn't manage a third child. Her ex-boyfriend had agreed to meet with us, too.

"There's just one thing I have to tell you," she said, as we drove to the coffee shop where we would meet Adam. "Adam has had serious epilepsy since childhood, and it's been hard to control. Because of the epilepsy, he has had severe learning problems. I want you to know that up front because I think it's important."

*She's such a sweet girl,* I thought, but my stomach sank, and I could taste the catfish we had for lunch rise into my throat.

"I'm not sure how significant that is, but it *is* important that we know, and we appreciate your honesty with us." Charles smiled softly as he spoke to her.

We met Adam, who was a nice young man. He shared that he was not ready to settle down, although he loved Maddie. We talked for an hour, and then we drove Maddie home. We let her know that we liked her but that we had already planned to meet with another person and would get back to her within twenty-four hours. We hugged and parted ways, and as the light reflected off her silver trailer, I could feel the metal's heat radiating through me. This way of becoming a family was so much more complicated than it looked in picture books. So many life stories were intertwined. I felt a need to tread very carefully.

We made our way to Baton Rouge, where we met Gina. Although she was also twenty-four, she was nothing like Maddie. She was a tall, slim redhead, chatty, with frenetic movements. Her shifting and indirect gaze left me feeling uneasy. Her speech was quick and pressured, and she didn't stay on any one topic for more than thirty seconds. It was not easy to feel connected to her. Her eyes were glazed, and although she denied any substance abuse problems, neither Charles nor I was so sure. But we wanted a baby and didn't want to lose an opportunity, so we asked her to call our attorney so that he could speak with her if she was interested. Charles and I both preferred Maddie, but we were ambivalent. We wanted to consult with experts before we decided.

"If we gave birth to a baby who had a medical problem, we would deal with it, right?" I said rhetorically, and then continued. "And if we wound up adopting a baby and there was a problem, the baby would be ours and we would deal with it, right? So is it bad that I don't want to go into something knowing that there is a real probability that our child would have significant medical problems? Is that so bad?"

Charles cocked his head, half-smiled, and gave me one of those looks that said, *Do you really need an answer for that?*

I knew I didn't. I just felt guilty about it.

When we returned home, I spoke with several pediatric neurologists, who each gave me the same answer: that there was a good chance that Maddie's baby would have some difficulties, so we had to decide going in that we could do it—that we wanted to do it.

With that, I realized I couldn't do it. I wanted the fantasy of having a normal baby, at least until the baby was born.

I called Maddie, and we cried together. I then gave her the contact information for our attorney. I knew he would have lots of couples with whom she could work. Happily, that eventually happened.

We had a few weeks of telephone contact with Gina, as did our attorney.

"Jim, do you think we should go with her? Di and I are not sure she's stable." Charles asked one day when we were in our lawyer's office.

"Just keep it going as an option; it will become clear pretty soon whether or not it will work."

"I guess you're right," Charles said. I didn't disagree.

There were a few more conversations with Gina, and then, suddenly, they stopped. No one could get in touch with her. One week passed, then another and then another. Then she called, upbeat and giddy, as if we had spoken only the day before

"Hi, Di. How have you guys been?"

"Hi, it's good to hear from you. We were starting to get worried about you," I said, trying to sound friendly, caring, and nonchalant—not pissed.

"Well, I got in a little trouble, but the good news is that now you don't have to worry about me."

"Oh? Do you want to tell me what's going on?"

"It's a long story, but my friend and I got busted for dealing." I didn't want to know what she had been dealing.

"And I'm gonna be in the slammer for the rest of my pregnancy. So you know I'll be clean." She let out an ear-piercing screech.

In the long silence that followed, I felt myself restrain every muscle in my body. *You stupid ingrate,* I thought. I wanted to jump through the telephone, scream, and shake her for being so cavalier about this baby she was carrying, this baby I so longed to have. I took a breath and did what I was good at doing. I became a therapist.

"Well, Gina, for the baby's sake and your sake, I'm glad that you're going to be clean during the rest of your pregnancy, but I don't think this is going to work out for us."

"Why not?" She was stunned.

"Gina, we didn't know you were using drugs. You said you weren't, but obviously you were. That wasn't the truth. There's no way I can trust you, and I know Charles will feel the same way. So we're not going to continue with plans to adopt the baby. It would have been great if things could have been different, but I'm sorry. I hope things work out for you. I really do."

"You fuckin' bitch." I flinched as the sound of the phone slammed down in my ear.

I left a message for Charles, and then I called our attorney, Jim.

It was good that we had our group, and a place to cry and laugh about these difficult experiences that all of us were having. And we carried on.

There were times when Charles and I were talking to four pregnant women at a time, only to discover that three of the four were scamming us or playing some kind of sick joke. There was Katie from Michigan. There were a few things that sounded odd when she spoke about her husband, but it wasn't until we got a call from him that it became clear. I answered the adoption line late one night and heard a male voice.

"Hello, is this Diane?"

"Yes, it is."

"My name is Israel, and I believe that you've been speaking to my wife, Katie, about adopting our baby."

"Yes, I have." Charles walked into the room as I was speaking.

"I need to tell you something. I'm really sorry about this. We have one daughter, who is three years old, and we are not putting her up for adoption. My wife is not pregnant. I don't know why Katie did this; I just found out about it. There is no baby. I am very sorry."

"I appreciate your call. Thank you," I said, and I robotically placed the phone down. I turned to Charles and said, "There was no baby, Katie was playing us."

Charles's face turned bright red. I had never seen him that angry. He picked up the phone and redialed the number. Katie must have picked up the phone because Charles railed into her.

"How dare you do that to my wife? What kind of sick person are you to play with people that way?"

Other candidates tried to extract money from us. After a while, we recognized the signs of a scam and quickly ended our interactions with these women.

One day in late September, as the days grew shorter and the air grew cooler, I saw the flashing light of the answering machine. There was warmth in the husky, female voice that left a tentative message asking for a return call. Janice, a woman in her late twenties, was divorced and had an eight-year-old son. She was seven and a half months pregnant and in a complicated relationship. They couldn't afford another child, so they had decided to give the baby up for adoption.

"My mother is opposed to adoption because of that Joel Steinberg case that's been in the news." Janice sighed. "She's worried that every lawyer is a scumbag who will make an illegal deal with parents and then abuse the baby. But you don't sound like those kinds of people. I want to meet you as soon as possible because my due date is getting close."

She was anxious to meet us and our attorney, and we wanted to meet her, too. We bought her a ticket to fly to Washington, DC and waited for her at the gate. She looked just as she'd described herself; we knew her the moment we saw her, not only by her round belly but also by her long, curly auburn hair, the freckles across her nose, and her dark green eyes. She was pretty in a very down-to-earth way, and we both liked her immediately.

Charles drove to a diner close to our lawyer's office for breakfast. If our meeting went well and felt right, we could adjourn to Jim's office. We all talked openly about our lives and backgrounds, and we even talked about how it might be hard for Janice to give up the baby.

"I'm sure this is the right thing to do, and so is Ray. I'm sure it's a girl," she added.

There was silence, and then Charles asked, "Does that make a difference for you in terms of whether you give up the baby?"

"No. I know it's a girl, but if it was a boy, then the baby could sleep in the same room with my son, and we wouldn't have to move."

Charles and I looked at each other and knew it could go either way, especially since Janice's mother did not support her giving up the baby. Family support was, we were learning, crucial in a successful private adoption.

We went from breakfast to introduce Janice to our attorney.

He thought that this one was a good possibility. About ten days later, her boyfriend was in town on business, and he called and asked if we'd like to meet for dinner. It went well and further reassured us that the process was moving forward. But I couldn't forget that Janice had said, "If it's a boy, the two boys could share a room . . . but I know it's a girl."

We started to work on the nursery, but we also still took whatever calls came in on the adoption line. We already knew it wouldn't be final until it was final.

## Chapter Six

The leaves were in full fall color as Charles and I drove toward home one October morning after doing some errands. We turned onto our winding road and approached the one-lane bridge that crossed over the water where the Gunpowder River was narrow. There in the shallow water stood, with one foot raised, one of the largest white birds, with the longest legs and a long, stout bill, I had ever seen. It just stood there, wading. I had never seen a bird like it before, other than in books.

"Charles, what kind of bird is that?"

"It looks like a stork to me."

"That's what I thought. I don't think I've ever actually seen a stork before." I paused. "I don't see any baskets. We'd better get to the house quickly; in case he dropped something off for us." I smiled, not serious but hopeful. Charles smiled, rolled his eyes a bit, and squeezed my hand. Within moments we were turning onto our drive, but as we got to the door, it was obvious that there was no basket or baby waiting.

"Sorry about that." Charles hugged me, seeing that I was somewhat deflated. As we entered the house, the adoption line started ringing and I disengaged from his embrace.

"I'll get it."

"Hi, I wanted some information, please," a woman's hesitant voice responded when I said hello.

"Sure. How can I help you?"

"Did you place an ad in the *Atlantic City Weekly*?" she asked.

"Yes, my husband and I did place an ad. We're hoping to adopt an infant."

"And you're a child psychologist?"

"Yes, I am, and my husband is a physician." Those things were in the ad. "We both love children very much. Are you thinking of adoption for yourself?" I figured I might as well ask.

"Well, no. I just saw your ad this morning." There was a long pause. "You see, I just found out that my sixteen-year-old daughter is pregnant. She wants to give the baby up for adoption. We'll support her in whatever she wants to do, but she's adamant that she's too young to be a mother. Can I have her call you at this number when she gets home from school?"

"Of course. I'd be happy to speak with her. It sounds like she's really trying to make the best decision for herself and for the baby."

"She is. She's an honor student, a great musician, and an artist. She's wonderful, and I just want what's best for her."

"Have her call me. I'd love to speak with her. I'll be home today after five. She can call any time after that, okay?"

"Great. She'll call you after five. I like that you're a child psychologist, and you sound nice. It was lovely talking to you. Oh, by the way, my name is Beth, and my daughter is Joni. Thank you. Bye."

The connection ended, and several moments later I found myself still standing there, telephone in hand, smiling, with tearstains splattered on my shirt.

Charles was standing in the doorway. "What's up? You're smiling and crying."

At that moment, I couldn't explain anything. He came and held me, and we stayed like that for a long time. Then I told him about Joni.

At five minutes past five, the phone rang. It was Joni, who sounded as gracious and articulate as I expected.

"I hope you don't think I'm terrible, but I did think about having an abortion, 'cause I knew I didn't want to have a baby now. But it was too late."

"I don't think that's terrible," I assured her.

"Well, I couldn't do it, so I decided adoption would be the best thing. I just wanted to know the baby would have a good home and be loved as much as I love her or him."

She told me about Tom, her ex, with whom she had just ended a relationship. He was her first boyfriend.

"I won't say his name again. My mom and I just refer to him as the Jerk. I really like his family, though, and I know they'll want to meet you. They're great people . . . even though he's the Jerk."

We both giggled.

She seemed to have a great deal of insight for a girl who had just turned sixteen. I was certain her life had not been easy; I sensed that her wisdom was born of experience.

"What do we do first?" she asked, after we had talked for almost an hour.

"I'll talk to Charles when he gets home from work, and if he doesn't have to work this weekend and you're free, we could drive up and meet you. That's probably a good place to start. How would that be?"

"That would be great. Can my mom be there?"

I laughed as I said, "Of course, I would expect that she would want to be there. Why don't I call you back when Charles gets home? Meanwhile, think about any questions you have."

"Great. I can't tell you how relieved I feel having talked to you.

"Thanks so much."

"Thank you, Joni."

I sat on my bed, surrounded by three fluffy sheepdogs, and smiled. I couldn't wait to tell Charles about Joni and then to meet her. In the back corner of my mind, I thought of Janice and of her baby. But I already felt myself connecting with Joni.

That Saturday, with the mellow autumn sunshine in our eyes and feeling the sweet breath of crisp, fresh air, Charles and I started off for southern New Jersey. After we crossed the Delaware Memorial Bridge and country roads, the earthy, smoky scent of autumn surrounded us. The foliage turned redder and more golden as we drove farther north.

Joni and her mother were waiting for us when we arrived at our meeting place. She was a lovely girl with almond-shaped eyes of an unusual aqua color. She had a maturity far beyond her years. We took them to lunch at a restaurant named Vito's, and by the end of the day, we felt as if Joni were family.

For the next few weeks, I spoke to her almost every day. Most days she would call when she got home from school and wanted to talk about her day, about the baby, about the Jerk, and what it felt like to be pregnant and in school. She was excited to tell me about the ultrasound. I sent her some books about adoption. As much as I felt that she was bestowing a miraculous gift upon us, it surprised me that she experienced that same feeling about what we were doing for her and for her baby. Our baby. We wanted her to work through all of her feelings about relinquishing her baby and suggested that she see a counselor. She agreed and found someone to see. Our attorney paid the bill.

While I spoke to Janice frequently, there was a formality, a certain distance, that wasn't easily bridged. With Joni it was different, and it was she whom I grew to love. When I allowed myself to consider both pregnancies, I began to think that maybe we could adopt both babies. I didn't say that to Charles just then, though—we still had waiting to do.

Charles and I worked feverishly on the nursery. It was a soft and soothing palette of pastels. We decorated one wall with a wooden frieze of our little farm, and we sat in the nursery late at night and told stories to the baby we hoped would soon be there permanently.

It was the beginning of November. I was talking to Joni almost every day. In the meantime, Janice was approaching her due date, and then suddenly she didn't call for four or five days. Charles thought I should phone her, but I didn't want to push, so we waited. Then, on November 10 and 11, there was an unusually early snowstorm in Maryland. Everything shut down. We watched the world turn white, and we waited.

It was about one o'clock in the morning on November 12 when the adoption line rang. Charles answered and put the phone on speaker.

"Hi, it's Ray. I'm calling to let you know that Janice is in labor and is in the hospital. She wants you to wait until the baby is born before you come, so I'll call you as soon as we know something."

"Okay, sure. Send Janice our love." Charles stood there, the expression on his face flat.

I hugged him. My stomach felt as if it had dropped to the floor, but Charles looked devastated, so I said, "Hey, it's so pretty outside, why don't we get dressed and take a walk?"

Charles looked at me quizzically and then laughed. "Okay!" We threw on clothes over our pajamas, pulled on our boots, hats, and jackets, and walked out onto the unblemished white hills that shone brightly against the boundless black sky. The crystalline crunch of the snow beneath our boots was the only audible sound.

As we walked around the back of the house, we passed the trash cans and Charles pulled off the lids. "Come on, let's go for a ride down the hill."

"Yes, sounds great," I said, and through the snow we ran, toward the hill that lay beyond the horse pasture, with nothing but the reflection of the moon and the glittering stars on the white snow to guide our way. It was very dark, and a bit spooky.

"Charles, how about we go down on one top?" I suggested, as we got to the top of the hill.

"Why?"

"I don't know—it's dark; it's scary," I threw some snow at him, and he returned the favor.

Going down that hill was a great release, and we did it together, laughing the whole way down—all five times. By the time we got back to the house, our bodies were quivering. I made hot chocolate, Charles started a fire, and we fell asleep cuddled together.

We were awakened by the phone ringing at eight o'clock. It was Eliot. Ani had just given birth to a little girl. Charles didn't tell him that we might have a baby with the same birthday.

After taking the dogs out, Charles started breakfast. The comforting aroma of bacon frying on the grill and of coffee wafting through the warm, cozy house made the loud ringing of the adoption line less jarring. It was 10:00 a.m. Charles ran up the stairs and picked up the phone. It was Ray.

"Congratulations! You have a son!"

*A boy?* I thought. *She was so sure she was having a girl. Can she really do this?*

Echoing my thoughts, Charles said, "Really? The two of you are sure you want to do this?"

"Yes, we're sure. Do you have a name picked out? We need his name for the birth certificate. When can you get here?"

We did have a name ready. It was Jonathan Adam.

We arranged for a flight to Chicago late that afternoon. There were no connecting flights until the next day, so we made our way through the crowds of O'Hare, rented a car, and drove the three hours to meet our son.

As we drove, I thought of Joni. *I'll call her later tonight to see how she is.* But, amid all that was going on, I didn't.

As we walked into the lobby of University Hospital, Ray was there, waiting for us with a huge smile and a balloon that read IT'S A BOY!

"How is Janice doing?" I had to ask before I saw her; despite Ray's smiles, I knew she was struggling. She had a son.

"Oh, she's doing okay. It's hard, but she knows Jonathan is going to a wonderful home. We're both thankful for that. I just wish her mom would stop harping on her." My chest tightened.

We followed Ray down the corridors and onto the elevator to the maternity floor. After a few more turns, Ray pushed open a door. There sat Janice, her long, wavy auburn hair flowing over her shoulders, the freckles on her face more noticeable than the last time we'd met. She looked tired but smiled as we walked in. She rose, holding out her arms to welcome us. She embraced us with immeasurable gratitude and love.

"Do you want to see him?"

"Of course," Charles and I said together as Janice bent down over the Plexiglas bassinet hidden on the side of the bed. My breath caught like a leaf in a branch as she lifted this small bundle.

He was wrapped in a yellow blanket and wore a yellow knit cap on his head. She held him to her chest. She placed a kiss on his forehead and then placed him in my arms. She whispered softly, "Take good care of him."

"Always. Thank you." I nuzzled his soft neck and breathed in his sweet, soft newborn scent. I looked up. Janice, Ray, and Charles were crying, but Jonathan slept peacefully. I placed him in Charles's arms, and he was clearly transported. I don't know how long we passed the baby between the four of us, admiring his beauty. Finally, it was late, and Janice was clearly exhausted. She gently placed Jonathan back into his bassinet, and we agreed on the time we would return the next day. Janice would officially relinquish Jonathan upon her discharge from the hospital.

Charles and I made our way to a nearby motel. "What do you think?" he finally asked when we settled into the room.

"I think she's ambivalent. She wants to want to do this because Ray wants her to. Did you see the expression on her face change when her mother called? I'm not sure who has more power. He's such a beautiful baby."

"If we can just make it through tomorrow morning, we'll be home free."

"Not really, Charles. She can still change her mind."

"Oh, she wouldn't do that." Charles sounded sure of himself. I had real doubts.

Sleep evaded us, so we looked for a movie. All we could find was *The Terminator*. The action-packed film moved us toward the morning with some semblance of invigoration and hope. It also helped dispel some of that pent-up anger and frustration we were feeling. We were really into the action of the movie. It helped us to be more relaxed when we arrived at the hospital in the morning. Janice and Ray piled our arms with newborn formula, diapers, and a car seat.

"I can't tell you . . ." I started to say, as we stood by the car after packing it.

"I know." Janice raised her hand and smiled—a tight smile. "It's okay."

That was it. The waiting was over. As we drove from the hospital parking lot, our eyes remained locked on Janice until she was out of sight. I sat in the backseat with Jonathan.

He was a beautiful boy. When we got to O'Hare, we called my parents and then Charles's parents. They wanted to come the next day to meet their new grandson. They would all drive together from New York.

We said, "Absolutely."

Jonathan slept through most of the trip. His flaxen hair was so soft, and his eyes—his huge eyes—were the clearest blue. Charles and I took turns cuddling him throughout the flight. By the time we landed in Maryland, the temperature had warmed considerably and there was no trace of snow—only mud. We would pick up the dogs the next day.

All seemed to be in order, but as we drove home, I sat in the back with Jonathan, feeling my arms and legs becoming increasingly tight.

"So, who's going to carry our boy in?" Charles asked as he parked the car, certain, I'm sure, that I planned on doing that.

"Why don't you do it?" I said as I unbuckled his car seat. What I didn't say was that I had a growing feeling deep within me that I couldn't carry Jonathan into the house. Somehow, I knew I could not allow myself to connect to this sweet bundle of love, no matter how strong the longing. But once Jonathan was inside, my feeling of dread seemed to disappear, and I began to feel that maybe this was real. And Charles was so excited to have a little boy that he glowed.

We took Jonathan upstairs to show him his nursery. For now, he'd sleep in our room in a beautiful antique French cradle that I had found and refinished and covered in quilted eyelet. As Charles and I sat in the nursery, taking in Jonathan's scent and sounds, I noticed the flashing light of the adoption line's answering machine. Charles turned it on, and it was a message from Joni.

"Hi, guys. I haven't spoken to you for a few days. What's going on? I'd like to see you again. Miss ya. Please call when you get this." My heart sank. I loved Joni. She was depending on us.

"You should call her tomorrow and tell her that we were able to adopt a baby sooner, but that we know other couples who are trying to adopt and can hook her up with them. Our attorney can also help."

*Maybe we'll adopt both babies*, I thought, but I said nothing, and I didn't call Joni the next day. All four grandparents arrived early Sunday morning to see their grandson. My parents were floating on air. They kvelled and hugged and kissed him throughout the day. Jonathan took it like a trouper and slept. He opened his bright blue eyes and seemed to smile in response; then he drifted back to sleep.

"Di, are you okay?" my mother asked, when she had finally gotten me away from everyone else. "He's so beautiful. You're a mother, but you don't seem very excited. What's going on?" She looked into my eyes in the way only a mother can. She knew.

"I don't know. I think it just hasn't sunk in yet. I *am* excited and will be even more so as it feels more real." Then I just started to cry, and my mom and I sat on the nursery floor while she held me.

They left around five o'clock. Winnie, Dizzy, and Ginger were home and curious about this new little being in the house, while Charles and I settled in as new parents. I was changing Jonathan when the adoption line rang.

"Did you call Joni?" Charles asked before he picked up the phone.

"No. I haven't had a chance."

Charles picked up the phone as I lifted Jonathan from the changing table and stood beside him. He wasn't saying much more than "yeah" and "sure" and "I understand." His final response was, "Okay. Tomorrow at ten o'clock."

His expression was unreadable until he spoke. "That was Ray. Janice can't do it. She's been sick from this. She wants the baby back. They've already called Jim and told him she's coming tomorrow morning. I'm sure he'll call any minute." His face was filled with pain.

With Jonathan between us, we hugged. Then I lifted him up and said, "Hey, little guy, you're going back to Illinois." With all my years of training and practice, I had called this one right. I hadn't been able to bring Jonathan into the house because, despite having hoped differently, I knew what I knew. After crying with Charles, I called my mom and cried with her.

The next morning, carrying Jonathan in his car seat, we walked into our attorney's office. As if it were Macy's, I asked, in an uncharacteristically loud voice, "Is this the Return Department?" I knew Janice must be nearby. I just couldn't help it.

## Chapter Seven

I called Joni. Charles and I continued with the plan to adopt her baby in January. We worked, we saw friends and family, we made love, we did all of the things we always did, but for what seemed like forever, I walked through a dark abyss.

In early December, I had my first appointment at the IVF clinic. Afterward, as I made my way to the market, I couldn't help but notice a woman in the car next to me who had also been in the waiting room. When I got to the market, there she was again.

"Hi, my name is Diane. Were you just at GBMC?"

"Yes, I saw you there; that's so funny. I'm Shelly." And so began our friendship, the first of many I would develop while going through the process of IVF. Shelly, as it turned out, had an eighteen-month-old son, Robert, who was adopted. I began to feel more connected to the world around me. And, of course, there was Joni.

Joni had her own attorney in New Jersey, but she needed to meet with our attorney, too. Early one cold and gray December morning, as flurries fell, I left our Maryland cottage to pick her up and bring her to Washington for the meeting. Christmas was approaching. Giving presents unrelated to the pregnancy was not allowed; nevertheless, we stopped at a mall for a bite to eat and to enjoy the twinkling, magical lights and decorations of the season. I was able to buy Joni some things she could use during her pregnancy and while in the hospital. She picked out some cute night gowns and a robe and slippers. We giggled as we tested perfumes and makeup, and then she chose soothing lavender-vanilla bubble bath and bath salts. I didn't imagine that anyone would object to these. When we returned to New Jersey late that afternoon, we went and visited her ex-boyfriend's parents. They were welcoming and lovely and thrilled to meet me. Likewise, I was happy to meet them, see family photos, and hear family stories that I could share with our baby. By this time, I was feeling pretty sure that this would be "our baby." Mid-January was Joni's due date.

At our first adoption-group meeting in January, we had four new members. Dara and Rick had successfully brought home a little boy. Lauri and Bob had been working with two birth mothers who had delivered the same week, and they decided to go through with both adoptions, so they now had a son and a daughter. Amy and Larry had brought home a beautiful little girl. The remaining three couples were all hoping to have a family by the beginning of February. If it happened, we'd all have become families in less time than a full-term pregnancy took.

Joni's due date came and went. My closest friend, Allyson, gave birth to a little girl. January was warm and muggy. Joni was calling more often.

"Dr. Armon said he's not ready to induce me yet. You and Charles will be here for the delivery, won't you?" she asked every day.

"As soon as we get the call, we will be there as fast as we can," I always said.

Joni was scared, that was clear, but she was steadfast in her decision. On January 27 when she called, she sounded relieved when she reported what the doctor had told her.

"He said that if I haven't gone into labor before then, he's going to induce me on the first. I feel much better knowing that. Are you guys excited?"

"Joni, we are unbelievably excited. What about you? How are you feeling about doing this?"

"I'm terribly sad, but I'm really happy it's you and Charles. I can't be a mother now, and you'll be wonderful parents, so I'm happy."

"I know, Joni. Everything in life, if you really think about it, involves lots of different feelings. Nothing is ever just one way. As happy as Charles and I are, we also feel your sadness, because we really have come to love you and want what's best for you."

"I know you do, and I know you'll love the baby." And so the days passed.

"Try to relax, Di. It'll be soon," Charles kept trying to reassure me. But the time was going too slowly. When I was away from the house, I checked the answering machine for messages constantly.

It was warm and rainy that Saturday. Charles and I were doing things around the house; I was buying time.

"I have to go over to Sears and pick up some brackets so I can hang the shelf in the nursery. Do you want to take a ride?" Charles asked, trying to make the wait easier for me.

"Sure, let's go." I was already out the door.

It was late afternoon. Charles found the brackets and was at the cash register as I walked over to a pay phone to call home and check for messages. This time, there was a message from Joni's sister, Rebecca.

"We're leaving for the hospital; Joni just went into labor. Come as soon as you can." It was about four o'clock when I picked up the message.

My feet did not touch the ground as I flew breathlessly from the phone to the register where Charles stood. I didn't have to say anything—he knew immediately.

We were home within ten minutes and called Shelly, who had offered to take care of the dogs when we got the call. We called our attorney and called our parents. We threw a few things in an overnight bag, and we were at the hospital by seven o'clock.

We wound our way up to the maternity floor and found Beth, Joni's mom, in the family lounge. She was involved in a conversation with another waiting family as we walked in; when she saw us, she grabbed us, embracing us closely.

"These are the baby's parents, Diane and Charles," she said to the people with whom she'd been speaking. It was so matter-of-fact, so real, said with such love.

Joni's labor was long and hard. Her sister, a nurse, was by her side through most of it; Charles and I spelled her when she needed a rest. As daybreak drew near, the doctors thought they might have to do a C-section. But then, suddenly, active labor began. Joni wanted us by her bedside when our daughter was born. She was delivered with her thumb in her mouth.

"I want you to be the first to hold the baby," Joni had told me, and so when our daughter, Elisabeth Anne, was born, she was placed in my arms. I couldn't take my eyes off this perfect, warm bundle that had been bestowed upon me. I held her for a long time and then passed her to Charles; his eyes filled with tears. We marveled at how alert she was, how strong she seemed. She held her head up and looked around. Her aqua-blue eyes were the same almond shape as Joni's, and her face was a perfect circle with plump, rosy cheeks. She had a little bit of strawberry-blond peach fuzz on top of her mostly bald head. She was the most beautiful, cherubic baby I had ever seen.

Joni was exhausted. Our reverie was interrupted when the nurses scooped up the baby and began to wheel Joni to her room. We hugged and kissed her, thanked her profusely, and told her how much we loved her. We told her we would be back later. We took one last look at our daughter and walked out into the sunlight.

Elli was born on January 31; it was sunny and seventy-two degrees in New Jersey. We made our way to a local diner, had some breakfast, and found a hotel where we could crash.

We took Elli home on February 2. Each hand-created birth announcement read:

*Gracious gift of God*
*Springtime in winter*
*Elisabeth Anne*
*January 31, 1988*

And each was filled with stardust to sprinkle all over the universe.

## Chapter Eight

We did go through with further attempts at in vitro fertilization. Elli was very much a part of the process and was loved by everyone at the clinic. Her baby picture was posted with those of all the other IVF babies on the bulletin board; everyone considered her one of theirs.

For three years, I continued to get pregnant, and for three years, with each pregnancy, I continued to have miscarriages. But I was already a mother, and the miscarriages didn't have the same conscious impact of the earlier failures. I wasn't enshrouded in blackness; there wasn't a sense of continual mourning. I was enjoying everything that motherhood entailed, so I didn't feel different from everyone around me or as if I were on the periphery of life, although I think the miscarriages continued to be hard for Charles. Each time, he would find someone to blame. One time, a friend who happened to be pregnant was visiting, and after I drove her to the airport, he went on and on about how her demands for attention and her desire for me to drive her to the airport were the reason I had lost my pregnancy.

One day, when we were about to start a new IVF cycle, Dr. Gonzalez asked Charles and me to sit down in his office.

"Charles, Diane, I know I've explained this before, but let's go over it again so we can make some decisions. The reason you keep having miscarriages, as you know, Diane, is because of the shape of your uterus. It is shaped like the letter *T*, and so the endometrial tissue and blood supply don't support implantation in many parts of your uterus. Unless the embryo implants in just the right place, where the tissue is thick enough, you miscarry."

"Dr. Gonzalez, I've been reading that there is now surgery that is very successful in correcting this sort of defect. Do you think I should do the surgery?"

"No. Diane, I am going to talk to you as if you were my sister. I will not do the surgery. You have already been through too much, and you've had too many hormones. You and Charles already have a beautiful family. Elli is a wondrous little girl. If you were my wife or my sister, I would say no surgery and I would say no more in vitro fertilization. I know we're just starting a cycle now, so we can complete it. But I wanted to meet with you to say this needs to be the last time."

The silence hung in the air, suspended. Charles squeezed my hand; he looked at me, softness in his eyes, and then looked at Dr. Gonzalez. "Thank you. Thank you very much for giving her permission to stop; otherwise, she wouldn't be able to, and I would keep going along with it."

Both Charles and Dr. Gonzalez looked at me. My throat was dry, my tongue thick, my skin cold, my hands moist. I breathed deeply. I don't know how long it was before I spoke. My voice cracked.

"Well . . . I hadn't thought about it that way, but I think you're right, and I don't think I'd stop if you didn't say 'no more.'" I squeezed Charles's hand back. As I breathed, I felt my body relax and panic all at once.

"We have this cycle to talk more about it. I certainly am available, but, Diane, Charles, this is really what I believe is in your best interest as patients and for your family. We'll transfer the four embryos this time, and we'll see what happens."

The meeting ended, and Dr. Gonzalez walked us to the door. "He really is a good man," I said to Charles, as we walked out of the office.

"I agree. I think he's great. There are probably lots of Baltimore babies named after him. But how do you really feel about stopping after this cycle if it doesn't work?"

I tried to smile but sighed instead. "I guess we're not so optimistic about this cycle, and that says something, doesn't it? I think I'm okay with it. I'm sad, but I'm okay. It's not like before. What about you?"

"I'm glad he gave you permission to stop. I'm fine with it. I feel blessed that we have Elli."

"Me, too."

Elli was eating lunch when we walked into the house. Our babysitter, Anne, renamed Nanny by Elli, sat drinking a cup of tea, while our now nearly three-year-old daughter, blond curls bouncing, bolted from the table to greet us.

We all chatted, and then I saw Anne out. When she was gone, I hugged Charles and Elli and left them working contentedly on an art project while I went off to see my clients. Seeing my husband and my daughter together that way, I knew I didn't need more than I already had.

---

SEVERAL weeks after that, I was sitting with Elli when the phone rang. It was the fertility center telling me that my bloodwork was back, and I was ready for my last attempt to see if I could get pregnant and carry the pregnancy to term. "Great, tomorrow. I'll be there," I answered, not giving much more thought to the now familiar next steps.

Charles dropped me off in the morning and returned later in the day to take me home. Then we waited. When we got my pregnancy test results, my blood levels were sky high. I knew there must be at least two embryos implanted.

The room was dark, and the only light came from the glow of the screen.

"From what I can see, there are three amniotic sacs; I see four heartbeats."

"Four?" Charles gasped.

"Well, if you look over here"—Dr. Braken pointed to the screen—"you can see a heartbeat in this sac, a heartbeat here, and then, over here in this sac, if you look closely, you can see two heartbeats. There's only one placenta and only one outer membrane. They each seem to have their own inner membrane. These are identical twins."

It was all a blur to me. I couldn't see anything.

"Dr. Braken, are you saying I'm pregnant with quadruplets?"

She laughed. "That's what it looks like. There are options, but it's early, so let's just see how things go. I'll make a copy of the picture for you." Charles and I just stared at each other; as always, we needed no words in order to totally understand each other.

We walked out of the darkened ultrasound suite in silence. I held the small, square, glossy photo, and we both stared at it with amazement.

"Maybe we'd better start thinking about an addition or getting a new house," Charles said, sounding panicked, on the drive home.

He drove over the one-lane bridge on our road, and we passed the entrance to what would be a new housing development near us. I saw a tightness in his jaw, and the muscle in his right cheek twitched. I leaned over and hugged him and kissed his cheek.

"It will all work out; it always does," I said.

We parked the car by the house, and Charles started over to the office, but then stopped and, looking out over the hills, murmured, "They're ruining everything."

I ran over and hugged him again. "It's not that close, and the view is still beautiful. It'll be okay." I walked into the house, where first the dogs, then Elli and Anne, greeted me.

"Mommy, I'm so glad you're home." Elli leaped onto me, and I was aware that as she jumped full force onto my waist, I protectively tensed my abdomen. I held her in my arms and kissed her, but I didn't like that I had responded with that tense feeling. It felt like a betrayal of Elli.

Later that afternoon, I got my mother on the phone. "Hi, Mom. I had the ultrasound this morning, and there's going to be an explosion in the number of grandchildren you and Daddy have. I'm pregnant with quadruplets. One is a set of identical twins."

"Oh my goodness, Di, you can't carry four babies."

"Mom don't worry. It will all work out." I could hear the sound of the air as she sucked it in. I knew what her next words would be.

"Di, I know it's exciting to be pregnant, but please—I don't want you to be devastated if this doesn't work out, so be cautious. Be realistic." Then she started coughing. "One minute, honey. Let me get a cough drop. Okay, I'm back."

"Mom, have you spoken with the doctor about that cough?"

"Yes, I have, and he says it's nothing."

"Well, I don't like the way it sounds. You've been coughing way too long. Charles thinks so, too."

"Don't worry. I won't neglect it."

"Okay, remember, we'll be coming to New York in three weeks for that wedding; I hope you'll see the doctor before then."

"Don't worry, I'll take care of it. Daddy and I thought we'd take Elli over to Nellie Bly on Saturday when you're here—she'll love the rides—and then we'll take her to Nathan's and walk on the boardwalk and maybe go out onto the beach. You and Charles can have the day to yourselves in the city."

"Oh, that would be great. Elli would love it, and so would we. I can't wait to see you. We should get in about nine o'clock Friday evening."

Three weeks later, we made our way to New York. Charles's parents did not know about the pregnancy. He never shared anything with them about the infertility, either. Elli slept for the entire drive, awakening as we crossed the Verrazano Bridge. The lights from the bridge and the traffic shone brightly through the windows.

"Lady Liberty . . . Mommy, Daddy, where is Lady Liberty?"

"I'm not sure we'll be able to see her, but tomorrow we'll make sure you get to," Charles assured her.

"I love Lady Liberty. Are we almost there?"

"Very soon. Do you see that sign? WELCOME TO BROOKLYN: FOURTH LARGEST CITY IN AMERICA. This is where I grew up."

"I love Brooklyn 'cause it's where Grandma and Poppy live."

Elli sang, and Charles and I chatted. The lights of the skyline were already bringing that familiar rush of exhilaration I experienced every time I came home. Growing up. Walking to the ocean. So many things influence who we are. I hadn't realized how much all that surrounded me—the energy of changing tides, the visceral and subtle nuances, the shifts in everything in my world—affected me.

Elli was thrilled to spend Saturday with her grandparents.

Charles and I wandered through Central Park, amid its tapestry of colors. We walked around the lake and along the paths, people-watching and dog-watching, as the aroma of roasted chestnuts and soft pretzels wafted through the air. We slowly made our way to the Museum of Modern Art to see a new architecture and design exhibit.

Then, ravenously hungry, we headed back to Brooklyn for dinner in Williamsburg at Bamonte's.

As we parked, we laughed at the thought of having four more babies. Our evenings of going to restaurants might be over for a very long time.

The seedy surroundings and boarded-up buildings would make a good backdrop for a last supper.

As we walked through Bamonte's doors, warm memories of having been in the homes of my friends' large Italian families as I was growing up engulfed me. The medley of accents, the warm camaraderie, and the sight and scent of large platters overflowing with thin slices of veal, ravioli, and gnocchi reminded me of my childhood—as if I were standing in the surf of Coney Island and being splashed by the waves.

The maître d' showed us to our table. There in the center were a dozen yellow roses.

This time, I got it. "Wow, even in Brooklyn I get flowers!"

It would have been nice to have a glass of wine, but I restrained myself, and Charles and I toasted with our glasses of ice water. The food was fabulous. We shared eggplant rollatini and baked clams and then had the house special pork chops with sweet and hot vinegar peppers. I was in heaven . . . and then, without warning, a sharp, cramping pain hit me. I got up quickly.

"Excuse me. I'll be right back." I made it to the restroom. There wasn't much blood, but the crimson stains on my underwear had begun, along with the end of my fantasy.

When I opened the restroom door, Charles was standing there. "Are you okay?"

I shrugged.

He put his arm around my shoulder and said, "I guess maybe we overdid it today." The muscle in his cheek twitched.

We paid the bill, took the flowers, and returned to my parents' house.

In the darkness of the car, I told him, "I'm spotting. It's not a lot, but this is how it starts."

## Chapter Nine

Crimson-red blood. It continued. Not clumps or clots—just enough to be a bold reminder that the threads of life were ever so delicate, and that there are never guarantees. By twelve weeks, two of the fetuses had vanished. The two survivors were reported to be doing well, but by week fourteen, there was only one.

No matter how prepared I thought I was, it always felt like death.

"You're fine," Dr. Clare assured me, then looked reassuringly at Charles, a stiffening in her gaze. Turning her gaze back to me, she went on, "But you will likely have bleeding throughout the pregnancy from the placentas. You don't have to go crazy every time you see blood. Your body is just sloughing off what isn't reabsorbed."

I laughed as I said, "Dr. Clare, you know I *will* go crazy, and I will need to come in every time."

"I know you will, and it's okay; you can come in, and we'll do an ultrasound, and I'll tell you the same thing."

During that meeting with Dr. Clare, I could sense a palpable tension between her and Charles, over who would be in charge of my pregnancy and the decisions that would be made about it. It was just something that I could feel as a presence in the room whenever Charles came with me to an appointment. He would become the reserved observer, judging the action with a critical and subtle, or perhaps not-so-subtle, eye.

Charles was always intense about what he felt or wanted. If something wasn't that important to me, I usually gave in. It didn't seem worth a battle. It had always been that way. But during this pregnancy, something changed. Not only was Charles involved and invested, but I sometimes felt as if he wanted to take over my body, to consume me. Armor—I needed armor to define and protect myself. Whenever a decision needed to be made, I felt my body tense. I found myself having to stop and deliberately think, *Is this what I want?* My immediate response was that I would have to hold my ground. The ideas Charles had often were ideas I did ultimately agree with, like working with a birth doula. I'm not sure why I resisted this when Charles originally suggested it, other than needing to assert myself, to maintain my own boundaries.

In fact, nothing became a matter of contention between us, but there was an increasing feeling that I needed to hold on to myself, hold on to who I was as a person, separate from Charles.

---

I continued to work part-time through my pregnancy, and I did panic whenever the crimson color appeared on my underwear. Physically, though, I was fine. I was due in mid-August.

Springtime does not last long in Baltimore. That was the case in 1991. The cold days of winter passed, and the heat and humidity of summer descended upon us almost immediately. It was early July. It had been close to one hundred degrees for a week. I put some things in a bag, and Elli and I drove over to the community pool. Elli, a real water baby, was splashing in the shallow end of the pool, wearing her water wings, as I stood near her.

"It looks like you're going to deliver within the next twenty-four hours," a tall, dark-haired woman standing nearby casually commented.

"I wish, but I have most of the summer to go."

"I don't think so." She smiled warmly.

"Well, all I know is that I'm uncomfortable."

We introduced ourselves, and she continued, "I guarantee you won't make it to August. I think it's going to happen within the next twenty-four hours."

She certainly sounded sure of herself, so much so that I thought, *Maybe she knows something I don't know.* So many little things made me realize how important my connection with other women was. It was that bonding around maternity that made her comments feel as if I was about to approach another rite of passage.

Standing in the cool water, chatting with this stranger, made the blistering heat of that July day more bearable. Elli and I stayed at the pool for hours and headed home in the late afternoon. Cuddling on the couch after dinner, her head on my stomach, I read her one of her favorite stories, *The Foundling Fox.*

"Mommy, I can feel the baby."

"Me, too."

"Mommy, did you know that when I was in Joni's tummy I kicked and kicked so hard because I couldn't wait to get out and be with you and Daddy?"

"Really? That is so funny, because when you were in Joni's tummy, Daddy and I were so excited, we were having a hard time waiting patiently for you to get here, too. When you finally arrived, it was the most exciting day of our lives."

Elli's blond curls were spread across my stomach as she peered up at me through her long, long lashes and smiled. "I love you, Mommy."

"I love you, too, Elli."

---

IT was midnight. Elli and Charles were both asleep, and I did what had become a nightly ritual. After having a large glass of milk, I let the water run in the tub. I lit a candle and turned off the light in our tiny bathroom. With the sounds of classical Japanese koto music surrounding me, I dropped my robe and let myself sink into the warmth. I closed my eyes.

About two hours later, I finally crawled into bed and settled in against Charles's side. His soft, regular breathing lulled me into sleep.

Then I was on a beach, gazing at the clouds.

Suddenly, a wave crashed over me, and my reverie was broken. The sheets were soaking wet. I was disoriented, and then I realized what had happened.

"Charles!" I shook him. "My water broke!"

"Are you sure you didn't pee?" he asked groggily, turning over on his side.

"Charles, my water broke! I have to call Dr. Clare."

"Okay. I'm up. Calm down, though. She'll probably tell you to go back to sleep."

"I don't think so. When your water breaks, I think you have to go to the hospital."

Dr. Clare did tell me that we needed to go to the hospital. I called my friend Shelly, and I called my parents. Shelly lived nearby and had agreed that if I went into labor during the night, she would come over and stay with Elli until she awoke and then take her back to her house. My parents would then come from New York, pick Elli up, and bring her home.

We arrived at the hospital at five thirty in the morning. My labor was long and became loud. By the time I asked for something for the pain, I was told it was too late.

"I don't want to do this. Forget it. I just want to go home," I screamed.

"It's too late now," Dr. Clare said; then she told me to push. Samuel Ian was born at seven o'clock in the evening on July 17, 1991. He was six and a half weeks early. He had no fat on him, but he looked exactly like Charles.

Still on the delivery table, I have a vague memory of Dr. Clare saying something about an episiotomy, and then of her looking at Charles and adding, "This time, we do it my way."

Labor was hard, but the high I felt after Sam was born was unbelievable. My body was without form, ethereal; I was clearheaded, full of energy and joy, and so in love with my beautiful baby boy.

Because Sam came early, he had to spend some time in the NICU. We stayed with him for a number of hours, and then, around midnight, Charles left, and I went back to my room. I called Allyson, and I called Gail. My parents brought Elli to the hospital later in the day to meet her brother. I felt complete with my husband, my children, and my parents all there. The night before I was discharged with Sam, Charles and I had the hospital's new-parent champagne dinner as our son slept in his bassinet beside us.

"To everything wonderful that lies ahead," Charles toasted. "*L'chaim.* To life." I touched his glass with mine. "To love," he added.

AFTER that, life was loud. Our two-bedroom cottage was crowded. Elli enjoyed being a big sister to her little brother for the first several weeks. Then she decided she'd had enough.

"When can we send him back, Mommy, and get a sister instead?" she asked over breakfast one morning. "He cries too much. Can I watch *The Little Mermaid?*"

"Sure, let's put it on, and it'll get easier, sweetie," I told her, thinking, *It had better get easier*. The first week, Sam slept most of the time and I got into the rhythm of nursing, and all seemed well, but then he started screaming whenever he wasn't nursing. He had gas and diarrhea and projectile-vomiting. Whereas with Elli I had felt like the perfect mother, now I felt totally incompetent. At night, I would nurse Sam and then Charles would hold him on his stomach, gently stroking Sam's back, and I would drift off for a short while, until the screaming started, and Sam needed to nurse again—the only thing that would really soothe him.

The pediatrician said it was just colic. This was more than colic. It took three months to discover that Sam had a milk protein allergy and that the most minuscule amount of whey in my diet would set off a horrible allergic reaction in him. Once that was discovered, life did get better—in some ways.

Living in a tiny house with two small children was tight. We needed more room. Charles was not pleased that I couldn't easily increase the number of hours I worked. My parents came often and helped a lot. Charles appreciated that. Charles's parents visited, too, but he was adamant that he did not want to leave Elli and Sam with them. "My mother is too dense and flighty. I don't trust her with our children."

I felt sad about that. Marcy wasn't a bad person, but, over the years, Charles's disdain for her had colored my perceptions of her. And then there was the evening when we left Elli with his parents for just a couple of hours while they were visiting.

Elli was about eighteen months old and liked to have her bath before bed. I told Marcy, "I wrote out the instructions for how to turn on the hot water in the tub. It's an old house, and the plumbing is kind of quirky, so you have to turn on the cold water first and then slowly turn on the hot water. You have to test it because it can suddenly shoot out scalding water. I never put Elli in the tub until the water is already in and the right temperature, because she could get burned."

"Oh, don't worry, I've given plenty of baths before."

"I know you know how to give a baby a bath, but this plumbing is old and unpredictable, so we really are careful with it. Just make sure you follow these directions, and there won't be a problem."

Needless to say, when we returned home, Elli was still up cuddled on the sofa, thumb in her mouth, holding her blankie and cuddling Ak, her favorite stuffed dog. She was no longer crying, but a big patch of bright red covered her leg and thigh—she had gotten scalded in the tub.

"I had no idea that the water would become so hot all of a sudden." Marcy was truly oblivious. Albert rolled his eyes at her and silently walked into the kitchen.

The burn was not that serious, but . . .

"This is what I mean," Charles uttered through gritted teeth later when we were alone in our bedroom. "She doesn't pay attention to anything. Never again!" And that was the first and last time Marcy and Albert were left alone with the children.

It would be quite a while before I allowed myself to see Charles's criticalness and need for control. His need to treat me with denigration and contempt increased once we had children. However subtle they might have been, he always delivered his blows with the deft strokes of a surgeon's scalpel. Once Charles was no longer the sole centrifugal force from which I moved outward, once I was a mother, I could no longer be good, because for Charles, "mother" equaled "bad."

"I can't be around her for more than an hour, and then I get a headache; I feel sick," he told anyone and everyone about Marcy. He saw her as weak and pathetic, vulnerable. These were things I saw and ignored from the very beginning, but there was a turning point when it got worse. There was a point when I *became* Marcy.

# Chapter Ten

Relationships evolve; they have a life cycle. Sometimes they grow and mature. Sometimes they have an early death. Charles's and my days of belly laughs and flowers became only occasional punctuation marks in the litany of our lives.

My parents had been married for fifty years. At first, Charles and I thought of having a party for them, as his parents had made for themselves. We decided, though, that my parents would appreciate something other than a party, so we decided on giving them a trip.

We walked into a Park Slope restaurant to meet them for dinner one night with Elli, who was a head-turner, even at four. The blue trim on her white dress, and her white straw hat with a blue ribbon, perfectly matched the color of her eyes. Charles carried Sammy, then six months old, to the table, where my parents were already seated. They were a handsome couple. My mother, at seventy-two, still had dark hair and was a stylish and beautiful woman who looked much younger than her age. My father, although a bit heavier than in his youth, still had the broad smile and quiet openness that drew others to him, no matter what their age.

Two dozen yellow roses were in the center of the table. Back then, Charles still never forgot the flowers. The waiter poured Dom Pérignon. Charles made the toast.

"To Marty and Rita, Mom and Dad, Grandma and Poppy, we love you today, tomorrow, and for eternity."

"I'll give the presents. Then you guess why you got them, okay?" Elli's words spilled out like Cheerios from the box that I had placed in front of Sammy. I put three small boxes and an envelope in front of Elli, each wrapped in glossy white paper and topped with colorful, curled ribbon. Elli pushed the first small, square box in front of my mother. "You open this one, Grandma, but it's for you, too, Poppy."

"You guys are too much. This is so exciting." The sound of my mother's giggles mixed with the crunching sound of the wrapping paper as she took the small, finely crafted, miniature ceramic Cotswold cottage from the box.

"This one is from Sammy. Right, bro?" Elli reached over and made a raspberry sound in her brother's face, and they both started laughing. "You open this one, Poppy." He pulled a small metal 747 jetliner from the box he had carefully unwrapped.

"Wow, guy, you already know about planes. We're going to have so much fun together when you get bigger." Sammy continued to giggle.

The next box held an old map. CITY OF MANCHESTER, 1920 was printed across the top.

"That's the year I was born, and that's where I was born." As my mother began to speak, that dry, hacking cough interrupted her words.

"Where are the Halls, Grandma? I'll get you one." Elli was waiting for permission to look in Grandma's purse for the cough drops. Charles and I exchanged glances as the coughing stopped, and Elli asked if they could guess the meaning behind the presents.

"Okay, I guess we'll have to give you the final gift." With great fanfare, Elli pushed the white envelope toward my mother. "You open this, Grandma."

They looked with astonishment at the three-week travel itinerary to England that fell from the envelope, along with photos of the cottage in the Cotswold's and of the hotels we had booked for them in London and in Manchester, the city where my mother was born and had not been back to in over fifty years.

*Will Charles and I be together for fifty years? Why would I wonder that?* I thought, as I looked at the blond curls surrounding my four-year-old's cherubic face and the dark curls atop her baby brother's head.

As was often the case, out of nowhere, Charles began to talk to my parents about moving to Maryland.

"The next time we visit after this wonderful trip, I promise we'll look around at places," my mom said, deftly steering the conversation in another direction. I knew that my mother did not want to leave New York.

As this subject began to come up more and more frequently, I wondered, *Does Charles want them to move to be more available for childcare?* I knew he wanted me to be working more, even though my part-time practice was bringing in decent money. He was terribly upset about the new houses that were infringing upon our isolated paradise, and when Charles became anxious, his obsessing about money, or at least about my spending, became worse.

We really did need more space, and we thought about moving, but Charles wanted to add on to our small cottage, rather than relocate. We worked with an architect, but since Charles was also an architect, the modest addition that we had planned began to grow in scope. Charles designed a huge and separate suite as an enticement for my parents to come and live with us. The design was fabulous; it was hard for me not to be drawn in by both his enthusiasm and his talent. One night we stood under a cloak of black sky, in our own cocoon of silence, as Charles measured the distance from our position in the field to the point where he wanted to place the circular window. There was something magical about that moment: the two of us, ensconced in the blackness of night, covered by a canopy of twinkling lights, the air a soft kiss of paradise.

Shortly after my parents returned from their trip, my mother began to complain of being tired. Her cough, which had by then persisted for several years, worsened. It was even hard for her oncologist to ignore. He had minimized and scoffed at our concern previously, seemingly because he was so pleased with himself for having saved her from breast cancer twenty years earlier.

"That narcissist." Charles shook his head when he spoke of the doctor. I had to agree—but Charles also had a way of giving everyone a diagnosis, as well as little self-awareness when he made accusations about others. These characteristics in Charles, which I saw only subliminally at the time, would become impossible to ignore as our life went on.

Now my mother was having headaches and nausea, and at times she wasn't sure where she was. Lying in a bed in New York Hospital, awaiting a final diagnosis, she whispered to me, "I don't know why they're all wearing white; I can't tell who the bride is." The rare lung cancer that she had had metastasized to her brain and throughout her body. My mother was gone, her words and smiles hidden behind an impenetrable mask. I so wanted to tear through it, but, even if I had been able to, she really was lost to me.

Charles still wanted them to move to Maryland, but my mother would not even consider it now. She was dying. She did not want to leave her home. She did not want to leave New York. My father would have loved to come, but he knew that was not what my mother wanted.

When I first got together with Charles, a colleague said to my friend Allyson upon hearing that we were dating, "He is so controlling." It was only later, when the blinders had been ripped off, that Allyson told me about this comment. For years, I needed to see it and not see it at the same time. I think it was then, though, for the first time in our relationship, that Charles and I started to argue, to fight. He became so insistent about my parents' moving that he would badger me about it all the time, until I would scream, "Stop it! You can't make someone do what they don't want to do." He had a hard time letting it go. Although the fights were only occasional at first and there were still good times mixed in, Charles always had to be right. He knew the truth, and he couldn't stop harping on it, no matter what the issue.

"You'd get your reports written much more quickly if you dictated them," he'd say.

"I know, but it doesn't work for me. I need to see and feel what I'm writing, it's just the way I process information and organize my thoughts. Thanks for the suggestion, though; I guess I could try it again." Sometimes I might, sometimes not. But he wouldn't give up on even something so simple; he would belabor the same points over and over again. I'd leave the room; he'd follow. Over time, it got worse and worse.

Charles had great ideas about what to do with the kids, but he did less and less with them. That was confusing because he acted as if he were involved, which in some way left me believing he was involved, too. Looking back, I know he was involved only from his armchair.

"I'm going to do art with Elli," he would say. He did nothing. She and I built a dollhouse, including the furniture. He was an architect, but he didn't do anything. He would go to Sam and Elli's games, soccer and softball, and be terribly critical of the coaches, but never did he offer to coach or even practice with the kids, who were both very good athletes.

---

THE plans for our house addition continued, and our excitement about it grew. Then the neighbors from the development started harassing us, believing that we were running a psychiatric clinic on our property. We were not and were completely within code to have a medical office as part of our home. The developer wanted our property because one of his lots was landlocked and accessible only through our land. He began stirring up trouble so that we would sell.

Then the numbers for the renovation came in. The cost was astronomical.

Charles was furious with the architect when he saw the budget. "We can't afford this. How could Les have gotten us into this mess?"

"Charles, it's not really Les's fault. We kept adding things on and making it grander and grander. We can cut it back. I'm disappointed, too, but we don't have to do all this."

"We sure are going to take our time paying him."

Charles never took any responsibility for things not going right. I was seeing that more and more.

"Charles, we can cut back on the project," I kept repeating, to no avail. But Charles was now furious not only about the development but also about the architect and the entire project.

After a lot of discussion, we decided to look around and see what houses were available, though we were disappointed about the prospect of giving up on the fantasy of our dream house and we knew that finding something to match it would be difficult.

Tim, our realtor, and I started looking at houses, and as we drove through the valley, in an area much closer to town, I saw a home on St. John's Lane that I fell in love with. The winding road and huge trees made it feel very much like a country property. The house had been built in 1753 and expanded, and now it was a lovely five-bedroom home with four working fireplaces and random-width pine floors. It was close to the road, because in 1753 the road had been a wagon trail. The floors slanted slightly, and the ceilings in the original part of the house were low; it had the kind of old-world charm that was immediately comforting and warm. Charles liked the house, too, and, after some negotiating on the price and finding new office space, we moved to St. John's Lane in July 1993.

That New Year's Eve, we received a telephone call. My father had had a heart attack and was in the hospital. By this time, my mother was terminal; two of her cousins were staying with her. On New Year's Day, I drove to New York, saw my father and his doctors, and then brought my mother back to Maryland. Charles was wonderful. He went up to New York and, with some relatives, took apart my parents' home, made all of the arrangements, and a week later brought my father back to our house in Maryland.

The temperature was frigid and the ground icy when my mother died on February 12, 1994. Elli had just had her sixth birthday, and Sammy was two-and-a-half years old. After the funeral, I had the urge to call her up and tell her all about it—who was there, what they said—and giggle, as we always had.

# Part Two
# August 1998–July 1999

## Chapter Eleven

The flock of birds was headed south.

"Momma, look—that little one, he's so far behind the others."

I pulled onto the shoulder of the country road so we could watch the drama unfolding in the sky.

"He's really trying to catch up, Momma. Is he going to be left behind?"

"I don't think so, Sammy."

"What if a hawk or a turkey vulture gets him?"

"His momma will make sure he's safe."

The sweet and subtle shifts in the August light always seduced me toward September's softness. Always. Not memories, just sensations: the cool afternoon breeze, the clear blue sky tinged with just a bit of northern gray, sounds becoming a bit more muted. Only now, years later, comes the realization that the gentleness is followed by a pervasive sense of dread.

We sat quietly, looking up into the pale blue afternoon sky, watching the lone bird working hard to reach the flock a long distance ahead. We just sat there and listened to the silence. We felt the cool, wistful breeze coming through the windows.

"Momma, look—I think he's catching up to them!"

"Wow, I think he is, too. He sure is fast. Amazing, isn't it?"

"Momma, that's the kind of thing that makes me want to cry happy tears."

"Me, too, Sammy. We should remember that little bird, okay?"

I was glad that Sam would have memories that brought happy tears.

I hoped Elli would, too.

# Chapter Twelve

I didn't want to be making this long drive into Washington. In truth, I wasn't that worried about the hardened area I felt on my breast. Hadn't I had a mammogram and ultrasound six months earlier; hadn't I seen the best breast surgeon in Baltimore because I'd thought I felt something? No, she wasn't concerned—nothing was there! However, I was semi-aware that, in what seemed like the previous day or two, my nipple had retracted. It was hard to keep it in the recesses of my mind, but I did—I always did. My façade of strength and invulnerability were second nature to me. I laughed to myself as I reflected on how most people saw me as someone who could handle anything.

Charles certainly thought that about me.

Dr. Sager was a big, bearish kind of man, with a full beard. He was intelligent and yet warm and willing to talk to me as an equal. It was nice to see him again. But I can't forget the look on his face when he started to do the breast exam and saw the retracted nipple. As I looked into his eyes, I could tell that there was no doubt, no question in his mind. Any doubt I had vanished when he spoke.

"Diane, you need to have a mammogram today. We could do it here, but I'd rather you had it done where they have your previous films. I'll call them and arrange for them to see you this afternoon."

My head was spinning, not quite attached to my body. The nurse chatted idly when he left the room. I didn't even notice that I had never taken my feet out of the cold metal stirrups at the end of the table.

"Diane, they can see you this afternoon, but they can't find your films. Do you have them at home?" Dr. Sager's voice came through a crack in the door.

"Damn. I guess I must. I can pick them up on the way there."

Once in my car, I called to let them know that I would be late and that I had to go home to get the films.

"Just get here by three," the receptionist said, clearly wanting to be helpful. "Dr. Braken is leaving early today because of Yom Kippur."

I said I was sure I could make it. After that, I called Charles. I have no memory of what he said, but I know he didn't offer to cancel patients or to be there with me. I think I was too numb, or dumb, to notice or even to ask. As with everything, I could do it on my own.

I don't remember the drive back to Baltimore. I must have been in a daze. I know I went home and got the films and got to the radiologist's office before three. I was escorted immediately to the dressing area. I was given one of those damn official blue plastic-paper gowns. I hated that thing. They must have taken twenty to thirty films—contorted positions, pain. I had become an expert at making myself oblivious to discomfort. After each set of films, they sent me back into the dressing room. At least there was a wide range of magazines to distract me. I never even thought to call Charles as I sat there; I suppose I already knew that, despite being a physician, he was not particularly supportive in medical situations.

Finally, Dr. Braken was ready to see me. I could tell when she walked in that she was shaken. We knew each other. She had done my first ultrasound when I was pregnant with Sammy, with the quads. Moreover, I knew she identified with me. We were about the same age; Elli and her son were in the same fifth-grade class; Sammy was in the same first-grade class with her younger son; we belonged to the same synagogue.

"Diane, I want to do a needle biopsy. We don't have to do it today, but since you're here and it won't take long, I think it's best done now."

It was an offer I could not refuse, as much as I wished to. The procedure was short, and Dr. Braken made casual conversation.

"You know, Diane, breast reconstruction is really great nowadays." Upon hearing those words, I knew it was bad.

She quickly caught herself and added, "Let's not put the cart before the horse."

But we both knew.

"It's Tuesday, and I expect to have the results on Thursday morning," she said. "I'll call you as soon as they come in."

By the time I left her office, it was close to four-thirty. The sky was streaked with pink; the streets already had the hush that falls as a holiday approaches. Within me, hollowness resonated in that quiet silence, a cavernous sense of emptiness and aloneness.

On the way to pick up Elli and Sam, I called my analyst, Dr. Putman. Up until then, I had been pretty stoic, but as soon as I heard her voice, the gentle presence of it, the floodgates opened, and I could no longer hold back my sobs. When I could finally catch my breath, I gasped, "If it turns out positive, and I know it will, if you tell me you think psychoanalysis will be too intense for me, it will be a death sentence for sure."

We chatted for a few minutes more and then hung up. I blew my nose, fixed my makeup, and, feeling sufficiently composed, started up the long stone stairs and entered the school, the together mom, to pick up her children.

The halls were quiet as I made my way up to the gym. There was so much life on the walls of the building. Life. My kids loved this place, and so did I.

"Momma, where have you been?" Sammy yelled, as he saw me approach the entryway to the gym. He jumped up from the floor, where he and two other boys were sitting, working on a Lego project, ran full speed toward me, and threw his arms around me. Being enveloped in his hugs was a delicious respite.

"Let's get Elli so we can head home. Do you know where she is?" I looked around and didn't see her anywhere.

"She's in the art room with Ally and Ezra. I'll get her." He was out the door before I could say a word. That was Sammy.

As I began to collect backpacks, sneakers, and sweatshirts, Sammy and Elli appeared.

"Mom, why'd we have to go to Extended Day today?" Elli asked as soon as she saw me.

I paused for just a second. "Oh, it was just one of those days that was filled with all kinds of adventures." I winked at her as I spoke.

"Oh, you and your adventures! What did you do?" She tilted her head, her light eyes flashing, her smile impish. She was so cute, and persistent.

"Elli, I just had some appointments that I had to keep. I didn't expect that they would take this long." It wasn't necessary to say anything to the kids just yet.

"Wait a minute—before we go, I have to show you this. Ally gave it to me. It's so funny." Elli stopped and as we all gathered around, she unzipped the front pocket of her backpack and pulled out a photo.

"This is Ally's golden retriever, Bo."

There in front of us was a picture of Bo, lying flat, front paws outstretched, a book in front of him. His eyes were downcast toward the book, as if he were reading, and over his head was draped a shawl.

"He looks like a rabbi praying!" Sammy shrieked, and we all burst out laughing.

He did indeed.

We would hang the picture on the refrigerator when we got home. Maybe Bo would watch over us. If nothing else, he would certainly keep us smiling.

---

THE sun was low when I pulled the Suburban into our driveway on St. John's Lane. Charles had just opened the door and walked out onto the porch, greeting the kids and then me as they ran, and I walked, up the flagstone path. I fell into his arms as soon as he was within reach, feeling his protective warmth, appreciating my belief that I wasn't alone. I just wanted to be where I was, with my husband and children, to feel ensconced in the safety of our home, which I loved so much.

Thursday, October 1, 1998, was unusually warm as I arrived for my session with Dr. Putman. Every fiber in my body was like a member of the militia on high alert, awaiting the results of the biopsy. As I walked down the steps to her office, I was acutely aware of everything around me. The soft breeze was uncomfortably prickly on my skin. The scent of the boxwoods that surrounded her office suddenly seemed nauseatingly like cat urine. I walked into her office, lay on the couch, and said nothing.

"Have you heard anything yet?" she asked after a long silence. Under other circumstances, she would not have spoken at all. I was glad she did. She would become the person who would bear witness to all that was to come.

A hollow-sounding emptiness echoed within my brain. "Not yet." My voice sounded distant, as if it were not a part of me. It was oddly muted, detached, and ghostly. There was more silence.

"I have no doubt"—I paused—"what it's going to be."

And then the sobs came from somewhere so deep within me that I could feel them resonating through every thin, spidery vessel in my body. I did know what the truth was, and I felt that there was absolutely nothing that could be said. Dr. Putman's just being there was more important than I could even have realized at that moment.

I spent the session aching, feeling unbearable pain for myself, for Charles, and mostly for Elli and Sam. "They're just too young to lose their mother; ten- and seven-year-olds should not be without a mother. I'm not ready to leave them." Every word caught in my throat. At that moment, I was so overwhelmed with fear, there was no room for other possible outcomes. And when it was time to leave, it was hard to get up from the couch. After pulling myself together, I laughingly refused to go. But I did, and as I left, I already knew. I drove to my office, where the flashing light on my answering machine indicated that I had one message.

"Diane, this is Dr. Braken. I have the results. Give me a call and tell the secretary to put you right through."

I took a breath and made the call.

She got on immediately. Her voice was soft, calm, and practiced. "Diane, it's cancer. Can you come in so we can talk about it?"

I canceled the rest of my workday and went to her office. The only thing I remember about the drive is the sensation of my toes tapping on the tops of my sandals. The streets of my life were passing before me. Other than that, I felt nothing.

I must have called Charles—Thursday was his day in Washington— but I have no memory of my conversation with him.

Dr. Braken and I spoke for quite a while. She was kind and supportive. I was calm, because I was in shock, and heard only bits and pieces of what she said.

"Diane, the first thing you're going to need to do is to meet with a surgeon. I would suggest you meet with at least three. I'll give you some names of both men and women, and you can see whom you're most comfortable with," she continued.

I sat looking out of the window, lost in the white, fluffy cloud patterns in the sky. A flock of birds, in perfect formation, was flying to warmth and comfort for the coming winter. I had to force myself to focus on the conversation. I knew that I didn't want to quite be there, completely in the room. I finally found my voice and said, "Okay, but I don't think it matters. I think it's more important who the person is."

"You know that you'll have to have a lot of tests and scans before surgery, and it won't be until after the surgery that recommendations for treatment will be made," she said, continuing to give me a lot of information. She talked about pathology reports and genetic testing. All words.

I left the office, got in the elevator, and walked from the dimly lit lobby of the building out into the sunlight. The shift in light made my eyes water. The burning sensation was intense, and I had the overwhelming feeling I couldn't see at all. Maybe my mascara or eyeliner had gotten into my eyes, or maybe I was going blind.

## Chapter Thirteen

Needle pricks and probes, tests and scans— that was my life for the next few weeks. My father and friends accompanied me to some of those appointments; others, I went to on my own. My schedule was so full, there were so many things to do and places to be, that I had little time even to think about cancer. Charles didn't accompany me for any of the appointments, but at the time it seemed to be okay. This had always been the way of our relationship. His practice always had priority. I accepted that. I think that at that point, most of my friends who were married to physicians had probably had similar experiences.

Charles did come with me to all of the doctor consultations, and that felt important. At those moments, when I stopped and thought about the diagnosis, I felt blessed that he was there for me. I recall walking out of one doctor's appointment and starting to cry as I thought of what lay ahead.

"Don't worry, we're in this together," Charles said, as I leaned against his chest and wept, feeling the safety of his embrace, believing his words implicitly—or perhaps believing them automatically, without thought.

Charles and I spoke about which surgeon to use, we agreed, and I decided to go with Dr. Carlton, because I liked her best and no one had said anything different than she had said. The impression was that it was a two-to-three-centimeter mass. The initial surgery was a lumpectomy with reconstruction on the other side to "even me out."

Charles came with me to the initial surgery but disappeared into the hospital library, so when the doctor came out to tell him how it had gone, he was nowhere to be found.

"I told them where I would be," he said incredulously.

Friends and neighbors were bringing dinners and arranging meal trains. I was in awe of how many people reached out with love and support. I mentioned this to Charles one night, how good and kind people were.

"Don't think it has anything to do with you. Cancer makes people nervous. That's why they're calling and reaching out— they're just anxious. It really has nothing to do with you . . . just say the word *cancer*, and people get scared."

I know that I heard him. I have never forgotten his words. Yet the moment passed, and I said nothing.

As it turned out, the lumpectomy was not adequate. Dr. Carlton called Charles before calling me. I felt okay with that. Unlike with other things in my life, I was feeling okay with being dependent. I didn't want to be in charge. At that moment in time, I wanted someone to take care of me.

"The margins were not clean," Dr. Carlton said, meaning that cancerous cells still existed in the remaining tissue. "We need to do a mastectomy."

The second surgery, two weeks later, was scheduled for noon. That morning I baked brownies and cookies and prepared dinner for that evening, I would return home the next morning. As I look back, I was acting as if I were going in simply to have a wart removed. My dad drove me to the hospital, and my friend Peg was to pick me up the next morning. I was pretty irritable with my dad. It was only much later that it became clear to me why I found his wanting to be there for me so difficult for me to tolerate: I wanted and needed my husband.

I arrived at the Women's Surgical Center and was surprised to find it a wonderfully nurturing experience.

"Here's a gown and a robe and some slippers, hon. I'll be right back after you change," Tina, a fifty-something nurse with soft eyes and a gentle voice, assured me. When she returned a few minutes later, she handed me a heated blanket.

"You may want to wrap this around yourself; it can get awfully chilly in here," she said, as she draped the blanket over my shoulders. At that moment, I had no idea what symbol of comfort a heated blanket, and those who offered it, would become over the course of the next year.

Tina was at my side for the entire procedure, and I felt nurtured and held in the womb of maternal comfort. The entire team was women, and it was as if I were being cradled and lulled. When I was rolled into the operating room, the resident gently stroked my arm, while one of the nurses rubbed my neck. A second heated blanket was placed over me to remove the OR's ever-present chill. The experience, as it was, made Charles's going to work that day, and his saying he'd be there by the time I was in recovery, less noticeable.

Charles did speak with Dr. Carlton after the surgery. I don't know what was said. I know only that Elli was there and that whatever she heard terrified her. She ran from the waiting room screaming, and it took hours for my father and then Charles to comfort her. I imagined it had to do with my prognosis. When I returned home, she was remote and distant. Thinking about this now both enrages me and leaves me feeling limp with helplessness.

Both surgeries were without complications, and I was up and about within days. I returned from the first surgery to find that friends had planted flowers in front of the house. Dinners were delivered by friends and by people we hardly knew. The world was a place where I really wanted to be. I felt intense gratitude for my husband and children, and intense fear that I would lose them all. About ten days after the mastectomy, I had to go and get the drains and sutures out, as well as hear the final pathology report. When my mother had had breast cancer thirty years earlier, she'd had three nodes and lived another twenty-five years in good health. So I prepared myself for some lymph node involvement—two, maybe three—and maybe a three-centimeter mass. Charles and I both went to work that morning, and my friend Liza, who was there at every step, took me to my appointment that afternoon.

I was becoming even more aware that Charles would never think of canceling patients for me. He was so unlike my father, who adored my mother. My father would have done anything for her. She was his priority. I knew that was not the case in my marriage. Charles liked that I could manage on my own. It would have been so nice to have someone to lean on. More and more, I could see it would not be that way. Did that mean he didn't love me? I wanted to think not, but those thoughts were harder and harder to push away. I could manage these things on my own. It was all so confusing.

"Thank you so much for being so good to Di," Charles said, as he took Liza's hand and squeezed. He appeared so genuine that the fact that he wasn't going with me seemed less odd.

We didn't have long to wait before Dr. Carlton called me in. "Isn't your husband here?" she asked, surprise in her voice and her eyes. Physicians usually paid more attention to a spouse's illness, if only to show that they understood what was going on.

After a brief silence, she went on: "Diane, it's not good. The mass was much bigger than we thought. It was over six centimeters, and you had ten positive nodes."

"How?" I gasped. "Six months ago, there was nothing there; the mammogram now didn't even show anything!" I couldn't hold back the tears, and she hugged me until they abated.

When I walked back to the waiting room, where Liza waited for me, I couldn't speak, but it was written all over my face. My thoughts drifted to my mother. Finally, I had outdone her, and it wasn't fair!

Liza drove me home in silence. There was nothing to say. I felt as if I had indeed been handed a death sentence. She dropped me off at the end of the drive. I unlocked the door of our two-hundred-year-old farmhouse, walked into what we called the music room, looked at the old family photos lining the mantel, and began to weep. It was then that I called Charles. When he came home, he held me and cried with me.

There wasn't much of a time lapse between each step. Once I got the results of the pathology report, it was essential that I start treatment as soon as I recovered from surgery.

Charles and I went together to meet the four oncologists I considered using for treatment. The recommendations were the same from all of them: surgery, eight rounds of chemotherapy, high-dose chemotherapy with a rescue stem cell transplant, and then thirty daily radiation treatments.

Treatment would take about a year. The decisions had to be made so quickly. I did think Charles was there for me, but then one evening shortly after the mastectomy, when he had returned home from work at his usual eight or nine o'clock, I started to talk to him, wanting to feel his strength, wanting the connection, the closeness. I was telling him something about wanting to find the preciousness in each day. He looked up from his plate and newspaper and with cold detachment said, "Is this cancer thing all we're going to talk about for the next year?

How about before you start talking, ask if I want to talk about it?"

I wanted him so much, I needed him so much, that I ignored so much. And after that comment, I didn't talk about my illness with Charles.

---

THE sun peeked briefly through the clouds one fall Sunday afternoon shortly after the surgeries. We took the children to the park, where they could ride their bikes and look for tadpoles at the water's edge.

Charles and I sat on a bench. It was quiet, and there was a slight chill in the air. I reached for his hand. The muscle in his cheek twitched.

"You seem so tense." I touched his hand.

He flinched. "I'm angry; I don't have time for this, and I can't do any more than I'm doing."

I withdrew. I hadn't done this on purpose. Confused loyalty left me swimming upstream. Alone.

## Chapter Fourteen

My grandfather was a dapper little Englishman and I adored him. He died when I was sixteen, but his presence has always remained with me. Several years after his death, I began to have a recurring dream. The first time I had the dream was after I had broken up with my first true love; I was twenty and devastated. In the dream, I sat in a darkened movie theater. On the large screen in front of me, as the credits began to roll, my grandfather's smiling face appeared. Then, just as quickly, before his image faded, he nodded his head and winked at me. The screen became blank, and I knew that he was telling me everything would be okay. The image was so simple and yet so powerful.

I had that same dream the night Dr. Braken said to me, "Diane, it's cancer."

For a long time, I told myself that the year before my diagnosis, things in my marriage were getting better. That year, Charles and I had more sex and moments of that old laughter.

But when I look back now and read my journal entries from that time, there is no doubt that things weren't getting better at all. Charles was more openly cruel, provocative, and sadistic toward me than ever before. By the time I got my cancer diagnosis in September 1998, my internal footing in the world was already terribly shaken.

Early in 1997, I was more in touch with my withdrawal and depression than I had ever been. I not only felt like a lunatic, unable to control my rage at Charles, but also felt wounded and filled with shame—shame and humiliation about the rage, exposed and shamed about my failure as a wife. That was when I started analysis with Dr. Putman and when I finally began to remove my blinders and touch with tentative fingers the depression that had been there for years. That was when I wanted something different with Charles, when I took those first, faltering steps toward knowing who I was—knowing myself. That was my first step toward saying, *I am me. I am separate.*

It was a while before I even told Charles that I had started analysis. I saw Dr. Putman four times a week, at a very discounted rate, so it was as if I were paying for only one weekly session. I didn't tell Charles because I knew he would disapprove. He would complain about the cost, even though it was drastically reduced and was a full business tax deduction. On the surface, money was always the issue. It did not matter how much money we made. Even before children, even though we did not have an extravagant lifestyle, according to Charles, we were always on the brink of "financial disaster," and he could always rationalize the "whys" of it. Beneath the surface, I believe, Charles's disapproval was really his need to be in total control of me. In his eyes, for me to be in analysis would mean that I would be moving away from him, and that was unacceptable.

As I told Dr. Putman about the rages, the loss of control, with frozen watchfulness I awaited her disapproval. It did not come. For the first few months of my analysis, the rages continued, even escalated. She was my witness, and I gradually began to bare my soul and share my shame.

"On Saturday, I found a beautiful bisque wall hanging at Great Finds and Designs. It was lovely, something my mother would have liked, and it was only thirty-five dollars, so I bought it," I told her. "That evening, I hung it in the dining room and asked Charles to come and take a look at it. He came in, and of course he didn't like where I had hung it. As usual, he suggested that I hang it on the opposite wall. He always does this. It's like he has to have things a different way, just for the sake of getting his way. But I did it and then called him back in. He came back into the dining room and said nothing, just looked disapprovingly at it and began to adjust how it was positioned on the wall. As soon as his fingers touched the corner, it came crashing to the floor." I paused.

"What happened next?" Dr. Putman asked.

"I just stood there; I didn't have a chance to say anything, because the first words out of his mouth were, 'If only you'd hung it properly, that wouldn't have happened.' There was no 'I'm sorry' or 'Oh, I know how much you liked that.' Nothing but telling me that it was my fault that it lay smashed in pieces, the pale colors shattered across the dark pine floorboards. That's what made me angry. I screamed, 'Damn you! You fuckin' bastard!' and I flung my arm out and it hit one of the dining room chairs. It went flying, and its back cracked in half as it hit the floor. Once again, I was the lunatic." I laughed as I told the story, but not because it was funny.

"You're very attuned to Charles's anger, aren't you?" Dr. Putman asked, after a long silence.

I wondered about that, and my thoughts drifted to how Charles's concern with money was becoming worse. Now when he fantasized about how we might escape financial ruin, he didn't talk of winning the lottery; he spoke of a "fiery crash on 95." The first time he brought it up, we were sitting in the family room.

"I suppose, more and more, I do see how much rage Charles has." I paused. I always felt a tinge of betrayal when I spoke of Charles.

"I don't think I told you about the 'fiery crash on 95,'" I continued. She was silent. "The first time he said it, I had no idea what he was talking about, so I asked him what he meant. He had this strange, sheepish smile but very casually said, 'Well, if my parents got into a fiery crash when they were coming to visit us, then we'd get my inheritance sooner, rather than later, and we'd have no more worries.'"

"He says it all the time now. It's become just words; I'm anesthetized."

As I shared that with Dr. Putman, part of me wondered what she was thinking. Did she stiffen and become numb inside, as I had when Charles had first said that to me? She remained silent.

I remember thinking at the time, although I didn't say it to Dr. Putman just then, *Isn't saying something so angry and aggressive kind of implicitly abusive to me, too?*

I pushed that thought far away, and in the gentle silence that followed, I felt no judgment from her. As I looked upward, I noticed Dr. Putman's gray tabby cat, Pumpernickel, walking slowly, leaning against the window directly above me. My breathe caught, my chest tightened, and I began to shake, not able to stop. I bolted from the couch to the peach-colored armchair that faced Dr. Putman. I had an urgent need for a real face to face connection. I remember her handing me a blanket to wrap around my shoulders.

When I found my voice, when the shaking stopped and the tears abated, I said, " I don't know what happened -it was when I looked at Pumpernickel outside the window – there was this intense panic, terror." I just sat there. Time and space seemed to come together, unsteady and disoriented. I was glad I could look into Dr. Putman's eyes. I needed help to feel grounded at that moment.

"You were talking about Charles' anger when you saw Pumpernickel outside the window."

---

Yes, for a long time after my diagnosis, I told myself that things had been getting better that year before I had been diagnosed. I'd been trying for so long to ignore the depth of Charles's anger, but it had gotten to be too much. He was a master at provoking me. He always spoke so calmly, so rationally, but the tension between us was palpable, his contempt and denigration so clear to me. He was persistent about anything he wanted me to think or do—about things that had nothing to do with him, I felt badgered, I'd leave the room, and he'd follow me. Then I would finally explode. After I raged, he was less tense, more relaxed, almost relieved. It was if my rages were the way he got rid of his tension. My stuff became the focus, and he felt better. I saw the pattern. Once I stopped having rages, his tensions and criticalness became unrelenting. And I was left with what felt like a permanent crack in my very being.

"Perhaps you're changing, moving between less productive ways of dealing with Charles and ways that will serve you better. You have said that in some ways, you and Charles are connecting more. There's more sex?" Dr. Putman's eyes were softly serious as she spoke.

Maybe that was it. I wasn't sure, but perhaps . . . Sex and anger: not unusual bedfellows.

I suppose one of the reasons I thought things were getting better that year was that I was making changes. While my rages continued for a time, they did eventually stop, and other things within me seemed also to be changing. I started to feel better about how I was handling things:

with more dignity, without the frustrated screams. I was beginning to feel more capable and as if I had some power.

I reacted differently when Charles drew our secretary into our marital dysfunction, having her send me nasty notes about bills and finances, treating me as if I were a child. I had a Pier One charge account, which I had used only once, to buy a table I needed for my office. It cost $129. The next month, I found a note in my office mailbox from Geri, our secretary, attached to the Pier One bill. She wrote, Please sign the note I have written on the payment stub. On the payment stub, she had written, Please close this account immediately and allow no further purchases using this account number.

I was enraged! But this time, I handled it well. I met with Geri and told her she worked for me as well as for Charles and she could not tell me what to do, and that from that point forward I wanted weekly updates on all of the financial transactions that went on in the office. Charles sat silently during the meeting. He never said a word.

About that same time in my work with Dr. Putman, I got in touch with how I had withdrawn in many ways from Charles, including sexually. I was excited to share with him this recognition of my sexual withdrawal and my lack of receptivity.

After one morning session when Charles was in his DC office, I called him. "Charles, I just finished my session with Dr. Putman. If you're free for lunch, I can drive down. I want to tell you about my session."

"I'm free at noon for a couple of hours. That would be great. I'll make reservations at Sushi Ya; I'll see if I can get us the tatami room. I'm excited to hear all about it."

As we sat in our small, private space, sipping hot sake, I told him things I hadn't shared before.

"You know, for a long time I felt that you just weren't really interested in me, and I withdrew. I don't think that I've been very receptive to our having an intimate relationship. I think I've worried that you'd reject me." I looked closely into his eyes and saw softness.

With that disclosure, with my vulnerability, came renewed sexual passion, and more *genuine* connection, than we'd known in years—a sexual passion that continued until my cancer. We had a fireplace in our bedroom, and that winter we made love often, with the flames flickering, the wood crackling in the background. I can understand why I thought things were getting better.

In reality, though, Charles's contempt and denigration were no longer subtle; his sadism was no longer disguised. Those traits were crystal clear to anyone wanting to see it—anyone but me. And, as I would find out later, everyone else did see it.

I began to see that there were ways in which I had glamorized Charles's idiosyncrasies for years; I had rationalized what looked and sounded weird and crazy as being interesting and unconventional. What I did not see though was the price I was to pay for this illusion. What seemed like freedom was manipulation and control I responded with depression, withdrawal, and perhaps even cancer. While in the past I could tell myself Charles was "offbeat" now it was harder to deny - his unraveling was becoming more apparent. Friends began to say, "You've been the glue that's kept his craziness from emerging fully." Whatever the difficulties were before, after I got cancer, I became the object of Charles's demons and their wrath.

The connection I still hadn't made was that my reaction in Dr. Putnam's office to seeing Pumpernickel in the window was a visceral trigger response to the trauma of Charles having killed Mr. Buttons years earlier. It would still take time to put that all together.

## Chapter Fifteen

After my surgeries, a week before I started chemotherapy, I decided to cut my long, dark hair short. I was preparing for what was to come. Everyone thought it odd that I was doing this on purpose. I had always hated myself with short hair, but I was going to be bald. So much was out of my control. This was one choice I could make.

I had been going to Edward for years and told him why I was cutting my hair. Edward's mom had died of breast cancer eight months earlier, and it had been very hard for him. We had spoken many times over these last months about how much he missed her. He was shaken when I told him about my cancer.

"Welcome, welcome, welcome," he greeted me, as I walked in.

Maisha washed my hair, and then I sat down in Edward's chair.

"So, we're going to cut it all off, right?" he asked, looking directly at me. I noticed that all the eyes in the shop were on me.

"Yes, very short," I said. Nothing could penetrate my calm façade.

Edward smiled, combed out my long hair, and then made the first cut. I saw at least ten inches of my hair spread across the white marble floor. There was silence, and then everyone in the room began to applaud. I took a breath, I smiled, and I felt tears on my cheeks.

A week later, October 30, 1998, Allyson got a sitter for her kids and drove down to Maryland to take me to my first chemotherapy session. I was hoping I'd be up for trick-or-treating with my kids the next evening. I wasn't. Within a few hours after I got home following my first treatment, I fell asleep and slept for the next forty-eight hours straight. Charles didn't take the kids out, but at least I had made sure that friends would be ready to chaperone them, if necessary, so they did get to trick-or-treat.

Then it was late November. In the air were hints of the coming, biting cold of winter. The color of the sky was fighter plane gray. Since I had already cut my hair very short, I didn't have to deal with long clumps of it falling out in the shower. When the little bit of stubble on my head started itching, I asked Charles if he would help me shave my head, but he refused. So I did it myself, first using an electric razor, and then, when that wasn't working so well, a straight razor. I then waited for the wig I had ordered. I wore hats and scarves. I wore a bandanna around my head, much as I had in the 1970s, only then it was with long hair flowing beneath it. It didn't look quite the same this time. The children and I laughed as they teased me about how weird I looked. Elli, though, was really bothered by my appearance—I could just tell. Being a preadolescent girl watching her mother's physical appearance change so dramatically was very hard for her—harder still because there was no second parent for either Elli or Sam to lean on. Charles helped with the necessary tasks, but he gave no emotional support to the kids.

That Thanksgiving marked the first time in many years that I was not making dinner. Instead, we were going to spend the day with Allyson and Harry and their girls in New Jersey. It's funny now, because in my journal I wrote about what a nice and relaxing day it was, a day that felt perfect. A year later, once scourging fires were openly ravaging my marriage—the same fires that I now know I held in my chest, that were the cancer itself—and then when I was in the depths of anxious depression, Harry noted what he remembered most from that Thanksgiving dinner. It was what Charles said, or didn't say, as we all gave thanks at the beginning of our holiday meal. The table was lushly set, the smells of turkey and whipped sweet potatoes wafting through the air. After giving a blessing as we all held hands, I suggested that we go around the table and each say something personal for which we were grateful. Allyson, Harry, and all the children, giggling, said something.

"I'm grateful my mom's wig will be here soon." Elli laughed and got up and hugged me.

"I'm grateful that we're all together for Thanksgiving," Sammy said. "I love it here, especially Uncle Harry's pool table." Then he added softly, "I just want my mom to be okay."

When it was my turn, I spoke of my gratefulness for Charles, Elli, Sammy, my dad, and my devoted friends. I spoke of the preciousness of everything I had in my life.

Then it was Charles's turn. He dropped my hand and said, "I have nothing to say, and I have absolutely nothing to be thankful for."

Funny thing was, I didn't remember any of this at all until Harry pointed it out a year later. What had astounded Harry, more than anything else, was that our children were sitting there, and Charles could not even acknowledge his thankfulness for them.

Charles had promised to go with me to my chemotherapy appointment, at the beginning of December. When he hadn't arrived at the house to pick me up, I called the office. Geri, our secretary, answered.

"Di. I'm on my way over. I'll take you." She hung up before I could respond and was at the front door within fifteen minutes.

"Where's Charles?" I asked, already knowing what she was going to say.

"He scheduled patients for the whole day. I'll take you." She was clearly upset. "I can't stand watching how he treats you. It's just not right."

"Listen, Geri, I really can go by myself. I feel fine until a few hours afterward, and then I just want to sleep."

"You shouldn't have to go by yourself," she insisted, so she took me for my third chemotherapy treatment, and we laughed and drank chocolate milkshakes and then laughed some more.

Several weeks later, she gave notice, saying she had taken a new job. Charles called and pronounced, "I think she had a hard time dealing with you having cancer," never thinking that it had anything to do with how he was treating me.

---

NOT long after that, I turned fifty. I had to convince Charles that we should go out for dinner. I made a reservation at a local restaurant; my father stayed with the children. By this time, Charles never allowed for the cost of a babysitter. What was really striking, though, was that when we arrived at the restaurant and were shown to our table, there were no flowers, not even a $3.98 bouquet from the grocery store. It was my fiftieth birthday; I was going through chemotherapy for cancer, an aggressive malignancy that was in part related to the high doses of hormones I took in order for us to have a family; Charles was not present at all; and, strikingly, there were no flowers.

I didn't mention it, but our conversation over dinner was stilted.

Afterward, we walked to the car; the snow was just starting to fall.

"Charles, we used to talk so easily to each other, about everything. You don't talk to me at all anymore. I miss being close to you," I said, watching my breath fill the air as my words floated in the cold darkness of the car.

"I can't talk to you. You're too preoccupied with your illness; you don't have time to listen to me," he snapped.

I didn't think that was true at all, at least not in the way he meant it. "Maybe you're right. I really don't want it to be that way. I do want you to be able to talk to me, even now—especially now."

We drove to a local bookstore with a café and sat in the car before we went in, while snow fell quietly on the windshield.

"There's something I haven't told you," Charles said. "For the past year, I've been bartering with this woman Haley in DC for acupuncture. She gives me acupuncture, and I provide her medication."

There was a long pause. I listened silently, feeling strangely hollow inside, with only the sensation of the soft leather of the seat on my back. I vaguely recalled that he had brought up this woman two years earlier, saying that he didn't think it would be ethical to barter these services, so he wasn't going to do it.

"I've been really upset about Haley. She was in a terrible car accident. She's in the hospital in very serious condition. I don't know if she's going to make it."

At the time, I transformed into a silent and supportive psychotherapist. But later, during that sleepless night, the thoughts that kept running through my mind, over and over, were *I haven't said I don't believe him, but I think I don't believe him. I'm not even sure what I don't believe him about. I want to believe him, but I don't believe him. And it's very significant that there were no flowers at dinner!*

I did not sleep at all. The next morning, Sunday, at breakfast, after the children had left the table and were off watching television in the other room, I said calmly to Charles that it surprised me that he had been getting acupuncture for a year and hadn't told me.

Like a toxic explosion, he spewed venom: "I knew you would disapprove, you phony actress! You surprised me last night, listening as if you weren't passing judgment. I should have known!" he shouted, as he slammed down the frying pan he was washing.

The reality was, I was not feeling disapproval, not in the way he thought—disapproval of him professionally—although I certainly should have been. In fact, I wasn't feeling anything. I was numb, knowing only that he had a secret life, one that likely involved much more than just the acupuncture, and that it was a life that I was not a part of.

Charles stormed off, saying he was going to the office. I ran after him in an attempt to tell him what I had been trying to say, but he wouldn't listen; he got in the car and drove off. I called him throughout the day, but I got no response. Deep within me, I knew that the final judgment was being written.

It was becoming harder and harder to keep those blinders in place while moving through my treatment in a balanced way. I was still seeing some patients, still actively involved in every aspect of the children's lives. I could not allow myself to see what was becoming so clear; I could not avoid seeing it, either.

## Chapter Sixteen

I made up a game to help the kids deal with my illness.
The kids, especially Sam, liked to play it most evenings before bed and it became part of our nighttime ritual. It was a tossing-target game called Chemo-Shark. We would toss shark Beanie Babies at a large piece of poster board on which I had drawn circles with huge numbers written in each circle. We pretended that we were killing the cancer cells that were invading Mommy's body. We would hold the sharks in our mouths and laugh as we racked up enormous scores destroying the bodily terrorists.

"Daddy, will you play tonight?" Sam would always ask.

And every night when Charles was there, his response was the same: "Not tonight, guys. I have some work I have to get done. You go ahead and play."

"Daddy, it's important that you play. The more cancer cells we kill, the quicker Momma gets better. Come on, play with us."

"No, you guys play. I have work to do."

"It's important, Daddy!" Sammy pleaded, and then got angry with him. "You don't even want to save Mommy!"

"Come on, Sammy, let's play." Elli would say, rolling her eyes as Charles walked into the other room.

It was hard to know he couldn't be there for me, but it was even harder watching him not be there for Elli and Sam. I had said to Charles over and over that I thought we could use my illness as an opportunity to reconnect, to find the great joy we had known early in our relationship, to grow together. Charles always replied, "We'll work on our relationship when you're finished with your treatment." That was the end of it.

Although all the doctors with whom I had consulted had strongly recommended that I have a stem cell transplant, Charles adamantly did not want me to. It would mean I would be out of work for a significant amount of time and therefore not bringing in income. At the time, I wasn't consciously aware that my own heart-wrenching indecision about the transplant was based on how much Charles did not want me to do it. I would decide one thing and immediately think of the myriad reasons why that was not a good choice. I worried about the risks of the procedure itself, from which I could die; I worried about the children and being away from them and the impact it would have on them.

---

IN January, in the midst of chemotherapy, I got the flu. I awoke one morning so sick I couldn't get out of bed. I ached all over. My exhaustion was painful.

"I have patients until nine tonight, so I'll grab something for dinner in Washington before I come home," Charles called out, as he walked from the bedroom at 6:30 a.m. He never asked if I might need additional help with the kids that day. I heard his words, but they hardly penetrated the thunderous fever within my head. I could hardly open my eyes; I knew only that I couldn't get out of bed and certainly couldn't get the children off to school. I reached for the phone and called a family who lived nearby to see if they could pick up Elli and Sam and take them to school.

"Sure," Daniel said, responding to my call. "Listen, Diane, I'm going to be working at home today, so please call me if you need anything at all. I *really* want you to call if you need anything!"

*How does he know?* I wondered. And I believed him; it was such a little thing, yet there was such genuine compassion in his words— something I never heard from Charles—that I hung up the phone and could not control my tears.

Later that morning, my dad drove me to the hospital, and I was admitted. I was there for a week. I spent almost the entire time sobbing and agonizing about whether to go through with the stem cell transplant. I had to decide by my fourth chemotherapy cycle, which was fast approaching.

Charles visited a few times. One day when he brought lunch, I said, "There's a healing workshop next Monday for women dealing with life-threatening illnesses. It's open to family members, too. If I'm out of here, would you like to go with me?" I asked.

"I don't know. Maybe. I'll have to see what's on my schedule." He didn't look up from the salad he was eating. A pale-yellow bit of bean sprout was stuck on the corner of his upper lip. The sound of the crunching vegetables was particularly irritating at that moment.

"It would be nice to feel as if you cared at all about what happens to me—"

Though I spoke the words calmly, he got up before I could complete my sentence and said, "Listen, I have to get back to the office." He smacked the top of his Tupperware container closed and started to walk over to the windowsill, where he had put his jacket.

"Charles, please don't leave just yet. I really wasn't trying to start an argument. I want things to be better between us." He looked at me and sat down stiffly on the wooden ladder-back chair, adjusting the purple-and-pink floral cushion as he sat down. We talked about some inconsequential things for another, perfunctory ten minutes; then he left.

---

MY indecision about the stem cell transplant continued to be painful. Charles was clear about what he wanted me to do, as were friends who called from all over the country. Even my first husband, Bram, who now lived in Texas, tried to help me through the indecision. I spoke with people who had gone through it themselves, with people who said it wasn't so bad, but also with one woman who almost died from the procedure and then had a recurrence nine months later. I spoke with experts. I listened to a Bernie Siegel's guided-imagery tape almost continuously. His voice was soothing; his words were gentle. But in each exercise, he would speak of finding one's path and said that one would just know, when one came to the juncture, what the right path would be. As I listened to these words, I would begin to sob again, because I *didn't* know, didn't have a clue about the path that was right for me. I was trapped in a mire of indecision so thick that I felt unable to breathe.

I was discharged from the hospital on Sunday, and the healing workshop was the next day. Charles did not go with me. When an older woman in the group began to share, tears stained her face and her voice cracked as soon as she started speaking.

"My daughter is dying. She's only thirty-eight, and she has three babies under five." Her pain oozed within me like blood from an open wound. "We thought she had beaten it. They found the first lump in her breast five years ago, right after my granddaughter was born. Now it's everywhere in her body. She is going to die, and her babies will be without a mother. My baby . . ."

My own sobs were deep; I could not restrain them as she spoke. Her anguish was my anguish. When I left the group, my breath was tight in my chest. I drove to pick up my children from school, feeling dazed. The February sky was flat and lifeless. I began to climb the long stone stairway, and then clarity. It simply occurred to me, without fanfare or drumbeats, *I will do the transplant.* I knew I had made my decision. I knew the path to take. I knew that even if it ultimately made no real difference in the outcome of my disease, I wouldn't look back and say, *If only I had gone through with the transplant, if only I had done it.* Elisabeth and Sam deserved to have every possible chance of having their mother alive.

I called Charles and told him that I had made my decision. Part of me hoped he would be as relieved as I was; I couldn't fathom that he would not want what was best for me. I hoped he wanted me to be alive above all else. He didn't answer my call.

The real answer to those hopes came several nights later. Arriving home late from his DC office, Charles told me he wanted to share something with me. I could tell that it was not just going to be a casual conversation. By this time, his sharing most anything with me, amid his alternating remoteness and disdain, was unusual.

"As I was driving home just now, I passed a bad accident on the Beltway. It looked like it was fatal." Pausing, he then continued, "I began to think that if I were to die tonight, it would be okay. I wouldn't want anything extraordinary done to keep me alive. The children would be financially secure; there's plenty of life insurance; they had a good start in life. It would be okay."

I said nothing. I knew from the silence that followed that there was a message I was supposed to hear in this. At that moment, I heard that message not only subliminally but also in my heart and in the not-so-deep recesses of my mind. I knew he was telling me that I, too, should be ready to die. He was telling me that the children would be fine, and that there should be no extraordinary attempts to save my life—in other words, I should not do the transplant. My life insurance would leave the children financially secure.

How strange, how bizarre, how terrifying—this was the man I shared my life with, and he didn't think my life was that important for him or our children. Over the years, I had worked with so many people who had lost a parent to death during childhood. It had never been anything less than traumatic, no matter what the age of the child or the circumstances of the death. He didn't understand that.

At that moment, I saw it clearly. For years, I had thought and felt that much of what Charles said and did was "crazy-making." Never had I thought he was actually *crazy*. Suddenly, I knew, really knew, that his functioning had deteriorated. As much as I still longed to believe that he was "normal," I wanted a way to explain the last twenty years of my life. Nevertheless, the truth was there.

## Chapter Seventeen

Charles's obsession with financial disaster was increasing. It made no sense, but I couldn't allow myself, and didn't have the energy, to get caught up in it; my focus was on survival and my children. Against our accountant's advice, Charles insisted that we file for bankruptcy, get out of debt. If we couldn't sell the house, we should just return it to the bank, move to a rental, and have the children start in public schools. Charles had always handled all of our money on his own; I had no reason to believe that he wasn't being realistic about our financial stability. And, given my health, I had too many other things on my mind to read between the lines, so I didn't think there was anything manipulative about what he was suggesting; I just thought he was exhibiting his usual craziness. So when he told me he wanted to move by the summer, I said simply, "How can I do that? I'll be in treatment until August. I don't have what it takes to pack up this entire house, to go through such a major change while I'm going through all this."

"Get your friends to help," he said. "They're willing to do anything for you, let them pack."

He was so envious of the support I got from my friends, the extent of it so great precisely because everyone else could see how little I got from him.

Eventually, I did agree to the move. Although I was in the middle of chemotherapy, about to have a stem cell transplant, he kept telling me that we would work on our relationship as soon as treatment ended, and I so wanted to believe him—I so wanted our financial life to be stable so we could resume our life as a family. At that moment in time, I could not conceive of the end of my marriage, despite what I was already beginning to see.

One night, around the same time he began to talk about the move and bankruptcy, Charles asked me to check if he had gotten a particular e-mail. I logged in to his account and happened to see several messages from a patient whose name I recognized, Marissa. I recognized her name because she occasionally called on our shared business line at home and I had taken several of the calls. Her voice was distinctive, to say the least: deep, husky, and gruff, with something tough and aggressive about it that contrasted starkly with her ultra-feminine name. Once, after I'd taken a call from her, I had asked Charles if she looked anything like she sounded. He'd laughed and said, "Yes."

I don't know why I did it—call it intuition—but when I saw several e-mails from Marissa, I opened one. I was shocked to see a note talking about an upcoming lunch date and signed, *x-o-x, Marissa.*

It seemed a little adolescent, and certainly very troubling.

Marissa's excitement about their meeting for lunch was clearly filled with titillating energy. For several days, I said nothing to Charles about having seen the e-mails. But I was worried. Not only was he betraying me, although I didn't think it was sexual at that time, but he was involved with a patient. He was putting our family at terrible risk. I finally confronted him, and he said, "I need someone to talk to. I can't talk to you. She has a lot of the same interests I have; she's a psychic, and she's interested in astrology and UFOs."

"You *can* talk to me. And if you don't want to, at least find people who aren't your patients; if you need a therapist, get a therapist," I told him. "Having lunch with patients is putting yourself and all of us at terrible risk. Promise me you'll end this relationship with this woman, Charles," I pleaded.

Charles said nothing and walked into the other room.

At my next session with Dr. Putman, I told her about what happened, and she gave me an ethics brochure from the American Psychiatric Association. I hoped that Charles and I could discuss it rationally. I had left it somewhere on my desk, and then I went into the hospital for a weekend preliminary mobilization chemotherapy prior to my stem cell transplant.

It was late on a Friday night, and I was already asleep in my hospital room, the poisonous drugs dripping through the IV as I slept. The phone startled me awake, and when I picked it up, Charles was raging. He had somehow found the ethics brochure on my desk and was furious.

"How dare you, you bitch! You don't trust that I know what I'm doing!"

On and on he went. I sat in the bed, tears rolling down my face.

When the nurse walked in, I threw up.

I returned home on Sunday. Charles reluctantly said he would end the relationship with Marissa; he did not. Every once in a while, I would check and saw that the e-mails continued. Now, though, they just weren't signed *x-o-x*; in addition to talk of alien abductions and UFOs, astrological and psychic readings, Marissa spoke of my being evil and wrong for Charles, a malignant force in his life, and of his great gifts, compassion, brilliance. Her own psychic intuition told her that if I chose to have the stem cell transplant, Charles must disengage completely, and I must go through it alone.

It was also around this time that I had my first contact with Victoria. It was very early on a Thursday morning, not long before I was to go into the hospital for the transplant. Charles was in the shower, preparing to spend the day in his DC office, when the business line rang. Rather than letting the machine answer, as I usually did, I picked it up. It was a woman, Victoria, a patient, she said, and she wanted to know if Charles was going to be driving the truck that day because she planned on bringing him the large plants, she had promised him. I gave the message to Charles, he told me to tell her that he was driving the truck, and that was the end of it. Charles would later tell me that it was *not* Victoria who called, *not* Victoria who had given him the plants, and that I was again delusional.

Two months after I was out of the hospital after my transplant, I would see an e-mail to Charles from Victoria—one of what would turn out to be many "good-bye" letters—and it ended with *remember to bathe the plants.* Charles's response to that letter began, *My dearest soul mate . . .*

The name was indelibly imprinted in my memory; it *was* Victoria. Nevertheless, I would for a time question myself about whether I was wrong about it.

How could I have been so stupid? It was all there, for so long, and I still believed Charles and I would work on our relationship when my treatment ended—or did I? Two weeks before the transplant, I said to Dr. Putman, "The dilemma is, can I stay in this relationship, unloved, for the children and stay physically healthy?"

"Can you?" she asked.

"I don't know. Or maybe I do know but am afraid to know. He's never even met the doctors who are doing the transplant. You would think that, especially being a doctor, he would want to meet them, have questions for them, but nothing!" The intensity of my voice said it all.

During all my research about stem cell transplants for breast cancer, I discovered a seminal research study that would determine whether funding for transplants for breast cancer would continue. The hospital room was dark, the temperature chilly, as I sat on a hard mattress, atop a crisp white sheet, with a needle in my arm. Tubing ran from my arm to an IV pole holding a bag of dark red plasma cells, dripping silently into my body. All of this was in preparation for my high-dose chemotherapy and stem cell rescue, which would begin a few days later.

I drank a chocolate milkshake, an indulgence I gave in to these days, as I half listened to the news on CNN while playing Scrabble online on my laptop. I stopped when I heard the broadcaster say that the findings on this research study were in and were not positive. There was no difference in survival rates for those who had had the transplant and those who had not.

I did not waver, though, in my decision to go through with the procedure, and I never mentioned this to Charles when he picked me up after the transfusion. I was not going to change my mind. He would just use the information to badger me.

Several days before I was to be admitted to the hospital, I had to go in for the stem cells to be harvested. I had already had the surgery for a central line to replace the port through which I got my regular chemotherapy treatments. I was told it was a relatively minor procedure, that I would just be lying in a bed, hooked up to a dialysis-like machine. They would turn the machine on, and about four hours later, they would have separated out the stem cells and I would be free to go. If they were able to harvest enough cells, that would be it. Oftentimes, though, people did have to come back the next day.

Even knowing it was a minor procedure, and having been through so much already, I was scared. Charles didn't offer to go with me, nor did he say anything to me as I left the house for the hospital early in the morning. When I arrived at the unit, the nurses had a huge tray of donuts, pastries, and drinks for the three of us who were there for harvesting. The two other patients, one man and one woman, both with leukemia, were there with their spouses.

"Is anyone here with you?" the nurse asked. I could tell she had noticed I was wearing my wedding ring.

"No, only me today." I laughed and shrugged as if other days were different, but beneath the numbness and fear, I felt alone, abandoned. I knew I could do it on my own, I was capable of it, but damn it, why couldn't my husband be with me, just like these others had their partners with them?

The man in the bed on my left was there for his fourth try. He was not able to produce enough stem cells for the transplant. We laughed as I promised him that if I had any extras, he could certainly have some. In about two hours, it was clear that I had produced an enormous number of stem cells. I was free to leave. I felt as if this were an omen telling me that I would be fine, I would come through the transplant, and I would survive.

I flew down the nine flights of stairs to the hospital lobby, ran to the pay phone, and called Charles at the office across town. When he answered, I said, "Charles, you won't believe how many stem cells they got. It will be okay—I know it!"

Silence. Nothing. "Charles, are you there?"

"Listen, Di, I'm really busy right now." *Click.*

I stood frozen, stunned beyond words. Whatever elation and hope I had felt just moments before gave way to anguished paralysis. I walked, deadened, to the underground parking garage, feeling the dark, cold, damp stone reverberating with my every labored breath.

The transplant was ultimately a non-event compared with the black hole that I had imagined it would be, though that isn't to say it was easy. The first two days of my hospitalization, I received massive doses of chemotherapy, doses much higher than regularly administered, high enough to destroy all the cells within my body, high enough to kill me, leaving me with no immune system, no blood counts, whatsoever. The stem cells were to rescue me from death. On the third day, those harvested stem cells were injected back into my body with a very simple and anticlimactic syringe. The whole procedure took fifteen minutes, during which the cells had to be administered very slowly so as not to throw my body into a state of shock or, worse, death.

Charles was not there. He did visit, but I don't recall his ever asking anything about the procedures. By day two of the chemotherapy, my appetite waned; by day three, as my blood counts dropped, I had severe nausea and vomiting, and eating was no longer an option. I was started on intravenous feedings. The inside of my mouth and throat became swollen and unbearably painful. Friends brought me ice pops and puddings, hoping I could tolerate something, but I couldn't.

Once the doctors finally found the right combination of medications to help relieve my pain and nausea and vomiting, I became confused and disoriented, in a state of delirium. I didn't know what time of day it was, whether it was day or night. In my confusion, I pulled the central line out of my chest. All I recall is the fast-rolling gurney flying through a pale green tunnel and the swinging doors of the OR as they rushed me back to surgery for the line to be reinserted. I felt crazed and frenzied, I was trapped within my mind, and I could not escape.

I wrote in my journal at some point, in a very tremulous hand:

*I wake up and before me is a magnificent table of mahogany and cherry carved woods. Perhaps it is not a table. There are huge candles and hanging crystals. Perhaps it is a coffin. Perhaps my own.*

I was like that for fourteen days, and then, although a bit of nausea and vomiting remained, and though I was still terribly constipated from the drugs, which was the worst part of all, my blood counts returned to normal.

On night fifteen, my grandfather visited again in a dream.

By day eighteen with normal blood levels I was ready to be discharged. By all standards, I had come through it very quickly. It was a

Saturday, and as had become the custom, my father, not Charles, was the one who came to take me home.

After the transplant I didn't return to work. First, I would undergo a period of recovery: four more cycles of chemotherapy and then thirty radiation treatments. I planned on returning to work when the children went back to school, new schools, in September. Since I had closed my practice, I would have to rebuild it almost from scratch.

Strangely, Charles didn't want to hire help when I went into the hospital or during my recovery. He still thought my friends ought to "pitch in," do it for us. He never realized that they had lives of their own; he was always more than willing to take a handout—a characteristic I was becoming increasingly aware of. Despite his objections, we did get some at-home assistance while I was in the hospital, and Camille was wonderful. She was organized and nurturing, she loved the children, and without her, along with friends who came regularly, I couldn't have gotten our house packed for the move.

However, I still can't believe I agreed to move in the first place. Only a crazy person would have consented to such a thing. I would pack for a few hours, take a nap, and then continue to pack for a few more hours—all this while I was still in treatment and in terrible gastric distress. I hadn't shit in weeks! Again, it was never right, according to Charles. If I said I hadn't taken a nap during the day, he would complain that I wasn't taking care of myself. If I said I was particularly tired and had slept for several hours, he would complain that I wasn't doing enough for the move, that he was doing everything. The truth was that other than working, which was decreasing, he wasn't doing much besides complaining about me and what I wasn't doing. Not for another two months would I begin to suspect increasingly that he was sneaking out of the office to rendezvous with Victoria.

The spring became summer, the children were registered at new schools, and we were about to move. Around that time, when I pressed the issue about Victoria and the plants, Charles told me that the relationship with Victoria, his "soul mate," had ended; she had ended it. He still wouldn't admit that she had given him the plants that were now in our living room.

One evening before our move, coming out of the house on St John's Lane, I walked onto the porch where Charles was sitting, hiding his cell phone as I opened the door. I started to ask him how he was feeling about the end of the relationship with Victoria. I was still trying to connect with him, still beating my head against a brick wall, but all I got was stony silence, and I retreated back into the house. He began going out for a swim every night, sometimes staying out for hours. Later I would discover that he and Victoria would rendezvous at our pool, on our porch—*under the stars*, Victoria wrote—while the children and I slept just walls away.

Damn it, I needed him, and he had no clue about being there for anyone, about love or compassion. It was as if there was nothing inside him; he was just an empty shell. I had had only glimpses of this earlier in our relationship, but for the most part, I had pushed it away. Now, I couldn't push it away anymore. It had gotten too big; it had become the elephant in the room. His sense of inadequacy was so disguised that I didn't fathom how fragile he really was.

By this time, it wasn't the blinders that kept me with him. A harrowing year of surgeries and poisons flowing through my veins, blasted directly at my body, had beaten me down. I weighed less than one hundred pounds; when I looked in the mirror, I saw the body of a concentration camp inmate. It was there, at the lowest point of my vulnerability, that I began to really discover Charles's betrayals, who he was and wasn't, but I had nowhere to go, nor the energy or money to get there.

## Chapter Eighteen

It didn't matter what I knew, what I discovered; I still longed to see Charles as different than he was. I didn't want to give up all the memories of our life together. But then, suddenly, I was forced to confront the possibility that he had always been unfaithful, even early on, even when I had thought things were going well for us.

I had just gotten off the phone with Anne, Elli's former nanny. I stood there, my mind replaying the entire conversation over and over again.

"Why does it surprise you?" she had asked, upon hearing of Charles's relationship with Victoria. "He's always done that!"

I stood there, silent. My grasp on the phone tightened; my stomach twisted like a wet, dank, wrung-out dish towel.

"Why do you say that?" I asked, not sure I wanted an answer.

"He was having an affair with Faith for years."

"What makes you say that?" I didn't think my trembling voice was noticeable.

"Di, she told me. Good gracious—he's a psychiatrist; she was his patient. Why would I think up such a thing on my own? It wouldn't occur to me in a thousand years," she said. "Faith told me she was waiting for him to leave you. It astounded me so that I came home and told John. I didn't know what to do.

"John said, 'Just watch the baby, nothing else! It's not your place.' He told me, 'Keep your mouth closed.' I suppose I did agree with that back then. Now I wish I had said something."

I felt a fluttering in my chest; it was a sensation I'd had for years, but I'd never known what it was until now. Dazed, I thought of his patient Faith. He had seen her for many years, up until fairly recently, and had always described her as "crazy." I thought, *Anne doesn't understand psychotic transference.* I still wanted to give Charles the benefit of the doubt. I wanted to trust him implicitly, as I had for all of our years together.

Then I remembered. Elli must have been an infant. It was before we moved to St. John's Lane, when we lived in the little cottage in the country and used an even smaller cottage on our property as our office. We were there for nine years. Charles started working with Faith close to when Elli was born. Anne watched Elli when I was working, and Charles did mention to Anne that she might recognize people who came on the property, because he knew she and Faith both went to the same church. We both reminded her about the need for strict confidentiality.

I remembered that Faith used to leave long letters for Charles in our mailbox. I would find them almost every day: fat envelopes, taped closed, *Charles* written in a chunky, childlike hand on the front. I didn't think much of it since our professional mail also came to the same address. One day, though, Charles left one of Faith's letters lying on the windowsill in the treatment room. I picked it up to put it on his desk, and I saw what at the time seemed to be a sexual fantasy. I only glanced at it, but I still have a clear memory of what I read:

*I love to suck your cock. I dream about it every minute of every day and wait anxiously for the next time I can have you come in my mouth, sucking you, loving you, having you become part of me.*

When Charles came home one evening, I told him, "Charles, I couldn't help but read that letter from Faith that you left in the treatment room this afternoon."

"Yeah, her transference is really intense, isn't it?" he said, as he got something from the refrigerator.

"Charles, I was thinking, after seeing the letter and knowing she writes to you almost every day, that maybe it's too intense; maybe she's acting out her wishful fantasies."

Charles looked up, considering what I was saying. "You're probably right."

"Maybe exploring the meaning of writing the letters would help her contain her acting out and gain some understanding of the behavior."

"I thought I was doing that, but maybe not enough. I'll work on it," he said, and the letters did stop coming.

However, Charles had then said to me, when he was about to have an appointment with Faith, "She's really jealous of you, Di, and I think it would be better if she didn't see you around."

Not only did I work in the same office as Charles did, but I also was his wife. As skilled a clinician as I thought myself to be, I questioned none of it. Maybe it didn't happen. Maybe in Faith's internal fantasy world it was true, and from that world she spoke to Anne, believing her own words. I will never know the truth about this. I do know, though, that had I ever questioned Charles, his indignation would have been of mammoth proportions. He would have been hurt beyond words.

"You're delusional," he would have said, truly believing his own accusation. Once more, I would have been cast as the villain, he would have usurped the role of victim, and this dynamic would have further justified his contemptuous disdain.

His disdain. I recall a time when I was standing in the kitchen on St. John's Lane, before my diagnosis. Albert, Charles's father, a slight, bearded man, mouselike in his manner but also meanspirited and critical, stood next to me by the kitchen island. Marcy, Charles's mother, was at the table, harmlessly chattering about the weather, as she often did.

"Marcy, cut it out," Albert chided her, speaking to her as if she were a three-year-old, with disdain and disrespect. Just a simple phrase, but the tone, the scorn, was so familiar. That was the first time I really heard it, the first time it really penetrated my solid internal wall and resonated deep within me. It was Charles. This was his model of what a marriage was, and this was the way he spoke to me now, the way he had spoken to me for years. It was at the root of my rages.

"He is such a bastard," I blurted out to no one but myself after my phone conversation with Anne. The call had stirred a flood of memories, and I was unable to contain them, remembering Albert and thinking of Faith. They spewed out effortlessly, just as they had all those times in the two years before I began my analysis. And I allowed myself, for just a moment, to imagine disemboweling Charles and his girlfriend Victoria with a carving knife that lay invitingly on the kitchen counter.

# Part Three
# August 1999–September 2000

## Chapter Nineteen

In July, we moved out of the house on St. John's Lane and into a rented townhouse. A small part of me was still blindly hopeful that our marriage was salvageable.

By the time I finished my thirtieth radiation treatment, close to a year since it had all begun, I had been through two surgeries, eight rounds of chemotherapy, and high-dose chemotherapy with a stem cell transplant. It was late August now, and we were taking a trip to Cape Cod. When we had planned the vacation, I hadn't even considered that a camping excursion after twelve months of treatment might be strenuous. Charles certainly had not considered it, either, or if he had, what it meant for me was of no concern to him. There was a conference he wanted to go to—that was what was important. At that time, I was just glad he wanted us all to do something together.

The sky was gray and foreboding—an omen, perhaps, of what was to come. Elli and Sammy were bickering in the back of the Suburban, their way of dealing with the heaviness that filled the truck. Packing up for the trip that morning hadn't gone well, and the tension between Charles and me was thick. I hadn't planned on saying it—the thought had never even crystallized— but as we drove, I found myself asking, "Are you still having contact with Victoria?"

Without a pause, Charles replied, "You didn't believe me when I told you I wasn't seeing Marissa anymore."

And so we drove for hours, saying nothing more. It was at just that moment that I knew with certainty that something had been irrevocably lost. On the radio, Barbra Streisand pleadingly sang, "What Kind of Fool"—words that couldn't have been truer.

After many hours of driving, we arrived at the campground. It was nice, in spite of the cold drizzle that fell as we unloaded the truck. In my excitement about Charles's desire to take a family vacation, I had found a place where we could camp in a big tepee. I thought the kids would enjoy it, which they did, even the pungent odor that woke us each morning, a nocturnal gift from the skunk that sprayed the tent each night. In retrospect, though, I wonder if the skunk was a messenger of the stink that was to come.

Charles went off to his meetings each morning, and the children and I ate breakfast, hiked, rode bikes. When he would come back, we went to the beach. He was remote and irritable.

"Daddy, we're going fishing today. Will you put the rods together that Momma bought?" Sam jumped onto Charles's sleeping bag before his eyes opened one morning.

"Fishing? You want to go fishing?" Charles slid deeper into his bag and went back to sleep.

"Elli, I'll get things together for fishing. Why don't you take Sammy down to the arcade with your bikes? When you come back, we'll have breakfast, and then we can go over to the lake," I said, knowing that fishing was going to be an issue for Charles— though I didn't realize just how much.

The kids washed up and dressed and then took off on their bikes. I got out the fishing rods I had bought at BJ's for $10 each and started to put them together.

Suddenly, Charles approached from behind and said, in his most formal and pedantic tone, "You know, Diane, it's just like you to do whatever you want to do, never thinking of me. You could have at least asked me if I wanted to go fishing. You know I hate fishing. What a waste of money. We don't have extra to spend, and you go and buy two fishing rods."

I didn't say it, but I thought, *He dragged me camping days after finishing a yearlong treatment for cancer, and I never think of him? My only mistake was agreeing to this!*

Sometimes at night I would awaken and discover that Charles was not in the tepee. I would walk out and see him sitting in the darkened Suburban with the engine running. I didn't notice that he was talking on his cell phone, or perhaps I just put on my blinders because I didn't want to consciously know what he was up to. However, several weeks after we returned home and the cell phone bill came, it became clear that in one week he had run up over $250 worth of calls to Victoria. This was the same man who complained about the $20 I spent on fishing rods for our children.

A weird sound in the truck started a few days before we were due to head home. The next-to-last day of the trip, Charles took the truck, as usual, to his meeting and came back with a rental car. The truck had died; it needed major work and wasn't going to be ready by the time we needed to leave. We decided that Charles would fly back to Cape Cod and then drive the truck home the following weekend.

"I wish we had the money so I could go with you," I said, thinking how nice it would be to have some time just to ourselves.

"Well, that just isn't possible!" he said, and he stuck to that response even when my father offered to pay for the other ticket and to stay with the children.

---

THE day after Labor Day, the children started back at school, and it was my first day back in the office. I had a couple of appointments in the morning, and to celebrate my return to work, Charles and I walked over to Eddie's, a local coffee shop, for lunch.

As we sat at the counter, on red leather stools, I heard conversations buzzing around us and tried to penetrate Charles's wall, but to no avail. He responded to nothing I said. When we walked back to the office after lunch, Charles a step or two ahead of me, I skipped to catch up with him, to put my arm through his, but he jerked his arm back. I withdrew, and we walked in continued silence.

Charles's office was on the ground floor of a small yellow house we rented. It was right next to the secretary's office and could be entered from there or the waiting room. He also had a door that led outside. Charles, Bernice, our new secretary, and I were standing in Bernice's office. I was facing the two windows that looked out onto the driveway, at the outside door to Charles's treatment room.

As I stood there, a woman appeared suddenly, walking up the driveway. She paused and looked at the white rental car that was parked there. She then moved on toward the door to Charles's office. I saw her only from the back, a medium-built woman, wearing an unbuttoned white lab coat, with long, dark, wavy hair reaching down her back. It had obviously been colored dark and had oxidized; it had the reddish streaks of hair that needs to be re-dyed. I was very aware of hair, as I had little more than fuzz.

As I watched her, I almost said something to Charles. When we'd lived in the cottage, we had often joked that it was diagnostic if someone came to the house, instead of the office, no matter how explicit the directions to the office had been. We'd said that the person always turned out to be schizophrenic. So now, as I saw this woman walk up the drive, stop by the rental car, and walk to Charles's office door—the wrong door—I almost asked, "Is she schizophrenic?" These were words that in the past had connected us. This time, however, I asked only, "Are you expecting someone?"

"Someone's just dropping off some medication," he replied, and said nothing more.

The next day was Charles's day in Washington. He left early. I got the children up and drove them to school. Elli was now in middle school, and Sammy was also in a new school. After dropping them off, I headed for home, not having to be at the office for several hours. I made a spontaneous left turn at Park Heights Avenue, even though I wasn't sure why. Two more turns, and I was at the office, all the time not really thinking and somewhat dazed.

I parked the car, unlocked the doors, keyed in the combination, and walked in. There were no lights on because no one was there yet; it was early. I went straight back to Charles's office and directly to the shelves above his desk. I reached up, pulled off the first book and looked for an inscription. There was none. Then I reached up again and there it was, exactly what I was unknowingly looking for: a letter from Victoria. Articulate at times and in tortured English at others, clearly trying hard to match the intellectual depths she imagined the recipient to possess, she wrote:

*My dear Charles,*

*Hovering just beneath the surface, caught in my throat, admittedly, but with increasing insistence, is the impulse, thought, perhaps feeling that next weekend's planned escapade to Cape Cod is not in my best interest and likely not in yours either, although I hesitate to speak for you . . .*

*When our relationship veered from its intended path, I lost my safe witness . . .*

*I and the others inside, with aching hearts and souls, cannot bear to watch your pain or endure our own pain . . .*

*I fear that you are not actively working on your relationship with Di for fear that your efforts might actually bring the two of you into alignment and place me in some psychological danger . . .*

*If it is our karma to join together, in body and soul, in this universe or another, so it will be . . .*

*I wish you love, Victoria*

These are only excerpts. I couldn't read the entire letter just then. With a deep well of emptiness echoing inside me, I walked into the secretary's office, turned on the copy machine, and made ten copies.

## Chapter Twenty

"Di, I stopped at Borders and got these books," Charles said, as he tossed two paperbacks on the table. He smiled as he sat down. "Our anniversary is in a couple of weeks. Let's get away. Camille can stay with the kids. You pick the place."

I glanced at the titles of the books: *Intimate Weekends for Two* and *Romantic Weekend Getaways*. It was hard for me to say anything. I looked at Charles incredulously; then, without warning, I got up and ran into the bathroom and retched out the dinner I had eaten an hour earlier. My head felt dazed, and my skin was cold and clammy. Then, spent, I lay down on the tile floor and curled up with my cheek pressed hard against the coolness, not daring to move.

"Wow, what happened? Are you okay, Di? That was weird!"

I looked up at Charles's smile as he now sat next to me on the floor, gently placing his hand on my back. I sat up, and he put his arm around my shoulder.

"I wrote something today that I wanted to give to you. It's from my heart and soul." He took a folded piece of paper from his pocket, and as we sat closely on the floor, his arm still around my shoulder, I read:

*Thanksgiving*

*I never knew before you, that I could talk heart-to-heart with my partner, and I never knew it was possible to laugh with one another as we did.*

*You made it possible to find the way out of my cult, by not pushing me.*

*Having children had been a theoretical goal, not a real wish, until you.*

*You endured unspeakable pain, unwavering, to bring children to us.*

*You have given of yourself to them, ceaselessly, lovingly.*

*You have given us all an enriching, lovingly beautiful house to enjoy.*

*At festive times, you have produced wondrous, rich meals, celebrations of life. And at other times, you taught me that restaurants are to be enjoyed.*

*You have helped me by modeling a truly thoughtful way of being a therapist. You have navigated into areas of cognitive functioning totally new to me.*

*And now you are modeling courage, in a way that can never be forgotten.*

*For these things from you, and more, I am forever grateful.*

*Forever yours,*
*Charles*

The words were there, but they sounded hollow. They didn't feel real or true. I wanted them to be true, I wanted to believe that he loved me, but I felt empty. In truth, there was no mention of love, only flowery words disconnected from real feelings.

"Di, I am forever grateful to you for so much. I really want you to know that."

"Thanks. It's lovely." And as I spoke, that same empty feeling came over me and I turned quickly to the toilet so I could throw up again.

Later that evening, after the kids were in bed, he again handed me the books. "Di, pick a place. It'll be fun, just like it was before the kids."

Why was he doing this? It was crazy-making. Nevertheless, I started looking through the books. Maybe he did mean these things. Maybe it would be okay. Maybe he did love me. Maybe he did want things to work out between us. Maybe he wanted to try.

At about ten o'clock, Charles said he was going to take Knaidl, our old yellow Lab, out for a walk. The kids were asleep, and I said that I'd go along with him.

There was a long pause. Then he said, "Di, I just feel like having some time to myself." He smiled, picked up his cell phone, put it in his pocket, picked up the leash, got the dog, and walked out the door.

"Damn you!" I yelled as the door closed. "You're such a sadistic prick! You're driving me crazy!"

And so it was.

The next morning, Charles came and sat down on the bed as I awakened. "Di, I know we talked about your waiting awhile before having reconstructive surgery, because of your loss of income if you're out of work. But I was thinking that even if it means being out of work a bit longer, you might feel better if you have it now."

I didn't understand this change. Suddenly he had become so solicitous, so kind and gentle . . . and then I saw an e-mail he had left out, which Victoria had written to him:

> *Bear, as much as I love you, and you say that you love me, I want to be sure that you have given your relationship with Di every chance it can have. I need to know that you have done that before I can give myself to you. Vic*

I found a bed-and-breakfast on Martha's Vineyard and made reservations for four nights. We hadn't been there for years, and, despite everything, I was still hoping; despite knowing, I was still wishing.

That same night, I went to the computer and found an e-mail that he had written to Victoria.

> *I love you, Vic. You know I will do all I can to be with you in time. I have made efforts with Di, but my love for you colors all else.*
> *Bear.*

## Chapter Twenty-One

At the end of September, we completed our filing for bankruptcy, which Charles had convinced me we needed to do while I was still going through chemotherapy. The day after we went to the courthouse to sign the final documents, Charles told me that he didn't think we should go away for our anniversary.

"I've been trying so hard, Di, and you're just so unresponsive to all of my efforts; it doesn't make any sense to spend all that money when you really aren't interested," he explained.

I looked at him and said, "Okay," feeling like an idiot; he had played me again.

About a week later, I was sitting in my bedroom. I looked up and was startled to see Sam standing on the landing above me.

"Mom, were you crying?" He peered down, his huge brown eyes, his curly hair, and the downturn of his mouth looking so much like his dad's.

"No, Sammy, I wasn't crying. What made you think I was?"

"'Cause you're so sad and I sometimes hear you cry when Dad yells at you." His long lashes accentuated the size of his wide eyes as he spoke.

"It does make me sad, but he wasn't yelling at me this morning. Did you think he was?" As the words came out, I knew things were only going to get worse.

"I don't know. I don't know when it's a dream and when it's real," he went on.

"I know things here haven't been so easy. First, I was sick, and then we moved from our house that we all loved, and now you and Elli are at new schools. It's been hard for everybody, even Daddy. I do get sad when Daddy yells at me, but I'm okay. When I think about you and Elli, that makes me happy—the happiest person in the world."

He stood looking at me, a calm expression on his face, and then said, "Mom, I don't like it when Dad yells at you or when he yells at us.

You know, when Dad dies, I'm not even going to give him a funeral. I'm just going to dig a hole and throw him in. I'm not even going to cover it with dirt!"

"Hmm. I guess you're kind of angry at Daddy." And though I knew all of the other things I should have said, the things about their dad's loving them in spite of how he was acting, I said none of them. "I know. I sometimes feel kind of angry at Daddy, too. It's not easy being angry at someone you love, is it?" I asked, not really directing it to Sam, who had silently disappeared, probably off to his room to build with Legos.

Elli, on the other hand, was the one who seemed truly lost, much more obviously devastated. Changing schools for her was much harder. She was remote and distant and didn't want to get together with her old friends; she also wasn't making any new friends. Elli was so very aware of Charles's comings and goings; she so wanted him to be the attentive father she remembered from when she was a little girl.

When we lived in the cottage, before Sam was born, Elli was about two. Her morning ritual was to help Charles make his coffee. She would toddle downstairs, right to the kitchen, where Charles would be waiting for her. She would go get the canister with the coffee beans from the pantry and bring it to the old dough table. Charles would lift her onto the bench and give her the measuring cup. She would scoop out the beans and put them in the grinder, and together they would giggle as she pressed the button and said, "Coffee ready soon, Daddy."

She loved her daddy so much.

She still had the same round face, the same perfect features, and the same white-blond curls, but without the smile, she no longer looked like a sunflower.

That evening, after my conversation with Sam, I realized that Charles had left open one account, with a $12,000 line of credit.

"We're obligated to close that," I told him.

With contempt, as if talking to a stranger, he replied simply, "We need to have funds available for emergencies." Then he left the room.

The next morning, there was a letter on the pillow next to my head. I kept many pieces of paper, but I can't seem to remember where that one is. I do recall that it very clearly stated that Charles had no interest in continuing our marriage and that we had "no chance of reconciliation." He went on to say he would speak only with a third party, "in relation to matters regarding the children."

I heard the door close as I read the letter. I threw back the covers, rushed to the door, and screamed at his back as he walked down the path, "Get back here! Don't you just leave this for me and walk away! You planned this!"

But walk away is just what he did. He got into his car and drove off to work, without even glancing back. I ran back into the house, sobbing. Then I put my wedding ring in my jewelry box and called Dr. Putman.

## Chapter Twenty-Two

"Charles, next Saturday I have a doctor's appointment in Washington, and I want to meet a friend for lunch afterward, so I would like you to be with the kids for the day," I said, catching him one morning before he left for work.

His response surprised me: "Sure, that's not a problem. I want to have more time with the kids." And so I made my plans for the following week.

After my appointment that morning, my old friend Donna and I met for lunch. It was about four o'clock when I got on I-95; traffic was at a standstill. I would have been about an hour from home if it had been moving, so I decided I'd better check on the kids. I dialed my cell, and Elli picked up on the first ring. "Where are you, Mom? When are you going to be home?" she screamed into my ear; I could hear Sam yelling loudly in the background.

"Calm down. What's going on? Where's Daddy?" I tried to keep my voice steady as I looked out the window at the gridlock of cars surrounding me.

"He left a long time ago for the office and said to call him if we need him. Sammy won't listen to me, and Dad's phone is busy, and I can't get through. I've been calling him over and over again for over an hour. Mom, when will you be here?" she pleaded.

"I'm on my way, but it may not be for an hour. I'll get through to your dad. Put your brother on the phone."

"Mom, it's not my fault," Sam said when he picked up. "Elli took the remote for the TV and broke it, so I punched her, and then—"

I interrupted him, "Sam, right now I don't care whose fault it is. I want you to go up to your room—play with your Legos, read a book; right now, it's calm-down time, away from Elli. Do you understand what I'm telling you to do?"

"Yes." He breathed deeply. "Okay, Mom. I love you."

"I love you, too, sweetie. Please put Elli back on and then go upstairs."

"Here, Elli, Momma wants to talk to you. I'm sorry for punching you," I could hear Sam saying to his sister as he handed her the phone.

"Yeah." The sadness in Elli's voice was palpable.

"El, I think everything will be calm now, and I will get through to Dad, but you call my cell phone if there are any problems at all. I'm going to hang up so I can call him, okay?"

"Okay," she replied, and the connection was gone.

I dialed Charles's cell phone, but he didn't answer. Then I dialed his business line at the office, and it was busy. Unsure what to do next, I settled on calling my friend Allyson in New Jersey.

"Allyson, I went to DC today and Charles was supposed to be with the kids. Instead, he left them at home and has been on the phone at the office for hours—with 'Vic,' I'm sure." *God, I can't imagine what they can talk about for so long. Oh, I know: Should they or shouldn't they have a relationship?* "Anyway, the kids are going crazy. They can't reach him, neither can I, and I can't break into his conversation 'cause I'm on a goddamn cell phone. Can you call the operator and have her interrupt their telephone sex and tell him his kids need him?" I swallowed hard as I finished speaking.

"Oy, he is such a bastard! Of course I'll call. I'll get back to you. Love you, Di. You don't deserve this!" she said as we hung up.

Finally, the traffic started to move, and I decided to stay on the highway and hoped I wouldn't get a speeding ticket. I passed the remnants of the accident off to the left on the shoulder. As I sped by, Allyson called back to let me know she had gotten through and Charles had said he would go home to the kids. Even knowing that, I still pushed the limit with my foot on the gas. Forty-five minutes later, I pulled into the driveway, thinking Charles's car was probably in the garage.

"Hi, Mom. I'm glad you're home." Elli put down the book she was reading, and Sammy rushed down the stairs from his room as he heard her speaking to me.

"Where's Dad?" I asked, looking around, seeing no evidence of his presence.

"Oh, he called, but everything was quiet, so he said that he would stay at the office and just use a different number for his phone calls; that way, we could get through if we needed him." Elli smiled. I knew that she knew something was going on with her dad. "Why don't you both get dressed, and then we'll go out and get some dinner? How does that sound?" I asked, just wanting not to be in the house when Charles returned.

"Yeah, can we have sushi?" Elli asked, while Sam ran upstairs, shouting, "Pizza, pizza, pizza!"

"We'll decide on the way. Let's just get going, 'cause I'm starving!"

Within fifteen minutes, we were in the car and heading out the gate of the townhouse community. Just as we pulled through the gatehouse, out of the corner of my eye, I saw Charles's Suburban pull in the other direction. I kept my eyes straight ahead and kept on driving, not noticing a thing.

"I think I just saw Daddy drive in." Sam twisted in his seat to look back.

"I doubt it," Elli replied.

We all agreed it would be fun for us to try the new Japanese restaurant in town, where there was a rotating sushi bar. I thought it would be different enough to help us put the last few hours behind us, at least for a while.

By the time we arrived home several hours later, we were all laughing and telling funny stories. There stood Charles, a forced smile on his face, very much in control. He gave the kids hugs and told them he thought it was time they got ready for bed. I didn't know whether the kids knew the subtleties of his moods and his tones of voice, but I certainly did.

"Will you come up and read to me?" The words tumbled from Sam's mouth.

"Sure will, and then I'll come in and we can talk, Elli." He sounded so smug and sure of himself as Sam raced up the stairs.

Elli was looking at me, rolling her eyes. "Sure, Dad." She turned to him and smiled sweetly; then she, too, climbed the stairs.

Charles turned to me. "Can I ask you why you couldn't wait for me to get home for dinner? Then again, you never think of me; it's always all about you, isn't it?" He spoke calmly and rationally, in the tone he used whenever he wanted to provoke me into a rage.

I looked at him, smiled, and said, "We were hungry and didn't know where you were or when you'd be back. Nowadays, we never know when you'll return," I still had that tight, frightened feeling in my chest, the feeling that I was being told I was a bad child, that I had again done something wrong. The only difference was that now, despite the feeling in my chest, I was beginning to notice the fogginess in my head, which had served to blur my thoughts and perceptions of what was really going on. Now I could respond in a way that at least presented the illusion that I felt okay inside.

"You're a master with words, Charles," I said matter-of-factly, as he climbed the stairs. He looked back with a smug, puzzled look. As I turned and walked into the bathroom, I felt awful, but this time I did not rage.

I walked over to the toilet and lifted the lid. It hadn't happened for a long time, but once again there it was: a bowl full of shit. The same thing had happened when we were living on St. John's Lane, the year before I got sick.

Charles always took a long time in the bathroom in the morning; one morning, a while after he left the bathroom and I went in, I saw that he hadn't flushed the toilet. Not thinking it was anything other than forgetfulness, I flushed it down and forgot about it. Not too long afterward, it happened again, and then again and again. I don't know how many times it happened over several months before I began to suspect that this gesture was not quite forgetful or accidental. Eventually, I was being confronted with a bowl of his shit several mornings a week. I finally said something: "Charles, you must really be deep in thought lately when you're in the bathroom in the morning, because you've been forgetting to flush the toilet."

I was trying to be sensitive to his feelings, but that wasn't how he heard it at all. Within a day, he had moved his things into the hall bathroom and began to complain that I had thrown him out of our bathroom in the master suite. That wasn't true at all. I was just asking him to try to be aware and flush the toilet! Now, again, this was how he was letting me know he was angry.

The next day, I received an e-mail from Charles:

> Di,
>
> I have given it much thought, and I think I would do much better with you, and perhaps you with me, if I moved into the basement. We don't even have to say anything to the children, and I can still use our bathroom, but I can use the basement to relax, work at home, and sleep. I think this will be a much better option than how it has been.
>
> Charles

His arrogance was beyond belief; nevertheless, each thing he did always surprised me—I could still never quite believe it.

By Monday evening, he was sleeping in the basement. I still had little energy, but I was trying to build my practice and feeling as if I were a rat on a wheel, going nowhere. At the end of the week, I called Allyson and said, "I am so tired. Charles keeps telling me I'm doing nothing. He thinks I should have a full caseload of patients already. What should I do?" My head was spinning. The dread I felt now was in some ways worse than the dread I had felt a year earlier when Dr. Braken had said, "Diane, it's cancer."

"It's one o'clock Friday afternoon, Di. The kids will be done with school at three, right?" Allyson didn't wait for a response. "I want you to throw some things in the car for you and the kids, pick them up from school, and come here for the weekend," she stated firmly.

"I don't know." I could feel the viselike grip on my chest. "Charles will be upset 'cause the kids will be away all weekend."

I was about to say something else when Allyson cut in, "Goddamn it, Di, so what? You've got to stop thinking about him. He doesn't think about you. He doesn't think about anyone but himself. You'll stay home and he'll be off doing whatever he does all weekend . . . so pack the car, pick up the kids, and come here!"

I took a deep breath and said, "Okay." I did call Charles, but he didn't answer, so I left him a message on his answering machine saying that the kids and I were going to New Jersey for the weekend.

I still couldn't just leave, just like I couldn't just change the locks on the door or throw him out.

The kids were excited when I picked them up. They loved going to see Aunt Allyson and Uncle Harry and their three girls, who were all very close in age to my kids. As we drove, we listened to *Harry Potter* on tape, and the escape into Hogwarts was a magical respite.

It was so nice to be with Allyson and Harry and the girls. There was no tension. The kids played; we laughed and talked, drank wine, went out to eat. That Friday evening, Charles called, just to say hello. He called again Saturday morning. Then he called again Saturday evening. When he called at noon on Sunday, his tone was a bit less friendly. "When are you planning on leaving?" he asked, with the clear annoyance of a parent to a teenager who has already missed her curfew.

"I'm not sure. We were going to take the kids to a local fair, and I thought we'd head back after that," I said casually, feeling a sense of panic wash over me.

"You always do what's good for you, don't you?" he quietly admonished me, and then hung up.

"Ready to go? Kids are already in the van." Allyson stopped and noticed the phone in my hand.

"You know, maybe we ought to leave now." I shrugged, my stomach in knots.

"He always does this to you, Di. He's the most controlling person I've ever met. The kids are in the van, and we are going to the fair. You can't let him scare you."

"You're right," I agreed, and she was, but, although the gray matter in my head may have known it, I still felt as if I were going to throw up.

It was about four o'clock by the time we had the car packed up and were ready to head home. The kids were all outside, and Allyson called me back into the kitchen. She was holding an envelope.

"Listen, Di, this is a gift. I want you to use it for one thing and one thing only."

She opened the envelope and took out a check, showing me that it was made out to me, Diane Pomerantz. She continued, "I am giving you this check for three thousand dollars because tomorrow morning I want you to start making phone calls so that you can consult with and retain an attorney. You need a lawyer. This is the retainer."

"Allyson, I can't take this." I tried to hand it back to her, but she wouldn't take it.

"You can and you will. This isn't Harry's money; it's my money from my own account, and I want you to have this money so you can get an attorney, *now*." She wrapped her arms around me, and we both cried. I told her that I would pay her back, but again she told me that this was a gift, a gift of love and friendship.

There wasn't much traffic, and both of the kids fell asleep on the way home, which made it easy for me to drift off into imagined conversations with Charles, with Victoria, with Victoria's estranged husband, being very clear with each of them about what I saw and what I knew to be true.

It was almost nine o'clock when we pulled through the gatehouse and then into the driveway. The kids had already awakened, but Sammy, still tired from the long weekend and the drive, moved slowly toward the front door. Elli ran in, saying, "Hi, Dad. I have to use the bathroom," as she sprinted up the stairs. Sam walked in ahead of me, looking very tired.

"Your mom sure didn't think about how it would be for you guys to get home so late when you have school tomorrow, did she?" He laughed as he tousled Sam's hair and walked with him upstairs, shaking his head slightly with not-so-subtle disapproval.

"Sam, get ready for bed. I'll be up in a few minutes," I called upstairs, and then I walked into Elli's room. She was already sitting on her bed in her nightshirt, drawing, when I walked in.

"Mom, I hope you and Dad don't get into a fight." She looked up from her sketch pad.

"I'll do my best to avoid it, sweetie," I said, though I knew Charles was ready to fight.

By ten o'clock, the kids were asleep. I was sitting in bed, reading, when Charles walked into the bedroom.

"Do you think it was really fair of you to make it so I couldn't see the kids at all this weekend?"

Although I knew how close to the edge he was and I could have avoided what came next, I said, "Come on, Charles. You spend very little time with the kids on any given weekend. Even when you're supposed to be with them, you leave them alone and go off to the office or wherever you go to be with Victoria. What are you making such a fuss about? What, was Victoria not around this weekend? Is that what the problem is?"

"Don't you dare ever mention her name. I don't want to hear her name come out of your mouth." He walked out of the room and smashed the bedroom door. I heard the wood crack and his fist go into the wall as he screamed, "This should be your face!" He came back into the bedroom. "You fuckin' bitch. You'll pay for this!" he shrieked, grabbing some things from the bathroom and storming back out. His raging continued; he shouted every foul word there was, all the words that so offended him when I went into my angry rages. His ranting went on and on, until finally he retreated to the basement, probably to share more about my black, evil soul with Victoria.

When I awoke and walked out of the bedroom the next morning, I noticed a picture hanging in the hallway outside the bedroom. I didn't recall having hung it there. I looked more closely and saw that it covered the hole in the wall that Charles had punched the night before. Never before had I consciously been physically afraid of Charles, but now that was changing.

After I took the kids to school the next day, I started my search for an attorney.

## Chapter Twenty-Three

By November, Charles had deepened his relationships with his female entourage even further. He called these women, including Victoria, his "four muses." He and Victoria were still spending countless hours on the phone and emailing and writing letters, discussing whether they were going to continue their relationship. If it hadn't been so crazy, it would have been funny. Nevertheless, I couldn't stop reading the communications between them. Everyone told me it was toxic for me to do so. I just couldn't stop. I couldn't believe what was happening—he even called me his "childhood friend" in one message.

By the time I called Calvin Jones, a well-regarded divorce attorney in town, I had already met with a number of other lawyers. I wasn't sure what characteristics I wanted in an attorney, but when I met Cal I knew he was someone I could work with. He spent over two hours listening to my story, he didn't charge me for the consultation, and then he said he wouldn't charge me a retainer, either. He was outraged by what Charles had been doing.

"Diane, the thing is, it's not in your best interest or in the best interest of the children for him to lose his license, so we have to be smart in the way we play this, okay?" Then he told me everything he wanted me to bring to him within the next few days. I left his office feeling as if I had someone in my corner, someone who would take care of me. That feeling wouldn't last long.

The kids and I made tacos for dinner, which they always enjoyed doing. Knaidl was under the table, waiting for all the droppings. It was a warmish evening, so the three of us took our bikes out after dinner and rode around the community.

"Too bad Daddy never gets to do fun stuff with us," Sam called out as he did a wheelie, almost tumbling over. I shuddered.

Elli rolled her eyes as I looked at her and shrugged my shoulders, not saying anything as we pedaled behind him.

Charles arrived home at about ten. Sam was asleep, but Elli ran downstairs to greet him, and then he went up to her room and read to her for a while. I was in my bedroom when he came in and sat on the corner of the bed, smiling, and said, "You know, I've been thinking about you working. I think it will be too much for you to work full-time right now. I know we need the money, but not that much. You need time to heal."

No decision I made would be right. I just looked at him, smiled, and said nothing. I breathed deeply and quietly. I had already made my decision. Living the way I was living now was more stressful than any full-time job could possibly be. No, I knew exactly what I was going to do. I had gotten an attorney, I planned to have my reconstructive surgery in December, and then I would get a job, to begin as soon as I recovered from my surgery. I wanted to be working by February.

My friend Pam was a social worker, and she worked in a very well-established group practice. She told me that someone was leaving the practice, they needed a new person, and they would love to have me. I decided I would do it. They would provide me with patients, and I wouldn't have to do marketing or pay office rent. The percentage of money I would bring in was fair. Charles was pleased with the arrangement. Conscious or not, my decisions were still driven by his response.

Why I kept telling him what I was up to, things I should have kept to myself, was something I continuously kicked myself for doing. But he was such a part of me, it was so ingrained in me to talk to him about anything and everything, that I still did so, even knowing what I knew, even when it was not in my best interest.

My mood was still awful. Panic attacks were the norm, and, although I managed to function and do all of the things I had to do, it was only on the surface. I was having a lot of fender-benders—at least four—and many more near misses. I always felt very disoriented afterward. I also was falling a lot, though back then I didn't know why. Dr. Putman kept saying it was a result of my inattention because I was so anxious. I wasn't so sure. It seemed to me like something else. Perhaps, I thought, the cancer had spread; perhaps it was already in my brain.

Charles certainly didn't make things any easier. Some days he said he thought I should work part-time and have the reconstructive surgery now so I would feel better about myself. Other days, it was as if he had never said that at all, and he went on tirades about money and how if I wasn't working full-time and had the surgery or was out of work, it would put us "on the brink of financial disaster." No decision I made would be right.

Since that was the case, with the encouragement of my reconstructive surgeon, Dr. Kealz, one of the many doctors in my support system who went the extra mile for me, I scheduled a tram flap procedure for December 3, 1999, six weeks away.

Feeling energized by the warm conversation I'd had with Dr. Kealz, I began doing some of the paperwork that had been sitting untouched on my desk. Before long, the phone rang. It was Charles, and his voice was filled with controlled wrath. "I just checked the balance in the checking account, and it's overdrawn by five hundred dollars. Someone made an ATM withdrawal and caused an overdraft. I expect you to correct what you caused."

"Charles, I don't know what you're talking about. I haven't used the ATM. I don't remember the last time I did. Either this is a mistake, or someone has gotten into the account and something fraudulent is going on." My chest tightened as I felt that old rage at being wrongly accused, but I was calm. "If you want me to take care of it, I most certainly will," I continued. "I will be over to the office in a few minutes to get all the information, and then I'll go to the bank." With that, I hung up the phone and drove to the office.

Charles didn't have much more to say when I arrived. I told him that I was going to get to the bottom of it and that I had not been to the bank or withdrawn any money.

For some reason, Charles had set up our accounts with the executive/professional division of the bank, and when I arrived, I asked to see the manager of that division. She was a lovely, middle-aged woman, kind and quite solicitous. I explained the situation to her.

"Don't you worry at all, Dr. Pomerantz. Let me handle this. I will get to the bottom of it, and as soon as I do, I will call you directly, okay?" She seemed to know more about what was going on than I did.

"That would be wonderful," I said. "I really do appreciate your help with this. Thank you for being so kind. I'll wait to hear from you." We shook hands, and I left the bank. When I arrived home, I called Charles and left him a message saying that the bank manager was looking into the situation. I did not hear back from him.

The next morning, as I was leaving Dr. Putman's office, my cell phone rang. "Dr. Pomerantz, this is Mrs. Dahly from Bank of America. Can you talk?"

"Yes," I said, aware of the hesitation in her voice.

"Well, I do know what happened, and I really am very sorry; I hate to have to tell you this. Dr. Pomerantz, first of all, it was not an ATM transaction. We have the entire transaction on tape, and it was completed over the counter, last Friday, at 12:47 p.m.

I'm telling you the time because it's recorded. Your husband, Dr. Mandel, came into the bank and withdrew all of the money from the account and that caused the overdraft. Believe me, I've had to do this before, but it's never easy. I am so sorry, Dr. Pomerantz."

I already knew I had not caused the error. My anger was at having been wrongly accused. But this, I had not expected. I still felt blindsided by Charles's more and more clearly conscious manipulation and gaslighting.

When I was able to find my voice, I told her, "I'm sure it isn't, but I do appreciate all of your help. Thank you so much."

It was hard to see through my tears as I tried to find my attorney's phone number. I finally got connected through directory assistance. When the receptionist answered, I said, "Is Mr. Jones in? This is Diane Pomerantz, and it's very important that I speak with him right away."

"Hi, Diane. What's going on? Sue said you sounded very upset." I was surprised when Cal got on the phone so quickly, and I blurted out what had happened.

"That sick bastard. I have to tell you, this is one guy I would like to find on a dark street corner and teach him a thing or two with my fists. Where are you now, Diane?"

"I'm in my car on the side of the road. I was going to do some errands when I got the call from the bank manager. I don't have any patients until later this afternoon." My voice was flat. I felt like a zombie.

"Why don't you come over to my office? I'm going to call your husband and give him a piece of my mind."

I said that I would drive over and that it wouldn't take too long to get there. I didn't allow myself to think about what it meant that he would be calling Charles.

Cal was standing by the receptionist when I entered the office. We went into the conference room and sat at the huge cherry table, and Cal just shook his head. "Your husband is really a sick puppy. When I called, he said he had forgotten that he had been to the bank last week, that he certainly hadn't done this intentionally; it was an honest mistake. I had to stop him when he started going on about how you distort everything he does and how he wanted me to know the 'truth' about you."

"There's another problem, though, Diane. It's not really a problem for me, but it may be for you in terms of how you feel about my representing you. When I was speaking with your husband, he brought up the name of his 'friend' Victoria Morgan. Until then, I hadn't realized that the woman you've been speaking about is someone I've been representing for a couple of years regarding a legal suit she filed against someone. It's not a very active case, and it's not a conflict of interest for me in any way to represent you. But will you feel that you can completely trust me when you know I have a relationship with this other party? There are so many boundary violations already going on here with your husband and this woman that this may complicate things for you."

Cal went on. "I want you to think about it. I don't want you to say anything to Charles. He is not your friend—remember that. This is a decision that you must make, and I will help you make it. If you want to continue to work with me, I will do my best for you. If you decide it's better not to, I will help you find someone I know will be right for you."

I sat there, stunned. This bitch was worming herself into every crevice of my life. I felt like strangling her.

"I think that I can handle it, but I'd better take some time to really think about what to do," I told him. "What about the money?"

"Let's schedule some time on Friday, and we can discuss all of these things then. I don't want you to get into any discussions with Charles about anything of any substance. He's a manipulator."

CHARLES came home that evening after Sammy was asleep. He went up to Elli's room and sat with her for a while. He then went down to bed in the basement, never saying hello or in any way acknowledging anything that had transpired that day, never acknowledging my existence.

I moved back and forth between hatred and compassion. Part of me thought he must be in great pain to be doing the things he was doing. Everyone reminded me, "He feels nothing for anyone but himself—remember that." I did try to remember, but still, I sometimes forgot—until the next reminder he gave me. And those reminders were definitely becoming very frequent.

By the next morning, after another sleepless night, I was feeling angry at myself for any compassion I had for his pain. *His* pain? That was absolutely crazy! I was the one who had gone through a year of treatment for cancer and faced death. The children had faced the potential loss of their mother. None of us had his support. Yet *he* was in pain? A line I had read resounded in my head: *The terrorist usurps the role of the victim in order to gain control.* That was Charles: manipulator of all with whom he came into contact.

I decided to stay with Cal Jones for the time being. There was so much going on in my life, I didn't have the strength to pursue changing lawyers just yet, and there was no hurry.

I did know that Charles was trying to contact many of my doctors in different ways. I found out that he would refer patients to them and then want to discuss me with them, using his physician status to show he was the more believable party. One of the doctors he targeted was my internist. At one of my appointments with her, she casually said, "Diane, I had a call from Charles last week. He wanted to refer a patient to me, but it was very clear that that wasn't his motive. He seemed to want to talk more about you. I want you to know that I cut him off and told him that I thought the conversation was inappropriate and I wouldn't engage in it. I also told him that I could not accept any referrals from him. Have you gotten an attorney yet?"

"I have, but this whole thing feels like it's more than I can handle," I told her, adding, "I made an appointment with Dr. Berry, a neurologist my oncologist recommended, so can you give me a referral?"

"Yes. Just make sure she sends me whatever findings she gets, okay?" She jotted down some notes, and I left her office.

I was still trying to get my practice going, and as part of that process, I was giving a presentation at a local parents' group. I was having trouble focusing on getting the material organized, and I knew that I likely would be winging it. Then, a couple of mornings before the presentation, I had a strange experience.

I had made breakfast for the kids and was having this fantasy that Victoria would show up at my talk. Just then, Charles came into the kitchen and said, "Di, I was wondering if you'd like me to come to your talk on Wednesday night, for moral support."

"Sure," I responded automatically, but he kept talking.

"Not that I would learn anything new," he continued, and it became clear that he was offering for some ulterior motive, clearly not to give me moral support.

"Why don't you think about whether it's something you really want to do, 'cause if it is, it should be for moral support. If you really don't want to do it, that's okay, and it would be better for me if you weren't there." I smiled as I spoke calmly.

"I really do want to go, Di." His reply came much more quickly than usual.

"Great," I told him, and I casually walked out of the kitchen, calling to the kids to get their things together so I could drive them to school.

There was a pretty big crowd at the talk, which was on attentional problems and learning difficulties in children. The format was informal, and Charles was an active participant, which made the presentation go well. Perhaps that was part of his motivation: to be onstage himself. Nevertheless, I did once again feel a connection to him.

On the drive home, continuing to feel that bond, I said, "Why don't I get a sitter for Saturday night? Maybe we could go to a movie, have dinner, have some time to talk?"

The silence was deafening and felt eternal.

Finally, he responded, "I'll have to think about it."

"What is there to think about?" I asked.

Another long pause followed. Then he said, "Well, if I say yes, you'll just want more."

I found myself thinking the words I had shouted at him in my rages: *You bastard, drop dead, I hate you*, but I said nothing and just sat with the understanding that I did not like this man very much at all.

## Chapter Twenty-Four

Charles was definitely sliding down a slippery slope. I knew from what I read in his journal that Victoria's estranged husband supported her quite well and that she was in good financial circumstances. He made it clear in his writing that she had money and would provide for him financially. "I don't want to give up the money," he said. "If I go back with Di, anything Victoria gives me will become a loan."

Everyone told me not to read it, but I felt compelled. Everyone told me he was leaving it out for me to read, and I knew that was probably true. Nevertheless, I kept reading. I was determined that before we separated, I would make a copy of his journal. I wanted it for court. I wanted it as a record of my sanity.

Charles was seeing fewer and fewer patients, and he often forgot about people he had scheduled. Sometimes he would be on the phone—with Victoria, I'm sure—and a patient would sit in the waiting room for an hour or more before asking the secretary where he was. I couldn't wait for the surgery so I could move my office. I was also so glad I had a different last name.

More and more, I was hearing from people what they had seen for years, what I had seen, what I had felt, what I had ignored. Person after person said, "We would come to your house for dinner and leave at the end of the evening so disturbed by the way Charles spoke to you" and, "We wondered how a smart, strong-spirited woman like you would tolerate being treated that way."

I heard it from everyone, and I knew this treatment from Charles was what had culminated in my rages.

One day, I had an appointment with a couple who were concerned about their six-year-old son. They began to tell me their worries, and as I listened, I sensed a hovering part of me that was aware of how disdainful and condescending the husband was toward his wife.

Nevertheless, she continued speaking, laughing, being kind, and acting as if she didn't notice the way she was being treated. I thought simply, *She is me*. Next, I considered their son and what it must mean for him, a small boy, to see his father treating his mother that way. What it must mean for him to see his mother acting as if nothing were wrong with how she was being treated. Then I thought of my own children. I already knew raging was not the answer, and—as much as part of me wished for something different with Charles, despite my ambivalence, despite wanting my children to have an intact family—I knew that we had passed the point of no return.

"Listen, Di," he said one evening, "you aren't pulling your weight around here, and you haven't for years. You've had Camille helping with the house and the kids since your stem cell transplant—what more do you need? You should be bringing in money. I want you to start paying some of the bills. I also want you to think about getting your own health insurance."

I was astonished, or maybe I wasn't. He had absolutely no concept of what a family was or what it took to make a family work; he just didn't want to support us. He didn't want to spend his money on anyone but himself. Camille, helping? Yes, she was. She had been helping out in our household since I had been in the hospital for my stem cell transplant—just a little thing like that, no big deal.

"Send the bills to my lawyer, Charles," I said, as I walked into the other room, where the kids were watching a movie. I sat between them and took a handful of popcorn, asking, "So, what did I miss, guys?" I had no intention of discussing finances with him. He could have his attorney discuss them with my attorney.

It was a few days later that I got a message from Dr. Kealz's secretary to give her a call. I thought it was to get the details about the surgery, which was coming up soon.

"Hi, Kenisha. This is Diane Pomerantz. You left a message for me to call you?" I said when I called back.

"Oh, hi, Diane. Listen, Dr. Kealz wanted me to call you right away because there's a problem with December third. There was something that she didn't realize was on her calendar for that date that can't be changed, and she thinks the surgery is going to have to wait until mid-January. She said she would call you to reschedule it. She'll call later today or tomorrow. She wanted me to tell you she's very sorry about this."

It took a few seconds before I could find my voice. I said, "Okay, I'll wait for her call. Thanks." That old numbness was there again, the numbness that came when my feelings were just too intense.

*Has Charles somehow found a way to interfere with my surgery? Has he gotten to Dr. Kealz?* I wondered.

I don't know how long I sat there, but the ringing of the phone brought me back.

"Hi, Di, it's Pam. I wanted to know if you'd like to stop by and meet the other people in the practice. I know you know Frank and Maria, but you can meet the others. We're having a lunch meeting on Friday at noon. We thought you could join us; can you make it?" she asked.

"I think I can, sure, that'll be fine, but there's something else I need to talk to you about. I don't know what to do. I'm really glad you called when you did."

I had met Pam a year earlier through a mutual friend. We had been introduced because we were both diagnosed with very aggressive breast cancers within a few days of each other. We literally went through our treatment together and supported each other. We had a lot of other things in common as well. Besides following the same treatment protocols, we were both therapists, our kids went to the same school, and we had both gone through fertility treatments. She was also married to a physician, but the similarity stopped there. Her husband was the most supportive man on Earth. He was on staff at the hospital where I had gone for treatment. He knew all my doctors.

Through tears, with panic in my voice, I said, "Pam, Dr. Kealz had to change the surgery from December third. Charles is badgering me about doing it anyway and now is starting to talk about not wanting me on our health insurance. I'm scared that if I put off the procedure, I may not have insurance. I don't know what to do. She's going to call me about rescheduling, but I'm in such a state of panic, I can't stand much more of this." I couldn't control my sobs.

"When Shelby gets home, I'll talk to him about this and see if there's anything he can do. Try not to let yourself 'what if' about everything. Just let it be, and let's see if there's anything to be done, okay? I'll call you after I talk with Shelby."

"Thanks, Pam. I really do appreciate it, and I'll see you on Friday," I reminded her as we hung up.

Although I should have known better, when Charles came home that evening, I automatically told him that my surgery had been canceled, though I didn't say anything about my conversation with Pam. He actually didn't even know who Pam was.

"We can't afford for you to be doing the surgery, and you know that. I don't see how you would even consider such a thing. It's completely selfish. But it's just like you . . ." He would have continued on, as he always did, but I interrupted him.

"I guess there really isn't anything to discuss, then," I said, and I walked into the bedroom.

A few moments later, Charles walked in behind me and sat on the side of the bed.

"Di, I don't think there's any rush for us not to live under the same roof. What do you think?" He looked at me.

Did he actually want to know what I thought? *Sure, he comes and goes as he pleases and has an intimate relationship with his patient-lover, and I'm here cooking, cleaning, and taking care of the kids.*

"I can't see how it would work for me, Charles," I said, with no expression in my voice, working hard to stay in the state of "transitional space" that I had been practicing in a meditation class I was taking.

"Well, maybe we could have some sort of agreement," he said. Then Sam bounded in and was clearly surprised to see us both in the bedroom, sitting and talking on the bed. Elli walked in behind him, her face flushed, saying, "My stomach is hurting, Mom. I feel so sick." I got up to tend to her. Feeling her head, I knew she had a fever, and that was the end of the conversation. I often felt saved by the children.

That same night, Charles slept upstairs. He just got into bed and went to sleep as if he had been doing that every night. I said nothing. I was getting too tired to try to figure out the "whys" of everything he did.

I took my pillow and blanket and slept in the family room. I was finding that there were moments when I felt more powerful, but I also found that when I allowed myself to feel my strength and power, I quickly became frightened. I didn't want to be a single parent.

The next evening, Charles got home earlier than usual. Being home for dinner was very rare for him, even when things were okay; this night, he was home at five. The kids were thrilled, and we all had dinner together, though I found Charles's cheerfulness annoying.

After dinner, I worked on homework with Sammy, and Charles helped Elli with her science fair project.

After the kids were in bed, Charles came into the bedroom. I stayed calm, despite my irritation with how he was trying to play me.

"Di, I was thinking that maybe we should talk to someone together, a marital therapist. Maybe we should try to talk about things with someone before we go any further with all of this. I know I said I wouldn't, but maybe we should." The muscle in his cheek twitched as he spoke.

"I'll have to think about it, Charles. I don't know what your motivation is, and to be honest, at this point I'm not sure that I even want to do it. I'll think about it and let you know."

"Okay." He looked down, picked up his phone from the dresser, and went downstairs to the basement.

I sat there, recalling the year before I had gotten sick. I had been working with an adolescent. Her father was seeing Charles in therapy. Charles would tell me how "crazy" the wife was and how the two daughters hated her. That wasn't what I was hearing from my adolescent patient. One day, I started hearing from Charles that the father was planning to leave his wife. Charles had advised him to go into counseling with her so that he looked as if he were doing everything, he could to make the marriage work; he told the husband how to hide his assets; and he told him ways to get around some of his professional indiscretions.

Back then, I was surprised at how easily Charles seemed to come up with these solutions. Back then, I was disturbed because I felt as if Charles was manipulating this patient and working to break up this man's marriage. Back then, when I met with this man in a parent meeting about his daughter, I found myself thinking, *His words sound like "unmetabolized Charles."* I think I may even have said something to that effect to Charles. What I was thinking now, though, was that Charles had done a dry run with that patient. So much of what had gone on with that patient, so much of what Charles had told him to do, Charles himself was now doing.

I also read in Charles's journal that Victoria had set up a "healing fund" for him. *What a joke,* I thought. *He needs a healing fund to support his activities to heal from his trauma.* Had he always been this way? I really didn't think he was this crazy. I also saw in the journal that he had been having his patients pay him in cash. I was sure he was squirreling away money.

No, I was not going into any kind of counseling with him. I was getting out. I just needed the means to do it.

I got a message from Pam the next morning saying that Shelby had spoken to Dr. Carlton, the surgeon who had done my mastectomy, and she was trying to work out the surgery schedule with Dr. Kealz. Despite all the pain I'd experienced in the past year, there had also been so many moments like this, so many moments of kindness and friendship, and they all made a difference.

# Chapter Twenty-Five

One Sunday in early November 1999, I sat on the deck with a cup of tea, reveling in the vivid orange, yellow, and red colors of the fallen leaves, which made the glare from the sunlight even stronger. I loved this kind of morning. Charles, wanting more time with the kids, had taken them for a hike, and I expected that they would go for lunch afterward and be gone all day. I had a day to myself. I might go get a manicure, something I hadn't done in over a year. Maybe I would even get a massage. I felt like being good to myself. Of course, Charles would say I was being selfish. Fuck Charles. No, I wasn't even going to think of ways he could ruin my day.

After I went into the house, had a nice, leisurely breakfast, and read the paper—something I never did—I showered, dressed, and started to plan my day. It was eleven o'clock, and just as I was about to call the nail salon, the door opened and the kids flew in, with Charles following. Elli picked up a magazine and a banana and flopped into a chair. Charles went down to the basement.

"Back already?" I asked, as Sam jumped onto my lap.

"Yeah, the trail was boring. We should have taken our bikes or scooters."

"Well, didn't you see some interesting stuff? I thought you were going to have lunch at the Wagon Wheel."

"Nah, Daddy said he had to get back to do work." Sam sighed, adding, "Like he always does."

Charles was suddenly standing there. I looked at him and then at the kids. "So, what are you guys going to do for the rest of the day?"

"Well, I have to get over to the office. I have a load of paperwork to do. I'm really falling behind."

"Oh, I thought today was a day you were all going to spend together." I began to stack the newspaper. Charles picked up his coffee mug, and I noticed the shine of his wedding band on his finger.

"I figured that if we took an early hike, at least we'd have some time together, right, guys?" By now, the kids were in the family room, negotiating which TV program they were going to watch. "I'm going to get going so that I can get my work done. See you all later." Charles stuck his head into the family room but didn't get much of a response.

I stood in the kitchen, looking out at the spectacular colors glittering in front of me. Through my tears, the shapes and colors were both tantalizing and frightening. I sat down and took some deep breaths and then went into the family room.

"It's a beautiful day. Finish this show, and then we'll turn off the television and talk about some plans for the day."

Sam didn't respond, but Elli followed me into the kitchen.

"You know, Mom, Dad always does this. He says he's going to spend the day with us, but then he spends just a little time and goes off to the office or wherever he goes. Sam really feels bad. I don't like it when Dad hurts him like that."

"Does it hurt you, too?"

"I'm older. He's my little brother, and nobody hurts my little brother, not even Dad!"

"I think it's wonderful that you care so much about your brother, but you don't have to worry about him. I can take care of both of you. I promise we'll all be okay. Now that you're not doing anything with your dad today, what would you like to do?"

"Well, I'd really like to see Jenna. I haven't seen her for so long, and I really miss her. Can I invite her over, and can we pick her up if she can come?"

"Yes, to both, cutie-patootie."

"Oh, Mom, you and your names!"

"What's wrong with my names? They're good names; they're funny names; they're special names!"

"Oy." We laughed, and she went off to call Jenna, her dear friend from her old school.

I heard the TV show ending in the family room, and I walked in and said to Sam, "I was thinking, since it's such a beautiful day, we could go to this new corn maze I heard about. It sounded neat. I think they even have a hayride there, and they make their own apple cider."

As I spoke, Elli walked in, saying that Jenna could come over. "Can Alex come with us, too?" Sam asked.

"I can call Kara and see if that's okay."

"Yeah! Gimme five!" Sam slapped my palm and raced upstairs, almost knocking his sister down the steps.

An hour later, we were on our way. There was just enough nip in the air to let us know that the seasons were changing. The girls helped me manage the boys through the corn maze, we went for a long hayride, and we made and ate candy apples. Luckily, it was a day without injuries or battles. By the time we walked to the van, I had four tired kids who were juggling a few pumpkins, several sacks of apples, and a couple of jugs of fresh apple cider. The sun was just setting as we pulled off the highway a few miles from home. The van had not been feeling quite right the entire drive back, but then, just as I got off the highway, it lost all power and I drifted onto the shoulder. By then, the temperature was dropping precipitously. I had a broken-down van with four tired and hungry children in it, and I had very little battery power left on my cell phone.

*Oh, shit,* I thought, trying to drown out the four voices behind me. I didn't know who was saying what: "What's wrong, Mom?" "Why did we stop?" "Call Daddy."

Although I did not want to call Charles, I knew I had to. We didn't have AAA. I had always had it when I was single, and we had continued to have it for years, but recently Charles had refused to keep paying for it. We had towing coverage only on our auto insurance. And now it was a Sunday evening and I had to find someone to come and tow me.

I called and I called, and I called Charles, leaving message after message after message on his cell phone, his office phone, and our home phone. Part of me still wanted Charles to rescue me, to be there for me, as he had in the early days, though those days were quickly fading into the dark recesses of my mind. I tried reaching my dad. He wasn't home, and he didn't have a cell phone. I finally called Kara, Alex's mom, and she came with a charged phone, by which point my phone was dead.

"Keep the phone with you, and don't worry about the kids," Kara said. "Rob was ordering pizza as I walked out the door, so everyone will be fine. You have the house phone number, but here's Rob's cell number, too. Call when you get towed, and I'll come pick you up." She hugged me, then turned to the back and gathered everyone into her van. Elli didn't move.

"Mom, I don't want you sitting here by yourself," she whispered anxiously.

"You and Jenna go with the boys. I really will be fine; a tow truck will be here soon. I want you to go." I hugged her, and they left.

About two hours later, I reached my dad. I had not been able to get a tow truck. He drove over and helped me unload the van. We locked it up and went over to Kara's house to pick up Elli, Jenna, and Sammy. Fortunately, there was no school the next day, so being off schedule was not so terrible. I would deal with the van in the morning. I could tell that my dad's distress about what was going on was increasing but that he was trying very hard not to say anything.

Charles never responded. He never asked what had happened. He never even asked where the van was when he got home at eleven o'clock that night. He just wasn't interested. Of course, that would change when he saw the bill for a new transmission.

Later, our attorneys asked us to give them lists of people they could call to testify, if needed, to our individual competence as parents. I gave a list of names to Cal, after making sure that the people I listed were okay with my giving their names. Charles, on the other hand, just gave a list and didn't ask anyone. Kara was one of the people he put on his list.

One day, as Kara and I sat at her kitchen table while Sammy and Alex were having an army battle in the other room, I told Kara that her name was on Charles's list.

"You mean he put me on his list without asking? I guess it shouldn't surprise me."

"I thought you might want to know," I told her.

"Well, actually I'm glad. I'd be happy to testify for Dr. Mandel. I have a great number of things I'd like to say that will give the court a clear understanding of the kind of devotion he has for his children."

"Like what?" I asked.

"I would love to tell them about that frigid night when he refused to respond to your calls for help when your car broke down and you had four children, including two of his own, in the car, and they sat there for over an hour before I came to help you."

---

NOVEMBER dragged on. I remained unable to stop reading the emails that Charles left out. *She's despicable; I can't stand the sight of her; hearing her voice makes me sick*—these were just a few of the things that he wrote, and I read. I was still trying to understand what was going on; why did he hate me so much? I still felt out of control inside, although on the outside the lack of control wasn't showing. There were no more rages and only occasional sarcastic comments on my part.

When Charles's birthday arrived, Victoria and his other "muses" made him a party in his DC office. That morning before he left for work, he was unusually friendly. It angered me, but I said nothing. The kids wanted to make him a birthday dinner, and so I agreed that we could.

Charles was becoming increasingly strange. I called him throughout the day to find out when he was coming home and to make sure he would be home for dinner. When I finally reached him at about four thirty in the afternoon, his response to my comment on how hard it was to reach him was to say, "Mercury is in retrograde, so all communication is hard." He said he would be home by six thirty.

Charles did arrive home at about the time he'd said he would, he did put on the birthday hat the kids had put at his place setting at the table, and he was polite, but he was so tired that he could hardly keep his eyes open. We had not been at the table very long when he said, "Thanks for a great birthday dinner. I'm so tired, I'm going to go downstairs and just have some quiet time." He gave each kid a quick hug and, in a detached, spaced-out sort of way, got up and went down the stairs.

A bewildered silence permeated the room; then Sam bolted from his chair and ran to the top of the stairs. "Daddy, you didn't even open your presents." He stomped down a couple of steps and called,

"Daddy!" If Charles heard Sam, he didn't respond; he had closed the door behind him.

Sam ran back to the coffee table, where the children had placed gifts for their father. He grabbed the package he had carefully wrapped, and, before anyone could say anything, he stomped on it and kicked it across the room. There lay the wooden birdhouse that he had so carefully painted—smashed, splinters of bright colors lying across the dark wooden floor.

Sam burst into tears and ran upstairs to his room, slamming the door behind him, Elli looked wide-eyed at me and ran up after her brother, and I followed behind them. I found Elli sitting on Sam's bed. Sam was buried under his covers, crying, and Elli was sitting and rubbing his back, saying, "It will be okay, Sammy. Dad's just being dumb. He'll be sorry when we just don't give him presents anymore." She kept rubbing her brother's back. Other than Sam's quiet sobs, there was silence for what felt like a very long time.

Then, slowly, Sam's dark curls emerged from under the covers. His eyes were puffy and red. "Why doesn't Daddy love us anymore?" He looked at me, waiting for an answer.

It was very hard to look at the pain in his eyes, as well as in the questioning face of his sister. I knew I had to distance myself from my own anger, my own pain.

I took a breath, moved from the rocker, and sat on the bed. I pulled both of them close. "I don't have all the answers. I don't understand a lot of what Daddy has been feeling lately or a lot about why he has been acting the way he has been acting. But there is something I do know. Your dad does love you as best as he can. Right now, for whatever reason, he might not be able to show it the way you would like him to, but it's because he's not able to. I want you both to know that it has nothing at all to do with either of you. People sometimes have problems dealing with their feelings. I think Daddy is having a lot of confused feelings right now, but I do know he loves you." I hated him for doing this to my innocent, beautiful children.

"He has a funny way of showing it." Elli rolled her eyes.

No one spoke. We sat in silence. Charles and I had not talked about separation with the kids, but I now knew that it was coming very soon.

I also knew that I might have to tell them first and on my own. His instability was more and more obvious. His moods shifted up and down, depending on whether he and Victoria were "on" or "off" on any given day. Perhaps his birthday party had not been as wonderful in fact as it had been in fantasy.

"Hey, you know, just because your dad wasn't up for a party doesn't mean we should let a great chocolate cake go to waste. First one down gets extra icing." I smiled, and all three of us got up and rushed down the stairs to the kitchen.

Sam was subdued, but we were all enjoying our cake and milk, when suddenly Charles walked into the kitchen. "Hey, no one invited me for my own birthday cake?" He laughed.

I was uncertain whether I detected some sheepishness in his voice.

More likely, that was wishful thinking.

"Should we open some of those presents that I saw in the living room?" He winked at Elli just as she turned her head away.

"Would you like some cake?" I offered, seething that he was playing head games not only with me, but now with his own children. I needed to get out and get the children out. Living in this house of lies was crazy making for all of us.

"Hey, Sam must have had a pretty busy day—look at him!" Elli and I turned as Charles walked around the table and knelt down on the floor, gently picking up Sam, who was fast asleep.

"Come on, guy," he whispered softly. "Let me get you into bed." He gently lifted him up, and as he carried him, he turned and said, "I'll be back in a few minutes."

It was at those moments that I saw the old Charles. The problem was, I didn't know whether that person had ever been real.

## Chapter Twenty-Six

Although the house we now lived in was spacious, the layout felt confusing and "schizophrenic." The shades of pewter-gray sky filtered through random windows and made odd and disconcerting patterns on the walls. Sounds echoed off the high ceilings. The multiple staircases up and down gave me a feeling that dangers lurked in hidden places. Perhaps it was just my state of mind. I had felt so comfortable, so nurtured, in our old house; now I had no sense of protected containment. I didn't feel as if I had a home. Of course, I didn't have much energy to get things organized now, nor did I want to do that, since I now knew that this place would be temporary. Had I known what I now knew, I never would have agreed to the move from our house on St. John's Lane.

I always had liked the fall, knowing that Thanksgiving was coming. Until the previous year, when I had been in treatment and we had spent the holiday with Allyson and Harry, I had always enjoyed planning a festive meal and inviting family, friends, and anyone who had nowhere else to go. This year, I didn't have the energy. This year, it was enough just to get through each day.

"I spoke with my parents this morning," Charles announced when he returned home from the office late one evening. "I invited them for Thanksgiving. Have you invited your dad yet?"

Usually my responses came quickly, spontaneously. It wasn't that way anymore when I spoke to Charles. There was a long, drawn-out silence. Then I said, "No, I didn't invite my dad. He was invited to his friend Lydia's, and I told him that he should go there because it would be more enjoyable for him. It really is too much for me to be making Thanksgiving dinner, Charles. I would really rather not have company under the circumstances." I paused, avoiding looking directly at him.

"Well, we could go to a restaurant, so you don't have to cook," he said.

"The truth is, Charles, I really don't feel like entertaining. I would prefer not to have company at all. You have been very clear that you have no interest in being with me, yet you want to pretend that we're a family for Thanksgiving? I'm sorry, I don't want to do that."

Charles looked incredulous. "You don't know how to show any gratitude, do you? After all that my parents have done for us, you can't even make Thanksgiving dinner. You are unbelievable!"

Even though I knew that everything Charles said was a distorted projection of his own feelings, I wound up questioning myself, feeling guilty and feeling like I was being bad, just as Charles wanted me to feel.

In the end, Marcy and Albert did come for Thanksgiving. They stayed in a hotel, and instead of cooking, I ordered prepared food. I don't know whether he told his parents anything. They were as disconnected and oblivious as ever, but at least this time Charles did not leave me to entertain them for the entire visit, as he always had in the past.

I did still work for his approval, though, and at times I did still want to connect with him—I suppose in part because of my loneliness—but I knew that, despite his not always looking crazy on the surface, Charles had serious problems and that his actions toward me were mean and sadistic. I knew I couldn't stay—not if I wanted to remain healthy, not if I wanted what was best for our children. It wasn't that I didn't want to stay—I loved being married; I loved being a family. Whether I loved Charles was uncertain—but I couldn't stay given the way it was, and I knew in the depths of my soul that it was not going to change.

"Momma, Grandma and Grandpa are leaving. You gotta come out to say good-bye." Sam ran in through the garage, pulling on my shirt to follow him.

"Okay, okay, I'm coming." I followed Sam out, hugged Marcy and Albert, and waved along with the kids and Charles as they got in their car and drove off. It had just started to snow.

Unusual as it was, both of the kids wanted to watch the same movie, *Star Wars*, which meant I could get some things done in my office upstairs.

"What do you think about trying counseling?" Charles appeared suddenly in the doorway, an inquisitive look on his face.

I looked at him, expressionless. "Why do you want to go into counseling?" I asked, thinking about the things he said about me in the e-mails he wrote to Victoria and in his journal: *The only reason it's good she hasn't died is so that she can provide childcare . . .*

This was what he thought of me, of his children's mother, and he was talking about counseling. I should have been enraged, but I think I was beyond that.

"I don't think it's a good idea, Charles," I said, after a very long wait for him to answer my question without him responding.

"I guess it's not." I'm sure I saw relief on his face.

Charles looked at me and said, in a softer tone than he had used in quite a while, "I really didn't want this to happen. You didn't do anything wrong. It was destiny."

I didn't say anything, though I thought, *He's fuckin' crazy, and he's making me crazy, too! Destiny? Pendulums? He has been making decisions by using a crystal pendulum. He doesn't just find it an interesting curiosity; he truly believes it gives him the right answer without him having to consciously think anything through.* As much as it pained me to see him this way, I knew I had to get out with the children as fast as possible.

I could see the impact on Elli most clearly. She was always feeling ill, one physical symptom after another; the school nurse was always calling. Her withdrawal was intense; her moods shifted with the moon. She would refuse to do her homework. This usually bubbly, artistic, athletic child with a myriad of interests was now taciturn and sullen. She was always bored. She could never find anything to do. She would slam her bedroom door and hide. I would find my things and her brother's things hidden in her room. One night, Charles had said he would be home for dinner by six, and so we waited. At about six fifteen, the phone rang, and it was Charles, who said he had an emergency and would be home by seven but that we should start dinner without him.

"He's such a damn liar!" Elli yelled, as she ran up to her room, refusing to unlock her door so that I could speak to her.

The entire year I was in treatment, Charles really did nothing to help the kids deal with any feelings they had about my illness. Sammy was young and didn't have much understanding. Elli, though, was terrified, I know. She developed an acute fear of heights after going up in the glass elevator in the hospital to visit me when I was admitted for my stem cell transplant. After that, she wouldn't go near a hospital again and would white-knuckle it if she had to use an escalator or elevator. Driving over a bridge was terrifying for her. Her fear of bugs caused chaos in the entire household.

I walked down to the basement after Charles had come home one evening. It was one of those nights when he did not bother to say hello.

"I'd like to speak with you about something, Charles," I said. "Have you noticed how Elli has changed? I'm really concerned about her. She is so withdrawn and is not adjusting well to her new school.

Maybe we should have her see someone. What do you think?" I asked, preparing myself for an attack on my judgment in one way or another.

Charles turned from his computer and glared at me. "I think she's just a typical eleven-year-old girl going into adolescence. That does not constitute a psychological problem that requires psychotherapy."

"Charles, she has been through, and is going through, a lot. She's a really sensitive kid, and she's at a very vulnerable age. My illness, moving, changing schools, and the changes that our family is going through are major for all of us. They're having an effect on our daughter." As much as I tried to remain calm, I knew the intensity in the tone of my voice was increasing.

"She's fine. You call yourself a child psychologist? You're driving us into financial disaster. All you want to do is spend money. Why don't you just spend more time with your children?" he yelled, then added, "I want to go to bed. This is the end of the discussion. Please go upstairs."

I breathed deeply, turned, and walked upstairs. We were not yet separated, which meant I was not yet obligated to get his permission to do what I wanted to do in terms of medical treatment for the children. I was going to find someone who took insurance so that Elli had someone with whom to talk. It might not be the person I would choose if I had unlimited resources, but I was going to do it anyway, despite Charles. I was a child psychologist. I *did* know what I was seeing. My daughter needed some help.

## Chapter Twenty-Seven

Only as I saw my marriage falling apart did I really begin to think about and feel the physical consequences of my disease. More and more, I felt deformed, and it was hard to separate my distorted self-image from the profound sense of rejection that I experienced. One thing was certain for me: I would not leave my marriage before I had reconstructive surgery. I didn't know what lay ahead for me, financially or in any other way. Physically, I was determined to feel whole.

The actual reconstructive surgery had neither the drama nor the intensity of the surgeries of the previous year, although the place and many of the players, including me, were the same. Actually, I wasn't the same now. Two weeks after my diagnosis, a little over a year earlier, I had written a letter to an old friend: *I'm also very lucky to have Charles, who is a wonderful partner and friend and parent. Our whole experience with infertility took its toll on our relationship, but in this past year we have been able to do some real healing. I am truly thankful that we are sharing our lives together.*

Looking at that letter now, I realized how much denial I had been in as I'd tried to confront my diagnosis, and even during the previous years of my marriage. True, the problems had worsened since then, and they were to become even more pronounced, but at that time I'd needed not to see what I'd really known was there.

When I awoke from surgery, out of recovery and back in my room, I realized that my dad, who had brought me to the hospital, was gone. The surgery had happened at eight in the morning; by the time I opened my eyes, I could see through the window that the December sky was black. The room was empty, and the only sound was the slow and steady drip of the IV.

A nurse walked in and asked if I wanted a heated blanket. I nodded and smiled, remembering how soothing those blankets felt when they came out of the warmer. I put a hand to my chest tentatively. Even through the bandages, I felt the curves of symmetry. I left my hand on my chest and enjoyed the feeling of my body, of my heartbeat, through my fingers. At that moment, I knew that my decision to do the surgery had been the right one. I felt like a whole person again. I had trusted myself. I knew I needed to feel this way when I left my marriage.

An unappealing tray of yellow broth and jiggly green Jell-O sat on the bed stand next to me, and my stomach quivered. I reached over to put the stainless-steel cover over the dishes, to hide them from view. I didn't want that visual unpleasantness to disrupt the calm I was feeling at that moment. As I stretched out my arm to reach the tray, I felt the first sharp pains in my chest and abdomen. I flinched quickly and drew back toward the pillow, catching my breath.

Just then, Charles walked in, carrying a Christmas shopping bag. For an instant, my feelings toward him began to soften. I thought of all the years that he had brought me flowers, and I smiled.

"My patient gave this to me today," he began. "It's not anything I want, so I thought I'd bring it here to brighten up your room."

"Thanks," I said, as he handed me the bag and I unwrapped the first of two ceramic figurines. I knew which patient had probably given this gift to him. Dara had been giving Charles ceramic painted statues every Christmas for years. They were usually dogs or cats or elves or gnomes, sometimes Santa himself.

The first figurine I unwrapped, as I sat there in my hospital gown, with my IV pumping, was an Irish setter. His only remarkable feature was his wings. He was an angel. I sighed. "Thanks. It's cute."

It was clear that Charles had already opened and rewrapped both of these, so he knew what they were. It was upon opening the second statue, which was larger and heavier, that I found my head becoming light. As I unwrapped it, I could see out of the corner of my eye that Charles had started to unpack the bag I had brought to the hospital. I felt my chest tightening. I didn't want him going through my things. He kept looking at his watch. I continued to unwrap the object. I found myself confused by what I held in my hands. It was an old, gray, and wrinkled woman in ragged clothes. She had a crumpled shopping bag at her feet and sat on a dark, broken wooden bench. On her back were wings.

*Where could someone even find such a thing?* I would later wonder. But at that moment, my only thought was, *My husband has brought a bag-lady angel to his wife's hospital room to make it look cheerful. This after she has gone through a year of treatment for cancer and her doctors have predicted that she has a very poor prognosis.*

Charles picked up the statues and placed them on a table by the window, near the pictures of the children that I had packed.

"Thanks for setting up the room, Charles," I said flatly. I closed my eyes and tried to meditate.

"It's what I'm good at," he replied, as he went on chatting mindlessly but not really engaging directly with me at all.

Feeling very tired and really wanting him to leave, I did not open my eyes and finally fell asleep. When I awoke a while later, he was gone.

When it was time for a shift change, a new nurse came in to introduce herself and noticed the statues on the table.

"What in the world are these?" she asked.

"My husband thought they would cheer me up." I smiled weakly. "Do you like them?" she asked, and I shook my head no.

"They're bizarre. They need to be out of sight. How about I put them in one of these drawers, and when you leave, you can take them"—she paused—"if you want them, or you can throw them out. Not that I'm suggesting anything." She smiled.

---

MY five days in the hospital passed quickly. Although the recovery from this surgery was supposed to be difficult, I had a relatively easy time. The side effects from the painkillers were the worst problem I had, and when those were stopped, I felt fine. I had a sense that my body was whole again. The children and I called back and forth, my dad and my friends visited, and Charles came once or twice, but there was no connection between us.

On day five, December 21, Susan and Peg came to pick me up and take me home. I don't think Charles even offered. As we were packing up my things, I took the figurines from the drawer where they had been since the night the nurse had placed them there. Both women looked shocked when they saw the statues, which I had begun to put in my bag.

"What are those?" Peg asked, with horror in her voice.

"A gift from Charles, to brighten up the room." I chuckled.

"Well, you sure as hell are not taking those with you," Susan said.

She took them from my hands and threw them in the trash can.

"That is so perverse. He is so sick and so toxic for you!" Peg added.

The bag lady and Irish setter angels were thus left behind. I would later regret that I had not taken them with me. I would have loved to be able to take them to court, in an attempt to show how sadistic and crazy Charles was. Perhaps it also was a way to prove to myself that what I was experiencing was really happening.

I arrived home and found the house empty, except for Knaidl, who happily licked and nuzzled me. After I settled in, Susan and Peg left, and the echoes and chill of the house enveloped me. Immediately, anger at Charles overcame me. My breath was shallow, my palms were wet, my head was light, and my thoughts were dark. I felt such hatred for him, for his desertion, for his sadistic callousness. I recalled his saying to me, just a week before the surgery, when I confronted him about how he dismissed me, acted as if I didn't exist, "What do you expect me to be, Jesus Christ?"

"No, I expect you to treat me with the same compassion that one would show toward another human being, especially one who is the mother of your children and whom you have shared twenty years of your life with. *That* is what I would expect, even if the 'love' is gone."

"You don't know me at all. Once I make the decision, I have the capacity to completely cut someone out of my life." He said this as if it were an admirable trait. As if being able to split off parts of his experience was a healthy way to cope with life.

That conversation, as well as visions of the bag lady and dog angels, flooded me, and I wanted to scream. I tried to meditate. I did scream, but it hurt too much, so I cried and fell asleep.

I woke up a couple of hours later when Elli, Sam, and Camille walked in.

"Momma's home, Elli," Sammy called, as he jumped on the bed where Knaidl and I had been sleeping.

Afterward, Camille took Elli and Sam out to choose a few movies that we could all watch together over the next couple of days.

Charles arrived home around seven-thirty. We had already eaten, and Camille had left. The kids, Knaidl, and I had a bowl of popcorn and were sitting on my bed, watching *Willy Wonka and the Chocolate Factory*, when Charles walked in. Sam lunged at him, so happy he was home, and Elli continued to watch the movie.

"I love this movie," he said, as he pulled up a chair. "I hope you guys are helping your mom. She's got to rest for the next few days, okay?"

"We know, Dad." Elli's eyes never left the screen.

"I know you do, but I want to make sure that your brother does, too." Charles had not even asked how I was feeling, let alone acknowledged my presence, since he had walked into the room.

After the kids were in bed, he walked through the bedroom where I was reading.

"I take it everything went okay with your discharge today?" he asked casually.

"Uh-huh, yes, it was fine, thanks for asking," I replied, trying to keep my distance. Yet his polite distance always drew me in. It always felt like an invitation to try to break through the wall. I would always wind up talking too much, saying things I should have left unsaid. This time, though, my anger was still close to the surface.

"I didn't bring those statues home," I told him.

"They certainly weren't great works of art." He laughed disdainfully.

"No, they weren't. I'm sure there could be a lot of therapeutic material to go over with a patient who gave those particular statues as a gift," I said. Then I continued, "They really were kind of perverse."

I saw an almost imperceptible smile at the corners of his mouth. "Perverse?" he questioned. "What do you mean?"

Perhaps the smile indicated his anxiety. I suppose my saying his "gift" was perverse disturbed him. Charles was never one to acknowledge that, just maybe, something he had done was wrong or inappropriate.

"Well, I believe that angels are divine beings," he said, after a long pause.

"Yes, I agree. Angels can be divine and beautiful beings—just not when they're a bag-lady angel and a dog angel. They lose some of their divinity and beauty when they are brought to someone who has been confronting death and is in the hospital." This time, I looked directly at Charles as I spoke.

He turned and walked out of the room and retreated to the basement.

Sleep did not come easily to me that night. Physical discomfort and strange dreams made me fitful. I awoke at 3 a.m. with images of being in a room near Harvard Square, listening to loud, disturbing music with violent lyrics. The thought that crossed my mind as I drifted back to sleep was that at least the music was a more controlled and sublimated way to express how angry I felt.

I awoke again briefly at four-thirty with a feeling of dread. I felt as if I were falling into the depths of the abyss, alone and abandoned but knowing that I needed to protect myself. Again, sleep overcame me.

At five-thirty, there were more disturbing images. This time, they were more directly about my relationship with Charles and how unsafe I felt in relation to him, how deeply I believed he could not be trusted.

It was 6:10 a.m. when Charles came into the bedroom and walked over to the bed. I must have just fallen back to sleep when I opened my eyes and saw him looming over me.

"Good morning," he said, very formally, and then paused. His tension was palpable. "I want you to know that my caseload is going down. It's ten hours below what it was the third week in November."

"The first two weeks of December, your caseload was quite good, as I recall. Thirty-one to thirty-three hours isn't bad," I countered.

His breathing quickened. "We're going to be in financial disaster again. We need to make plans now for sources from whom to borrow. We have got to work together on this."

All I could think was, *We need to work together? All I want is to get out of this marriage.*

"You had the surgery; you caused this problem," he said.

I was stunned. He had all kinds of personal luxuries: gym equipment, a gym membership, air-flow machines, leather journals, rock gardens, plants. His office was becoming increasingly lush. His children, on the other hand, didn't have money for groceries, and not because I had chosen to have surgery. He rejected every suggestion I made to reduce expenses.

I said, "Why not rent the two offices upstairs so the rent on the building will be less?"

He said, "It will negatively change the energy of the building."

When he finally stopped badgering me, I was spent. He left for his DC office, not taking any lunch with him.

My dad arrived with bagels for all of us and then took the kids to school. I called Dr. Putman. She was pretty upset that Charles was putting me through this right after having major surgery.

My sense of reality was being tested constantly. Who was this person I had been with for all these years? Had I ever known the real Charles? Maybe not. Maybe only at this point of real-life crisis was I seeing his true self—and it was crumbling.

## Chapter Twenty-Eight

The clock said 9:00 a.m. And the only sound I could hear was that of the wind howling. Icicles glistened in the sunlight through the shutters and dangled like crystal needles on the branches. Every few moments, they made a tinkling sound as the wind blew them and they shattered against the windowpanes.

It was December 24, the first day of winter break. I was sure that Elli was still asleep and surprised that I hadn't heard a sound from Sammy. It was the first morning since I'd gotten home from the hospital that Charles had not pounced upon me, like a lion in wait, at the crack of dawn. I knew he must have left already; he was never home this late. I still wasn't able to move very quickly, but I was more mobile than I had anticipated. I put on my robe and walked out into the family room.

"Hi, Momma. Come sit here next to me," Sam said, as he pushed a spoonful of Cheerios into his mouth. "Did you sleep good, Momma? Poppy came over and made us breakfast and said we could watch TV, but he wanted us to let you sleep, so we did." He smiled proudly.

"This guy is the best, and so is his sister, who is still asleep," said my dad, sitting on the couch, drinking the cup of coffee he had made for himself. "Did you sleep well, honey?" he asked, looking at me with questions I knew he was not asking directly.

"I'm better than I thought I'd be. I'm a little stiff and sore, but I thought I wouldn't be able to move, and I'm moving." I smiled as Sam jumped up to hug me.

"Dad, I made plans for Sammy to spend the day at Colin's house today. Elli is going to go over to Jillian's house. I think you've been to both places before; will you be able to drive them there? Their parents have already said they'll bring them home after dinner."

"Sure. You know I'd do anything for you, dear, anything . . ." he started singing.

"Poppy, stop. You sound awful," Sam teased, and we all laughed.

Laughing hurt, so I had to stop.

My dad and I walked into the kitchen alone, and he said, "I guess this stuff happens all the time, Di. There was a story in the paper this morning about a psychiatrist who was sued for breaking up someone's marriage." My dad shook his head. "I thought Charles was a smart man."

I smiled. "Me, too." I got up to get the paper but couldn't find it. "I guess he was smart enough to take the paper with him so that I wouldn't see the story." I shrugged.

We sat and chatted for a while, until Elli appeared, still sleepy-eyed. Even with her blond bedhead, she was an absolute beauty. I just wished she didn't seem so sad.

"Hi, Poppy. Why are you here so early?" she asked, as she hugged him and then sat down at the table and poured herself some cereal and milk.

"Because I wanted to bring my most beautiful granddaughter something I knew she would like." He went over to the refrigerator and got out Elli's favorite chocolate, cream-filled Krispy Kreme donut and put it down in front of her, smiling broadly.

"Oh, I love you, Poppy! It's my favorite!" Elli quickly took one more spoonful of cereal, put the bowl and spoon in the dishwasher, and then, with great drama, took her first bite.

"It's delicious. Thank you, Poppy!" She threw her arms around her grandfather's neck and then sat down, savoring each bite. My dad and I watched her and smiled.

By noon, my dad had left with the kids, and I found myself feeling very down. Lydia, my dad's friend, called and invited the kids and me to dinner that evening with her family.

"Thanks so much, Lydia. That would be so nice, but I don't think I'm up for going out yet," I told her.

When I hung up, my mood had plummeted even further. I knew that the kids and I would get lots of invitations, but while we were still all living together, Charles was going to feel excluded from those events. I told myself I couldn't allow myself to think about that. He had made his choices. Despite his depression, he was the one who said he wanted out of the marriage.

I had kept a fire burning all day. I loved the warmth and the fragrant crackling of the wood. I made rice pudding, my favorite comfort food on days like this. Then I just lay on the couch and listened to John Coltrane and Cleo Laine. *This is what it should be like when someone's just had major surgery*, I thought. *This is what a partner who cares should want for the person they care about.*

Elli arrived home around six; Sammy was still at Colin's house. At about six thirty, the phone rang. "I just finished with patients. I don't feel well. I don't even want to see the kids. I guess I could get home by seven. Call me when Sammy gets home; I'm sure I'll hear the phone." Charles's voice was dull, and he sounded lethargic.

Part of me wanted to reach out to him, but I didn't want to get sucked in. Either he was pulling more of his shit, or he really was very, very depressed, which I believed he was. In fact, I knew he had started on an antidepressant the week before. But by now I also knew there was manipulation in everything he said and did. I wasn't even really sure that he was at the office. Would he go to such extremes to make me feel crazy? He had certainly done it before when he'd taken the money from our bank account.

Charles arrived home at about seven-thirty. Elli and I were working on the wallpaper in a dollhouse we had built. Charles acted as if he didn't see her.

"I'm going up to my room to draw," she said, looking directly at me with puzzlement in her eyes.

"Okay. I'll be up in a little while, sweetie," I told her.

Charles seemed to be in another world. He lay on the couch, put his head on my lap, and started to ramble, pant, and cry. It went on for hours. He said all kinds of things in his ramblings and groans.

Some were apologetic: "I didn't mean to hurt you."

Many were veiled barbs: "The sickest have the most power."

And there were accusations: "The only thing I did wrong was to not stop you from having the surgery. I should have called your doctor in order to stop you from ruining us."

He said all this with the grandiose and manipulative drama of the decompensating narcissist. He really believed that if he had called Dr. Kealz or Dr. Putman, they would have paid attention to him. He was oblivious to how others saw him. Somehow, I was able to remain fairly detached. He certainly did not pull me in the way he had in the past. Nevertheless, I didn't stop him. I sat passively, the "good, acutely vigilant" therapist, and I listened. I listened to every word.

When he began to lament about money, I gently brought up ways to reduce expenses.

"Perhaps you could think about giving up your DC office. It's over one thousand dollars a month, and you use it only one day a week. You could rent space in DC for the patients who can't make the drive to your office here," I said, in a very gentle tone. His moans and panting became even more intense.

When I suggested that he get a job for five to ten hours a week for a short time, his groans became louder and he said, "You are on a different planet."

Every so often, he took a deep breath, sighed, and said, "I just need to get up. I'm indulging myself," but as quickly as the words fell from his lips, the groans, moans, and panting resumed.

"If only there was any way we could stay together," he said several times, then added, "but we're too different." I said nothing.

I suppose those were the moments when I might have been able to try to do something to save my marriage. I knew he was struggling with his decision. Nevertheless, as much as I didn't want to end my marriage, in the depths of my being I had come to realize that I could not be with Charles. The problems were much deeper than his relationship with Victoria. That relationship, that betrayal, I could get beyond. It was his ability to be so sadistic to me and so contemptuous of me that I could never surmount. I could never, I would never, trust this man again.

Charles finally fell asleep in the bedroom. I was so tired, I just wanted to collapse. I finally just lay down and fell into a deep sleep.

When I awoke and walked into the kitchen, Charles and the kids were sitting around the table, eating breakfast.

"Sammy said that he's going over to Jack's house for a sleepover, and Elli said she's spending the night at Leah's house. I'll drive them, and I was thinking I would go for a hike on the trail. I think it'll help my head." Charles's voice was still pretty monotone as he spoke; his facial expressions were flat and distant.

"Okay, that's fine," I said, thinking about the weather report, which called for temperatures below zero with the wind chill.

Charles did take the children to their friends' houses. I had another quiet day at home. The question of whether Charles was really spending the entire day hiking in this piercingly cold weather or was with Victoria pricked my mind frequently.

The sun had already set, and the evening had turned bitterly cold and icy by the time Charles walked through the front door.

"It sure is cold out there." He shivered as he moved close to the fire, taking off his gloves and hat. "It was a good hike; it was good for my head." He didn't make any eye contact as he spoke.

"I was concerned that you were out in that freezing cold for so long," I said, mostly to see what his response would be.

"I didn't even notice how cold it was. I just walked. I dressed pretty warmly. I think I'll have some of that hot chocolate you're drinking," he said, as he walked into the kitchen.

When he emerged, holding a cup of hot chocolate in one hand and a bowl of rice pudding in the other, he said, "I'm pretty wiped. I think I'm just going to go downstairs and pass out. Good night, Di." And down the stairs he went, leaving me once again feeling like a fool.

I had avoided reading his journal and e-mails for weeks, but after the previous night and his disappearance for hours in the freezing cold, I couldn't help myself. He left his journal out, and I did read some of it. He was "falling apart, making no sense," yet his writing was so lucid and the clarity with which he spewed his negative feelings about me, despite my attempts to soothe him, was still there. There was no evidence of the distress of the previous night.

Again, I was being conned. I recalled my first therapist, long before Charles even existed, referring to something I did over and over again by saying, "So, you're knocking your head against the wall; how long are you going to do it this time?"

Yes, that was me, doing the same thing over and over again, thinking—or not thinking at all, really—that the result would be different. Hoping to understand my world, to give myself a feeling of control, was what drove me to read Charles's journal and e-mails over and over again. I was always hoping to gain some understanding of, to find a way to believe, something that I found incomprehensible. However, I just needed to stop, and instead to use a scripted language for myself, to find a way to interact with Charles, until I was out. I needed to "fake it until I could make it."

The next morning when I awoke, Charles was in the kitchen. "I think I'll go out for another hike this morning," he said, not lifting his eyes from the newspaper. "What time will the kids be home?"

"Around lunchtime, I think. Lynn is coming over with Ally this afternoon, and I think Jack is going to spend the afternoon here," I told him in a very detached tone of voice.

"I'll be back by the time they get here," he said.

I nodded and continued making my oatmeal, and then I started a fire.

Charles and the kids got home at about the same time. Shortly after that, my friend Lynn and her daughter, Ally, came by. Elli and Ally took off to Elli's room. Elli and I had been working on wallpapering the dollhouse, and Lynn said she would drive me over to a nearby shop to pick up a few supplies we needed.

"Yeah, go on—get out for a bit. It will be good for you, Di. I'm going to be here, so go. I can watch the kids," Charles said, as if this were how he always acted.

This was my first trip out since the surgery. We weren't gone much more than an hour when I tried to call Charles but got no answer. I shouldn't have been surprised when Lynn and I walked back in to find popcorn all over the kitchen floor.

"Where's Daddy?" I asked Sam, as Jack looked on.

"I don't know," Sam said, with a bit of defensiveness in his voice. "He went to the office, I think."

I looked at Lynn and rolled my eyes. "So, what happened here?" I asked. "You know that you're not supposed to be doing things in the kitchen that involve using any appliances, unless someone older is with you."

"Well, Mrs. Mandel, we did ask Elli and Ally if they wanted to make popcorn with us," Jack piped in.

"Yeah, but Elli told us to get lost and not bother them," Sam said indignantly. "And she should get in trouble for that," he added.

"Well, no one is getting in trouble, but everyone is going to help clean up the mess. I'll set the timer for ten minutes. Let's see if we can beat the clock."

Lynn and Ally stayed a while longer, and then Lynn offered to drive Jack home when they left. Elli decided to make picture frames for the dollhouse, and Sammy continued building with Legos. I sat by the fire and let my mind drift wherever it chose to go.

I realized that Charles did believe that his dramatic purging of the previous few days was his punishment for how he had been treating me and the children. He had paid retribution. Now he was free.

When he got home a couple of hours later, I didn't say anything to him about his having left the kids home alone. I did ask, though, "Did you see Victoria today?"

He paused briefly, and then he said, "Yes."

It was a while before I said anything else. Then I said, in a soft but even tone, "Charles, the next time you feel really anxious or depressed, or the next time you're having a panic attack like the ones you've been having, deal with it with Victoria; don't come to me." I was composed; my eye contact was direct. I had no doubt about what I was saying. Not that I wouldn't have internal doubts in the future, not that I wasn't feeling excruciating pain at that moment, but I would deal with that agony on my own.

## Chapter Twenty-Nine

It was a new year. One and a half years had passed since I had gotten my diagnosis and started my yearlong treatment journey. I was still alive. The process of being in treatment had kept me busy. It had given me focus and direction and no time for depression. Now, without that focus, I was confronted with the unavoidable reality of what had become of my life.

The most recent surgery and Charles's intense response to it had exhausted me, taken something out of me. I felt as if I had taken steps backward. Although I got up each day, put one foot in front of the other, and did what I needed to do, I often awoke in the morning with the thought, *I wish I were dead.* The other thought that always followed was, *Help me, Momma, help me.* Although I was finding myself more irritable with the children, the third thought, the one that would finally get me out of bed, was, *My kids need me.*

Charles was giving me money for groceries only every couple of weeks by this time. I was juggling air in order to make ends meet and provide the things the children needed.

"If I give you money, you'll spend it," he said, when I told him that our children needed things.

When bills arrived, he started presenting them to me, saying, "How are we going to divide these?"

I looked at him in astonishment. We were still married. I had virtually no income.

"You can send them all to my attorney," I told him. "He and I will go over them and decide what to do with them."

"Just remember, I've been supporting you and the kids for years. Now it's going to be your turn!" He seethed with every word he spoke.

I just couldn't wrap my brain around why he hated me so much. I certainly hadn't been perfect in the marriage, but his hatred was beyond anything I could understand. His concept of marriage and of family and mine were universes apart. And yet I kept trying to understand.

That January, the temperature was frigid. The icicles hanging delicately from the tree branches, although pretty, never melted. The frozen fields were the tundra of my internal existence. The black ice on the road was impossible to see but an ever-present peril I always felt. The kids needed me, and I was there physically, but my emotional presence was not constant.

In an attempt to be proactive, I finally moved my office in mid-January and had my name removed from the sign outside the former office. I wanted my professional association with Charles to be completely erased. I was now part of a group practice. That was the first step. Once they began providing me with referrals, money would hopefully start to come in. Despite these steps forward, my racing thoughts were exhausting me. My head was filled with Charles and Victoria. In addition, I had just started taking antianxiety medication, which left me feeling as if I were moving through a sea of molasses.

It was in January that it also became clear that my patient Jeb was dying. I had just been discharged from the hospital after having my stem cell transplant, eight months earlier, when Jeb had called me and told me that he had been diagnosed with colon cancer. Now he was in home hospice care. It was so quick. He had managed to survive the hot and steamy jungles of the Vietnam War, but this was a battle he was not going to win.

After I had reopened my practice in September, Jeb had been able to make it to a few sessions, but then his worsening illness had made that impossible. So I visited him each week and we had sessions in his home. As he became increasingly ill, I visited him no longer as his therapist but as someone who knew him and with whom he had shared his life story.

A disabled Vietnam vet, Jeb had appeared in my office five years earlier. His unsteady gait was evidence of his shattered leg and pelvis, the outward remnants of an explosion that had killed his buddy in the foxhole where they had been hiding in the dark, humid, overgrown jungle outside of Saigon. He returned to the States broken and isolated. Flashbacks of the foxhole, of his friend's dismembered body, of his sergeant wearing a necklace of human teeth around his neck as he ordered Jeb to shoot into a village of old women and children, were constant. These were the images that filled every fiber of his being. It was not surprising that the woman he married before he went off to war found that he was not the same man when he returned. They divorced. Our work together was intense.

I wonder how much of the intensity of all the pain and horror I listened to each day I had absorbed. I wonder how not having had a safe and loving refuge in my marriage added to my cancer. I love my work, and I have always been really present for those I work with. When things were good with Charles, I think perhaps it was easier to detach from all that pain and horror. The pain of Daphne, who at eight watched her mother fall to the floor, bleeding from an aneurysm and then die in her arms. Then there was Eve, abused, who at eleven shot and killed her beloved grandmother. All of these stories, I heard and relived with the intensity of having been there myself. How much pain did I absorb? Did I not protect myself enough? Could I have protected myself more if I had had a loving and safe partnership with my husband? My marriage had certainly not been a refuge for me for many years.

Oddly, as much as Charles was contemptuous and disdainful toward me, he was still referring patients to me. One evening when he came home, he said casually, "Di, I was speaking with one of my patients today, and she's going to call you so you can see her sixteen-year-old daughter."

I paused. I wanted to be clear but not condescending, as he always was to me.

"I don't think it's a good idea, Charles. I think there are too many boundary issues that I don't want to get involved with."

Looking somewhat blank, he accepted what I said without objection. He went on, "You know, I sent a note to Jeb today telling him my thoughts were with him," then looked to see what my response would be.

When I had first started working with Jeb, I had referred him to Charles for a consultation for medication. Jeb did not feel comfortable with Charles—he found him to be arrogant—and so I referred him to someone else, with whom he continued to work with for his medication management.

"Oh, that was very nice," I said, thinking that it was much easier for Charles to show "compassion" for Jeb. Writing him a note required only hollow words; filling that empty space by giving of himself was beyond what Charles was capable of doing.

I still occasionally read his journal. Despite everything I knew, my insides still tightened when I read lines like:

*I find it impossible to be around her. There is nothing redeeming about her.*
  *I cannot stomach living under the same roof with her.*
  *I know that I can turn things around with Di if I choose to. The question is, do I want to?*

What arrogance. It was true that if he had not given me that letter in September, saying he wanted out of the relationship, saying that there was no chance of reconciliation, I probably would still have been where I was in my marriage. I doubt I would have initiated leaving. But for him to think it was up to him to be able to "turn things around" if he decided to do so? He had no idea with whom he was dealing.

## Chapter Thirty

My patient, Jeb, died. I attended the funeral and was very glad that I was able to be there. A few days later, the kids were already at school, and I was packing up my briefcase to leave for my office. I was startled as Charles came up behind me and said, "Di, I want you to know that I placed a call to your attorney, Cal. I plan on going in to see him with Victoria. I want him to hear my side of the story. You know, he has been Victoria's attorney much longer than he has been your attorney."

I was learning, albeit slowly, not to always let words fly from my brain to my mouth without a stop. This time, I breathed, then said, "Okay, I do know that, but he is my attorney also and he needs my permission to speak with you about me. I really have to go. I can't be late for my appointment. We can talk about this later if you'd like." I added this last part knowing I had no intention of engaging with him about this any further.

"Well, we'll see what happens when Cal calls me back." His voice was calm.

"Whatever. I have to go. I'll be picking up the kids. See you later." Grabbing my purse, briefcase, and bagel, I walked to the door, trying my best not to lose my balance, which wasn't so great at the best of times; with my insides churning and my head spinning, I knew I might fall over.

What a relief it was to get away from him and into the icy car. Seeing my breath cloud the windows as I fumbled with the keys made me know I was still breathing and alive. I knew that I would have to call Cal. I knew for sure that I needed an attorney who was completely separate from Charles and Victoria. As much as I trusted Cal, I realized that this would not work.

By the time I got to the office, there was a message from Cal. "Hi, Diane. This is Cal. I just got a message from your husband, and I need to speak with you. Give me a call as soon as you can."

I called back as soon as my session ended.

"You know that I would not meet with your husband, don't you?" he asked.

"I do know that Cal. But even knowing that, I'm not feeling comfortable with the power that he and Victoria think that they have, even if it isn't true. I think I do need to find a new attorney, even though I would rather not have to do that."

"I understand, Diane. I just want you to know that it is not a conflict of interest from a legal standpoint. From an emotional standpoint, I think you may be right. Let me come up with a list of people you can call who I think you would work well with, and why don't you come in tomorrow, and we can go over it?" he asked.

I checked my schedule and said, "Sure, I'll see you then." I hung up the phone, spinning again.

After meeting with Cal, I returned to my office with a list of names. I also had a few names that I had gotten from friends and colleagues. I began making calls. Not wanting to find myself in the same position, I asked each attorney if they had any connection with Victoria, not really thinking that that would be the case. I was astounded. Multiple attorneys in looking up the name found that either they or one of their colleagues in their firm had in fact represented Victoria in some legal action. I couldn't believe how litigious this woman was. I began to wonder about Charles. I remembered his saying during his ramblings after the reconstructive surgery, "I feel like I'm driving all of us off of a steep cliff."

Now when I thought of that, I wondered if, deep within, Charles believed he had made an error in judgment. He had taken a step down a slippery ethical slope, and he could not turn back because he feared the consequences would be even worse. At this point, it didn't matter; whatever ambivalence Charles might have been not my concern. My concern was to get out with my children.

---

DAN Wilson practiced in a small law firm. "He's a great litigator," Cal had told me. He certainly had the presence of one. Well over six-foot-three, with silver-white hair, a handlebar mustache, and a deep, resonant voice, Dan commanded attention, and I liked that. He was very nice, but I also could tell that he could be intimidating, if necessary. I liked that, too.

As we sat in his office, going over what had been happening and where we currently were, Dan began to speak. "There's absolutely no reason that you should not start looking for a place for you and the children to live. You do not have to wait for him to leave. There is absolutely no financial risk involved. Let me explain. Based upon everything you have told me, to remain in the same house puts you in grave danger of a recurrence of your illness. You can leave on the grounds of constructive abandonment. In other words, it would be destructive, or of danger, for you not to leave. There is no penalty for that under the law; it is for your protection." His voice trailed off as his blue eyes continued looking directly into mine.

I wanted so much to get away from Charles, yet just thinking of another move was paralyzing for me. The emotional and physical weight of the last move had been carried out only with grit, determination, and luck. I didn't have the confidence or strength of mind to think I could pull it off again less than a year after I'd moved to the rental house and then moved my office. I also knew the kids would be upset at having to relocate again. It was another challenge I didn't want to face.

One evening I said to Charles, "I don't know if I have the energy to go through another move so soon. It really might be better for the children and me to stay here and for you to move somewhere else."

Indignantly, he responded, "Well, you've been the one who's been saying you want to separate as soon as possible. I suppose if your father moved in here, perhaps we could manage to work it out."

*What you want is for my father to move in here so that you can pay less of the rent.* That is what I wanted to say, but I didn't because I was still not saying the things I needed to be saying.

Despite being overwhelmed at the thought of another move and despite not saying what I should have said to Charles, I did act. I called Tim Bloom, the realtor we had worked with before, and told him what was going on. My father was willing to put down a large amount of money—really, a good bit of his money— on a small house or townhouse for the children and me to live in, and he would live with us as well. I wasn't sure about that, but it seemed like my only option.

"What a bastard," Tim responded, after hearing what had been going on. "He sickens me."

Tim was a very solid guy. He and his wife had five children, and he was very devoted to his family. Over the course of selling our small cottage and finding the house on St. John's Lane, he and I had spent many hours talking about our lives and families and had become friends. So, with the dedication of a friend wanting to help, Tim helped me sort through locations, school districts, and prices, and then he, my father, and I began the search.

"Tim, there's part of me that wants to just find a place and not tell Charles and pack up and move and just be gone. I guess I can't do that, can I?"

"Well, you can, but I'm not sure it would be the best thing for your kids, and anyway, if they know, he'll know." Tim smiled as he spoke.

It was a snowy February as we drove around, looking at houses. Everything we saw was unappealing. My head was spinning. Then my dad said something that caught my attention.

"Your mother was really a smart lady." He had adored my mother. Even when things were good with Charles, I knew he didn't have that kind of love for me.

"She certainly was, but what makes you say that now?" I asked.

"She never liked Charles. She always thought there was something 'off' about him."

"Really? She never told me that."

"Of course she didn't. Your mother wasn't like that. If you were happy, she was happy. She always did the right thing and treated everyone the right way, and she treated Charles that way, too. Your mother was really something else." He shook his head, and I could see how much he missed her.

"Yeah, I really miss her, too. It's funny, Gail asked me how I thought Charles would have acted if I'd gotten sick and Mom was still alive. You know, the first words out of my mouth were, 'He wouldn't have done all this.' I don't totally know why I thought that, but I think it was because he saw Mom as strong. My being sick really scared him and brought out the worst in him."

"I don't know, Di. I think there's something very wrong with him. You know me—I'm willing to accept everybody, with all their quirks and craziness—but this goes beyond what I can accept. Your mother didn't think he treated you as well as you deserved to be treated from the beginning. She told me about a time when the three of you went to a restaurant and you lost your earring and started to look for it. Mom said that he just went on talking as if you weren't even there, as if you didn't exist. It shocked her, but your mother said, 'If he makes her happy . . .'" His voice trailed off as he looked off into the snow-covered streets and sighed.

## Chapter Thirty-One

Dad was looking so tired. The strain was getting to him. I found myself being irritable with him and then feeling equally guilty about it. I felt guilty about everything.

Sammy was scared. He would sometimes wind up in my bed at night, and I didn't always send him back to his room. Charles never failed to have something negative to say about that.

"Diane, as a child psychologist, don't you think it's inappropriate to have your son coming into your bed at night?" he would say.

"As a child psychologist, I think our son, who is functioning very well in all areas of his life, is demonstrating some anxiety at bedtime. If he feels comforted right now by being close to me, I'm not going to make a big deal about it. I will see how it plays out." As it happened, Sammy and I talked about his scared feelings and his nighttime visits stopped.

But Elli was angry and withdrawn and I was having trouble connecting with her. Charles, in his infinite wisdom, talked about the children's resiliency and about how wonderfully they were doing amid the turmoil that had become their lives. He was blind.

One day, a package arrived. It was from Gail. I had to laugh. Only Gail would have thought of something like this. As I unwrapped the paper, I found two fabric voodoo dolls in the box, named Charles and Victoria. The pins were included. Gail had known this would be fun, in a dark sort of way. I put my wedding ring around the arm of the smaller doll. It was pure pleasure sticking the colored pins into their genitalia and into their hearts, twisting their heads and stomping on their faces, all the while thinking of the most torturous things that could befall them. If I was going to be accused of having black strands of evil running through my soul, I might as well make good use of them and cast some spells and chant some incantations. Of course, I had to keep this hidden, or Sam and Elli would surely think I had gone mad. Gail and I, though, laughed raucously about it on the phone.

The roads outside were still covered with snow and ice. Dad and I went out again with Tim to look at houses. This time, he took us to a see a townhouse in a development where several houses were on the market. Although not aesthetically appealing on the outside, the house itself was spacious, had a great layout, and was in wonderful condition. The three bedrooms upstairs were huge, there were loads of closets and a full attic for storage, and the basement had a separate entrance and was large enough for Dad to have his own space, including a living-sitting room and bedroom and bathroom. This was a place where we could live comfortably. We would need to do some renovations in the basement to make it ideal for Dad, but not a lot.

"I like it. What do you think?" I looked over to Dad, who was standing with the owners and Tim, chatting and already forming a friendship with these people, as he did with everyone he met.

Joe and Donna, the owners, excused themselves, and my dad and Tim walked over to me.

"It's a nice place, much bigger on the inside than it looks outside, and they really have kept it up." Tim was looking in the living room fireplace as he spoke.

"They said they put in a new heating and cooling system a year ago, and there's a new washer and dryer. It's a front-loader. Did you see that, Di?"

I hadn't seen Dad smile like this in a long time.

"Joe and Donna said there are loads of kids in all of these houses, and they all play in this courtyard! It'll be great for Sammy and Elli. They've never lived anywhere they could just go outside and play with friends. I think this is the place!"

It did seem to be the perfect find. It was in a great school district, and it was even walking distance to Dr. Putman's office. I did have some reservations, but, later that day, Dad made an offer, which the sellers accepted within a couple of hours. The house Joe and Donna were building wouldn't be ready until June, so they wanted to close and then rent the townhouse back from us until then. That would work, because then we'd be moving after the school year ended, which would make it somewhat easier for the kids. At least, I hoped it would.

"Dad, are you sure you want to put so much of your money into this house?" I asked him the next day, as we ate lunch together. "You're using up all of your money on me. That worries me. You may need it."

"Di, what else am I going to do with it? It's yours. Believe me, I'm not going to need it. I'm almost eighty-five. The mortgage will be low, and you'll get money from Charles, and you'll be working. I won't have any rent to pay. I'll buy the groceries. It'll be fine. The money is for you anyway. You're just getting it now when you need it."

The sadness and tiredness in his eyes were so difficult to see that I stared down at the white clumps of feta cheese on my salad, rather than looking directly at his face.

"Oh, it's one o'clock, sweetie. I'm supposed to meet Lydia and take her to a doctor's appointment. Don't worry, it's all going to work out."

He gave me a big bear hug as he got up, and I walked with him to the door.

"I love you, Daddy," I called, as he walked down the path to his car.

Turning back, he smiled, but the sadness in his eyes was still there.

As much as my father tried to reassure me, I still worried about how the kids were going to deal with another move and about how they would feel about living with Poppy. Mostly I worried about how they would deal with not living with Daddy. Despite my feelings, they loved their father, and this would be hard for them.

They, particularly Elli, were already starting to see for themselves what he was like. As much as I wanted to help them, much of this was a process that they would need to experience on their own. I could be there as a support, but some of this would now be part of their own life journeys. *It's not fair*, I kept saying to myself.

The night that the offer on the house was accepted, we got hit with a big snowstorm and the schools were closed. After spending hours building snow forts and sledding, the kids and I sat in front of a warm, roaring fire amid piles of Lego pieces, seeing who could construct the most outrageous robot. Charles had weathered the storm and said he was going to his office.

"Mom." Elli paused and did not look up from the pieces she was pushing together. "Mom, are you and Dad going to get a divorce?"

I looked up to see Sammy wide-eyed, open-mouthed, fumbling with the pieces he was trying to connect and yelling, "I don't want to do this anymore."

"Okay, let's get comfortable and let's talk. Why don't we sit on the couch?"

"I'll sit over here," Elli said, pulling over a beanbag and a soft woolen blanket from a chair. Sammy cuddled close to me on the couch.

"There are some important things we have to talk about. You know that Mom and Dad haven't been getting along for a long time "

"Daddy didn't care that you were sick. That was mean." Sammy looked directly into my eyes; his own eyes full of tears.

"I don't know how your dad felt about my being sick, but I know he had a hard time dealing with it." I pulled Sam close, and Elli moved to the sofa and sat beside me, putting her head on my shoulder.

"These problems are painful, and they're scary for your dad and me, and I know that they are for you, too. But, to answer your question, Elli, yes, Dad and I have decided to separate at the end of this school year. We both love you, and we will both always take care of you. We also are grown-ups and can take care of ourselves, so you don't have to worry about us. Part of my taking care of myself is to make sure I remain healthy so I can be here for you." I stopped talking and waited.

"I'd like to go up to my room now," Elli said, getting off the couch and petting Knaidl, who followed upstairs.

"There's one more thing I want to tell you, and then you can go upstairs, and we can talk more later." Elli turned toward me. "Poppy and I have gotten a house that I think you'll really like. You won't have to change schools, and there are loads of kids around to play with. We can go by to see it and also go and buy something special for each of your new rooms, okay?"

"Can we finish building robots?" Sammy asked.

"Sure we can." I tousled his hair and picked up a couple of pieces, and he placed a lightsaber in the hands of one of the tiny figures.

ONE of the things that terrified me about separating was believing that Charles would try to turn Elli and Sam against me in subtle, insidious ways and then deny it was happening. Nevertheless, despite my terror and my fury, I would have to allow them to have a relationship with him. I would, though, protect them at all costs. That need for protection had already begun. I have to admit that both Charles and I weren't always so patient with the children during this time. My fuse was shorter than usual, and I raised my voice more often than I liked. But Charles was mean and physically aggressive, especially to Sam. I never laid a hand on either of the kids, so it surprised me when Sam started saying, whenever I did raise my voice, "Momma, don't hurt me."

Then I began to see it. One day I noticed that Sam's ear was red, and Elli told me that Charles had pulled him by the ear when he hadn't responded immediately. Another time, Sam had red marks on his arm. One day, when the kids and I were about to go out to a street fair after they'd spent the morning with their dad, Sam threw himself on the couch and started to sob.

"What's the matter, Sammy?" I walked over and rubbed his back.

The sobs continued.

Finally, through halting breaths, he whispered hoarsely, "Momma, don't let Daddy hurt me anymore."

"What happened?" I looked at Elli as I continued to rub Sam's back.

"Sam didn't get on the elevator fast enough for Dad." Elli scowled. "So he kicked him in the butt to make him move. I told him he better not do that again. Then he told Sam not to act like a wuss," she added.

I leaned over Sam and, hugging him, said, "I promise you Daddy will never hurt you again. I will take care of this today. But if either of you is ever scared or worried when you are with your father, you call me immediately."

Before we left for the fair, I wrote a letter to my attorney, Dan, asking him to send Charles a certified letter that put him on formal notice that if he hurt Sam again, I would report him immediately to the Department of Child Protective Services and the police. I hand-delivered the letter to Dan; he had a letter out to Charles by five o'clock that day.

Charles never mentioned the letter to me, although I knew he had received it. After that, whenever he got upset with one of the children, he always made sure to tell me exactly what had happened. He knew I meant what I had said. It was the mark of a true narcissist: they fear someone only when they think that person has more power than they do.

---

I didn't plan to tell Charles about the townhouse. I would have liked to just pack up and disappear, but I knew I couldn't put that kind of pressure on the kids. Also, it was still hard not to automatically tell him things, whether I wanted to or not. They just came out in moments of calm.

"Charles, I want to let you know that I found a place and I plan on moving in mid-June," I said one evening, shortly after the contract on the house was accepted.

"Well, since you found a place, I guess I ought to get an attorney." Charles shook his head as he continued, "I just don't know how I'm going to free up the money. I guess your dad is going to be paying part of the rent, right?"

"Actually, no, he's not. He's holding the mortgage, and I'm going to be making the mortgage payment to him. He's the landlord." We both had our therapist masks on, and so we were both speaking in neutral voices, not indicating anything we were feeling beneath the surface.

Suddenly, out of nowhere, Charles asked, "Do you think we want to have a miniature poodle?"

I shook my head, speechless. I walked into the other room, the thought, *Why does he keep asking about "we"? It's so bizarre* spinning circuitously in my head. Then I caught myself and once again remembered that nothing is random, everything is calculated, even the way the words in a sentence are ordered. Charles was in his mode of showing his "goodness" by finding a home for his dead acupuncturist's dog. If I was off balance, perhaps I would think he wanted to reconcile, and I would say yes to the dog. Of course, I would then be stuck with it.

It was no different from how he had gotten me to agree to file for bankruptcy during my cancer treatment. He hadn't been willing to talk to me about anything I saw happening in our relationship; he'd always said, "We'll work on it once you finish treatment." Then, within weeks of my finishing treatment and days of our signing the bankruptcy papers, he'd told me he had decided the marriage was over.

No, saying "we" as we were talking about separating was not a new thing; this was the crazy-making behavior of my marriage that had existed for years.

I walked back into the family room with a basket of laundry, and as I began to fold Sam's shirts, I looked over at Charles, who was just sitting quietly, with a half-smile on his lips. Perhaps he was meditating.

"So, about this mini poodle you've been talking about. I really have no interest in another dog, Charles. I think Knaidl is enough," I said casually, as I folded a shirt.

"Okay. I just thought it might be nice for the kids to have another dog, and Knaidl would have some company."

"There are a lot of things that would be nice for everybody, but I'm not taking on another dog right now." I continued folding and making piles of clothes, much more meticulous than usual.

Charles got up from his seat and started to walk toward the stairs. Just before he started down, he turned and said, "It's not a problem. I just thought you'd want to do it for the kids."

"No, not this time. This time, my decision is going to be based on what's best for me, which will in the long run be what's best for the kids," I said, as I put the folded and sorted clothes back into the basket.

Charles walked down the stairs, and I heard the door close behind him.

## Chapter Thirty-Two

"Daddy, can you and I camp out in our sleeping bags in front of the fireplace tonight?" Sam asked one cold March evening, pouncing into Charles's arms when he walked through the front door. He had been talking about camping all afternoon. "We have marshmallows, graham crackers, and chocolate, so we can even make s'mores. Please? Please?"

"I don't want to sleep in the family room, but the s'mores sound great to me," Elli added, as she walked through the foyer and heard what was going on.

"Sounds like a real possibility; it's Friday, and there's no school tomorrow. We'll get everything ready after dinner." Charles couldn't say much more because Sam was already off and running to get his sleeping bag and pillows to bring downstairs.

I had been pulling some baskets off a shelf when everyone came down for dinner. On top of the pile of baskets was a handwoven hat with a long orange toucan feather and woven birds and fish decorating it.

"Where's that hat from? It's really neat." Elli got up, took it in her hands, and looked at it closely. "These birds and fish are great."

"They are, aren't they?" said Charles. "Before you were born, I went on a trip to Hawaii. When I was on the Big Island of Hawaii—Hawaii is made up of a lot of islands—this guy, with a toucan named Toco, was making hats, so I got one. The feather is one of Toco's feathers."

"That's cool!" Sam exclaimed, as he took the hat from Elli to look at it more closely.

I was stunned. Charles hadn't gone to Hawaii by himself. We had gone together. He had bought the hat for me.

Yet here we were, and it had become his trip, his hat, his experience alone. When I spoke with the kids, even at this point, I always spoke about things we had done; I didn't exclude Charles. Again, I felt my anger building, at being treated as if I had never existed.

But then I had a realization. In my days of raging at Charles, I would say, "You are such a master manipulator of words." Now, though, I saw it much more clearly. When he wanted me to adopt the mini poodle, he spoke of "we." When he wanted to make sure I knew I did not exist for him, the spoke of "I." It was all manipulative, and I had to be aware enough to respond to the intent of the words, not the words themselves. With Charles, I could not be real. I had to always listen with the ear of a therapist, not a lover. So, this time, I handled it differently when he spoke of "his" trip to Hawaii.

"It was such a great trip. The sand on the beach was black from the volcanoes on the island, the water was turquoise blue, the food was wonderful, and Toco the toucan was hysterical! Wasn't he, Charles?" I smiled as I spoke.

Charles was silent. The muscle in his cheek twitched. I couldn't do anything about it when I wasn't there, but I sure as hell would not allow myself to be so blatantly discounted in my own presence and in my own home. It may have been insignificant, but I felt empowered, and for a few moments there was a conversation about *our* trip to Hawaii, though I didn't fool myself into thinking it meant anything more than that I had taken control and not allowed myself to be the victim of his denial of my existence.

In order to really be empowered, though, I still needed to find a way to copy his journal. There was too much evidence in it that I could use to my advantage in multiple ways. I especially wanted the pages where Charles had written about still writing prescriptions for Victoria and about her giving him money. These things would not look good in court. These things would be leverage in relation to his keeping his license.

Perhaps Victoria was out of town, because the day after the camping trip in the family room, Charles said he would take the kids to see a *Star Wars* exhibit that had opened at the museum in DC. They were thrilled, and I knew I had several hours to myself. They left at about noon, and I knew it would take them about forty-five minutes to get there. Forty minutes after they left, I called Charles.

"Charles, I gave Elli some money to get a present for Ezra's birthday party tomorrow. Could you make sure she remembers to get something in the museum shop?"

"Sure, no problem. Any idea what he would like?" he asked.

"I don't know; he likes to put things together, and he likes science, so anything like that would be fine. Thanks a lot. Enjoy *Star Wars*." I said good-bye, assured that they really had gone and would be away for a while.

I made another call. "Hi, Rick. I have the opportunity to copy the journal over the next few hours. Are you available right now?"

Rick was an old friend. He had been my service chief when I had worked at the hospital, and we had remained good friends. He was retired now. Both he and his wife had had some serious illnesses, and he had been one of the many who were a great support to me. He happened to have a copier that would work quickly, and he had offered to copy the journal whenever I brought it over.

"Come on over, Di. I'll put some hot water on for tea and make sure there's plenty of paper in the copier. You and Jane can chat while I do the dirty work. I'll enjoy it!"

"Okay, I'm on my way." I hung up, ran down to the basement, saw the journal on Charles's desk, grabbed it, and ran out to my car. My heart was pounding. I felt so much like the bad child. Yet I had to do whatever I could to protect myself and my children and our future.

The whole time Jane and I sat in the kitchen, I could hear Rick calling out to us, "This stuff is sick, really sick. When did you say you're moving? It can't come soon enough."

The feeling in my chest was like a rubber band being pulled, about to snap, the direction of its impact unknown but the danger very real. Even though I had been reading the journal for months and copying all of the e-mails Charles and Victoria had written to each other, somehow this felt worse—I think because, as always, I was still so caught up in how Charles would judge me. He would call me a "sneak," say that I had no boundaries. And, despite knowing what I knew about him, I felt guilty. He was right—I *was* a sneak.

"Here it is." Rick finally walked out of his study and handed me a thick, sealed envelope, along with the journal. "Put it somewhere safe;

in fact, you probably want to make a couple of copies, and don't leave any in the house. Give one to your attorney right away, okay? Do you want to stay awhile?"

"No, thank you so much, but I need to get this back to his desk. I'm too nervous having it out of the house."

Jane and Rick walked me to my car. We all hugged, and I thanked them again, then got in my Subaru and rushed home to return the journal to its exact placement on Charles's desk. As I drove off, I thought about Rick and Jane. Rick had not always treated Jane in the most respectful way. Then she had cancer, and shortly after that, he, too, was confronted with his own mortality with a cancer diagnosis. Their relationship changed. By now, I knew that would not be the case for Charles and me.

I was home a couple of hours before Charles and the kids arrived.

"Momma," Sam blurted out, as he came running into the kitchen, where I was sitting. "You should have seen it. They had the cockpit of the *Millennium Falcon*, and we got a virtual jump to light speed. It was so cool. Even Elli had fun!"

"Yeah, it was pretty neat. Did you know, Mom, that the idea for Darth Vader's helmet came from those Japanese feudal samurai movies? I love everything that has anything to do with Japan!"

"Wow, it sounds terrific. I'm sorry I missed it." I looked over at Charles as he was walking in from the car and said, "I guess you really struck gold with this exhibit. It sounds great!"

He shook his head, said, "I'm really worn out," and walked down to the basement and closed the door. The kids continued to share everything they had seen. I hoped I had left the journal exactly as it had been.

As was always the case, I still went through periods where I wanted to read his journal, to know what he was thinking, to understand him. The kids had enjoyed the *Stars Wars* exhibit so much, I was curious what he had to say about having been with them all day.

On Sunday morning, Charles said, "I'm going to go over to the office to do some paperwork. I have a lot to do."

"I guess you're not coming to my swim meet this afternoon?" Elli said preemptively.

"Oh, sure I am. I'm coming from the office. Just remind me of the time."

"Mom, what time do we have to be there?"

"You have to be there at two o'clock, Elli," I said, trying my best to sound nonchalant. We all knew that Charles had not remembered the swim meet and likely would not show up.

"I'll see you at the swim meet," Charles called out, as he walked out the door and left for the office.

"Yeah, right," Elli said, sarcasm oozing from her lips in perfect harmony with the rolling of her eyes. "Mom, do you think he's going to see Vic, his 'best friend'?"

I couldn't help but laugh, which made Elli laugh, and together we turned the heaviness into the kind of raucous, loving melancholy that sometimes only women, even mothers and daughters, seem to share. Finally, as we both caught our breath, I said, "I really have no idea where he's going, and to tell you the truth, sweetie, wherever he's going, it's okay."

"Yeah, Mom, and I hope Vic goes with him, wherever it is. They deserve each other." And then we laughed some more.

"It does make me sad, though," I said, putting my arm around Elli's shoulder, and then asked, "What about you, sweetie—does it make you sad?"

I could always tell when the tears were coming. Her cheeks would begin to get pink blotches, her jaw would clench, and then her beautiful, almond-shaped blue eyes would be brimming over.

"I'm getting used to it. He just isn't the dad I've always known. I don't know where my dad went." There was a pleading look in her eyes as she spoke.

"I wish I had an answer, but I don't. I do know for sure that your dad loves you and your brother. He loves you as much as he can love anyone."

"Yeah, I know. That's the problem. Mom, I feel like going and taking a bath, okay?" she asked.

"Sure. Just please clean the tub when you're done," I reminded her.

Sammy was watching a video, and so I did have a chance to go down to the basement and take a look at what Charles had written about the outing he'd had with the kids the day before.

The journal was on his desk, and I found the entry easily:

*I was glad that I took the kids to the exhibit. They seemed to enjoy it, but for me it was kind of boring. I could have spent the day with Vic, and had I known she was coming back from Texas a day earlier, I wouldn't have suggested going to the exhibit at all. Their mother enjoys doing things like that with them. I have broader things I can teach them.*

*Broader things to teach them?* What the hell was he talking about? That was his grandiosity. He didn't have time for the ordinary tasks of parenthood—those would be too mundane for his level of greatness. He was absolutely right about one thing, though: I *did* love doing things with my kids; it brought me joy and did the same for them.

"Momma, do you want to come up and play *Star Wars* with me?" Sam called from the top of the stairs. "You can be Princess Leia." "Sure, I'd love to play *Star Wars*. I'll be right up," I called back, as I placed the journal back where I'd found it and climbed the stairs.

Surprising all of us, Charles did make it to the swim meet, just in time to see Elli in the two-hundred-yard freestyle medley. She beamed when she saw her dad standing there, cheering, as she got out of the pool. I was glad for Elli that he was there, but for myself, I would have preferred he wasn't. I didn't like that it had to be okay with me that the kids loved him.

---

BY the last day of March, the financing for the house was already approved. Dad had made a large down payment so that my house payment would be low. The deed to the house was written as a living trust so that it would automatically be passed on to me without any sort of taxes or legal process when he died. He had thought it all out so that everything was the way he wanted at the closing.

Afterward, Tim, Dad, and I went out for lunch to celebrate. It was a clear, bright day and the scent of spring was everywhere, along with the colors of the crocuses and daffodils.

After lunch, Tim drove Dad home because I had to do some errands. As I often did, I took a shortcut down St. John's Lane. I loved that route; it was so peaceful driving beneath the canopy of towering trees, prisms of light hitting the glass occasionally. And seeing our old house still brought me a sense of warmth and comfort. My loving feelings about that home overrode all the losses that had occurred for almost two years now.

My windows were open to let in the cool breeze, the sun was shining, and there were no other cars in sight. I drove past our old house on the left and then the soccer field of the girls' school on my right. There was a gentle curve in the road, and then my next recollection was that I was sitting in my car, disoriented, in a ravine, going in the opposite direction, only an inch from a huge oak tree. Everything looked very familiar, but I wasn't quite sure where I was. I thought, *If I just sit here for a few minutes, I'm sure I'll figure out where I am.*

Two women came running to the car from the nearest house. "Are you okay?" a tall woman in her thirties, with a short blonde bob, asked as I sat there.

"We have more people going into this ravine than you would believe. We're trying to get them to do something about it," the older woman said.

"I think I'm okay, just a little disoriented," I said, as I opened the door and found I was able to move and was beginning to recognize where I was, although I still felt very dazed. The irony of where this accident occurred would come to me only later.

"I'm Christine, and this is my mom, Katherine," the younger woman said. "Would you like to come in, sit down, and make a phone call?" She was lovely.

"I think I can take care of it with my cell phone, but I appreciate it, and if I do need anything, I'll be sure to knock. Thank you so much. I think I'm okay."

"Well, I'll put a call in to the police," Christine said, "so they can get over here and get you towed and all. If you need anything, we'll be in the kitchen."

I thanked them as they smiled and walked back to their house. I then stood looking at my car. I had no idea how much damage there was. I now knew where I was, but I had no idea what had happened.

A police car arrived as I was standing there, and I explained as much as I recalled.

"Were you speeding?" the officer asked. "No," I responded. "Any alcohol or drugs?" he asked.

"No alcohol. I take some prescription medication for anxiety, but only what is prescribed," I told him, certain that he was thinking that there was some substance involved in this accident.

"Well, I'll call a tow truck, but I think you really ought to call your doctor right away to see what happened." He seemed to be softening somewhat as he spoke. "Do you know where you want the car towed, and do you have someone to call to pick you up?" he asked.

"The car can go to Heritage Subaru," I said, "and I can call someone to pick me up."

"Okay, I'll stay here until both the tow truck and your ride get here. You can sit in the back of the cruiser if you'd like." He pointed to his car, which was just a couple of feet behind us.

After sitting down in the cruiser, I tried to call my dad, but he didn't answer. Interestingly, I didn't even think about calling Charles. I tried a couple of friends who lived close by, but none of them answered, either. Finally, I called Peg. She was still at her office but was between patients. When she picked up the phone, relief and gratitude surged through me.

"Hi, Peg, I hate to bother you, but I just had a car accident."

"Are you okay?" she asked.

"I'm fine, but my car isn't, and I have no way to get the kids or get home. I didn't know if you were still seeing patients or if you might be done for the day and could help me out."

"Di, I have two more patients. I'll help afterward if you still need help, but you should make Charles take some responsibility. He is much closer to where you are than I am, and he is your husband and the father of your children. *He* should help you." I could tell that she was annoyed.

"I guess I've stopped even considering him as someone to ask for anything, but you're right."

"Call him and tell him to get his ass over there and pick you up and then pick the kids up. You've always done everything for him. Let him take some responsibility. Listen, I have to go, but call me back if you still need my help." She hung up.

I knew Peg was right, and I also felt as if I was taking advantage of my friends, asking too much of them. My rage at Charles began to swell, but I took a deep breath and called him anyway.

"Charles, I just had an accident. I'm on St. John's Lane, and my car isn't drivable. It has to be towed. I need you to pick me up, and then we're going to need to pick the kids up from school."

There was a long pause. Then he said, "Listen, I'm really busy. I don't think I can get away from the office right now."

"Well, what do you suggest I do? Walk to the nearest hospital? You don't even know whether or not I'm injured. The kids can fend for themselves, right?" That was certainly the mild version of what I was thinking and feeling.

Charles reconsidered and said, "Okay, I'll be right over," but never once did he ask about what had happened or how I was.

## Chapter Thirty-Three

I was diagnosed with a seizure disorder. The doctors were uncertain whether there was a relationship between my high-dose chemotherapy and the development of my seizures, but, after they did a complete workup, the findings were clear: it wasn't inattention, it wasn't stress; the anti-anxiety medication I was taking was lowering my seizure threshold. The neurologist took me off that medication and placed me on medication for the seizures.

The medication did help, and my inexplicable falls and car accidents stopped for quite some time. I didn't mention anything about it to Charles.

Dad went with me to look at cars, and I got a used minivan. Sammy and I picked Elli up from school in it, and he asked, "What do you think, Elli? Do you like it?"

"Hey, this is cool. I like the color. It would be even nicer, though, if we could watch movies in it," Elli said, as she looked everything over.

"That's what I said, too, but that would have been too expensive. Mom said she'll get us a DVD player for trips," Sammy added.

"Oh, that'll be good. Thanks, Mom."

As was the custom when we had tacos for dinner, we all worked together to prepare the meal. The kids chopped up vegetables and all the toppings and set up everything in bowls on the dinner table while I got the meat ready. It was a meal that we always enjoyed.

As we ate, I reminded them about the house we'd be moving to after their dad I separated. "Would you like to drive over there this evening?" I asked.

"Yes," they said.

"Can I bring my new clock to put in my room?" Sammy asked. "Of course, if you'd like to." The words were hardly out of my mouth when Sammy was upstairs, retrieving his clock.

So, that evening, with our new vehicle, the kids and I drove over to see the new house. They had both gotten funny alarm clocks for their new rooms, and they had shown them to Charles. That's how he'd found out that they knew about the separation. He had been furious with me that I had told them without discussing it with him. He had wanted us to tell them together. As if we did anything together. I wasn't doing it the way the experts said to do it, even though I happened to be one of those experts to whom parents turned to for advice about such matters. My advice to parents was never that black and white. There was always a context in which all decisions had to be made. Charles, on the other hand, always knew the "right" way to do everything.

He had distanced me so completely; I was nonexistent in his world. With that, I was beginning to function as if he didn't exist in my world. As much as I knew the "correct" way to handle telling the children, I also had a new understanding that in reality, life and theory weren't always the same. Decisions in life could not be black and white. It would be counterproductive to have a universal principle upon which someone always made a decision.

I hadn't really even planned to tell them when I did. It had just occurred in the natural course of my life with my children, with whom I spent every day. I had made that decision based upon their needs and our needs in our life. I was beginning to trust my own judgment again.

There certainly would be many times afterward when I would be encased in a knot of doubt, but the obsessive ruminating that followed had more to do with my unrelenting and unrealistic wish for Charles to approve of me and to love me.

"You call yourself a child psychologist?" Charles sneered at me in disgust after he learned that I had told the children about the separation and the move. He seemed to like that phrase—it had become a common refrain.

"I do, Charles. I also call myself a mother, and I also refuse to be the target of your sadism anymore."

He turned and walked away. At least now I could defend myself without raging. My insides, though, still felt as if a vise had a stranglehold around them.

The days were longer now, and so when the kids and I pulled up in front of our new townhouse that evening, it was still light, and the courtyard was a kaleidoscope of colors and a cacophony of kid noises. Laughter, the sound of balls hitting pavement, and squeals of both delight and frustration echoed in the air.

"Wow, do all these kids live here?" Sam's eyes were wide with excitement, his head out of the car window, as I pulled into what would be our parking space.

"I think they probably live somewhere nearby. I told you there would be a lot of kids to play with." I could tell they were nervously excited. "Let's go inside so you can see your rooms and the rest of the house, and then maybe you'll want to come out and meet some of the kids."

Before we could even open the doors of the van, children began to surround us.

A slim, dark-haired girl of about fourteen smiled as she walked over. "Are you the new people who are moving in? My name is Carol."

"I'm Sam, and this is my sister, Elli." He was already out of the car and ready to play. His sister stood by, taking it all in.

"There are so many kids around here," Sam said, as a boy smaller than he came over and introduced himself.

"Hi, I'm Bubba. I live in the end house over there. I'm six. I have three brothers and two sisters. That girl over there with the long ponytail is my sister Kaitlin—she's eleven—and that girl in the blue T-shirt, drinking from the water bottle, she's my sister Jenna. She's nine. My big brothers aren't here right now."

Pleased at this unexpected chance to meet the neighborhood kids, I walked over to the house, unlocked the door, and went into the kitchen, leaving Elli and Sam outside with an ever-increasing circle of new friends around them. Elli followed me in a few moments later.

"Oh, I like the kitchen," she said, as she walked through the first floor, opening doors and walking out onto the deck. "There's even a fireplace." She smiled. I followed her as she climbed the stairs to see the bedrooms.

"This will be my room." I pointed to the room on the left as we reached the top step.

"I like all the windows, and it's big. It doesn't look this big from outside. Where's my room?"

We walked past the hallway bathroom. "You and Sam will share this bathroom," I said, as we approached the two rooms at the end of the hallway. Elli walked into each room, carefully assessing them. The windows faced the courtyard, and she walked over and looked out.

"Sammy, come on in so we can choose bedrooms." He looked up and laughed when he saw his sister in the window.

"I'll be right back," Sam called to the kids he was talking to, as he ran toward the door.

"Hey, this is cool," I heard him say as he ran around the first floor and then up the stairs. "Momma, there are so many kids here," he added when he appeared. "This is great!"

"I want this room," Elli declared, standing in the room that was somewhat larger.

"I wanted that room." Sam glared at Elli.

I intervened to prevent them from arguing: "First, everyone can choose the color they want their room to be."

"Green, dark green," Elli continued. "I know exactly the color I want."

"I want blue, definitely blue," Sam said.

Deciding who would get the larger room was going to be more of an issue. I knew Elli really wanted the larger room and that she was also struggling more with her place in the world than Sammy was. Honestly, I didn't have the energy to deal with one of her moods.

"Okay, let's figure this out. Sam, you've been wanting bunk beds, right?"

"Oh, yes!" His face shone with delight.

"Sam, if you take this room"—I pointed to the smaller room— "we can paint it a great blue and put bunk beds on this wall. How would that be?" I asked, knowing that I had been a bit manipulative in getting the choices made in the least problematic way. I knew that Sam was much easier in these ways; he would love his bunk bed and his blue walls. I also knew I had avoided one of Elli's meltdowns.

"Great, Momma!" Sam shouted, as he ran downstairs to see the basement.

"Thanks, Mom." Elli hugged me and smiled, and then we followed Sam down to the basement. "Is Poppy going to live with us?" she asked.

"Yup, we're going to make the basement into his own space. But there will still be room for you guys to use the basement, too. We'll have the air-hockey table down there. How do you feel about Poppy living with us and about the move?"

Elli shrugged her shoulders. "It's just so many changes. I guess it will be okay," she said, as she started to explore the basement.

The doorbell rang, and the kids ran up to see who it was. I followed behind. There stood Carol, Bubba, and several others.

"We're going to play Capture the Flag. Want to play?" Carol asked, looking first at my kids and then at me.

"Can we?" they asked at once.

"Sure, have fun," I said, and they were out the door before I could say anything else. I smiled as I walked back inside and went out onto the back deck, just listening to the sounds of the evening air and the children's play on the other side of the house. Maybe this would work out. Maybe this would be a community for all of us.

There had been several women sitting in the courtyard as we drove in, and they had waved. I decided I'd go out and meet them. Becky ran into her house to get another glass and poured me some wine, and this group of women immediately welcomed me. Amy, Laura, Becky, and Ann were all divorced, professional women with kids who were the same ages as my kids. A new world of neighborly support was beginning.

It was nine o'clock when we walked through the door of our old house. Charles was already home. Elli said "Hi" to him and walked up the stairs to her room. Sam, upon seeing Charles, ran to him, climbing onto him, with tales of his new friendships.

"There are so many kids." Sam's face exploded with excitement; then he added, "And everyone plays together. It was like a hundred kids were there. Right, Momma?"

Charles smiled and seemed to listen attentively to him, without saying anything. His eyes were glazed, and my own tightening chest and suddenly foggy brain let me know that he was not pleased. It wasn't anything he said; it was the almost imperceptible tightening of the muscles in his jaw, the twitch in the corner of his mouth, and the slight stiffening of his shoulders that told me, without words, that his inner pressure was building. These nonverbal signs had for years kept me gingerly and unconsciously walking on eggshells. Now, at least I recognized what my body was telling me.

"Sounds like it was a busy evening." Charles spoke in slow and measured words. "I think it's pretty late, a lot later than you should have been out, so let's get up to bed." He put his arm around Sam, shot me that tight, forced smile again, and walked toward the stairs.

"Momma, are you going to come up and read to us?" Sam craned his neck under Charles's arm to look back at me.

"I'll be up in a few minutes, sweetie." I smiled at him. "Maybe Daddy wants to read to you tonight."

"I do," Charles quickly responded.

"Oh, good. Momma, maybe you can sit with us while Daddy reads," Sam said, with a tinge of hopefulness in his voice.

"Why don't you have some special time with Daddy? I'll come in for hugs and kisses before you fall asleep," I said.

I walked into Elli's room, hoping we would have a chance to talk about what she thought of the new house and new neighborhood. "Elli," I started to say, and realized that the visit to the house must have really drained her. The light was on; Vivaldi's *Four Seasons* was playing on her tape player. She had clearly started to get out of her clothes and into her pajamas, but there she lay, asleep, clothes half-on. Her still-cherubic face was surrounded by her blond curls; her old stuffed dog, Ak, was against her cheek, a bit of worn-but-remaining fur moving in a self-soothing way between her two fingers. I stood in the doorway, watching her, before walking over to the bed. I pulled the comforter over her and gently placed a kiss on her cheek. Eyes still closed, she smiled and whispered, "I love you, Mommy."

"I love you, too." I hugged her again, letting myself hold her for a bit as she fell back to sleep. I shut the light off, leaving on Vivaldi. I stood in the doorway, feeling gratitude for my beautiful children.

I walked into Sam's room, where I found Sam and Charles all sprawled out on the bed. Charles, half sitting, with his back against the footboard, was also asleep, holding *Harry Potter* open on his chest.

I pulled a cover over Sam and kissed him. Then, before leaving the room, I looked at the two of them, so peaceful as they slept. I turned on the night-light, shut off the lamp, and left the room, but I had a desire to hug them both and to lie together with them—something that would never be again.

The next day, in distant and formal tones, Charles told me that he was going to find a place for himself.

"Sounds like a good idea," I said, in my neutral therapist voice. I was just beginning to, sometimes, be able to stay disengaged. It was easier to do that when Charles was distant and formal with me. It was harder when he spoke to me in the intimately casual conversations of everyday life. At those times, I could still be drawn in. When I was drawn in, I always said too much, revealed my inner thoughts and feelings, only to then be surprised anew by the ugly words he wrote about me in his journal or in his e-mails to Victoria. Nevertheless, even though I still behaved in ways that were futile efforts to connect with Charles, and even though I was still knocking my head against a wall, the patterns were becoming clearer. Everything Charles did was planned and calculated. He always had an ulterior motive. I was thankful that I would soon be away from the critical and judgmental toxins that surrounded me.

I was scrambling eggs for breakfast when Charles walked into the kitchen.

"There are a couple of houses I'm going to look at today," he said, as if we were any married couple chatting about the day's events.

In the past, I might have asked him a question or made a comment, something that would have furthered the illusion that all was fine in this house.

"Oh," I said casually, as I dumped a handful of cheese into the pan, never looking up from the stove.

"Once I find a place, I'll take the kids over to show it to them. We still have to figure out the schedule of when they're with each of us. I do want them with me half of the time."

I could hear the challenge in his tone.

"You're right; we do need to do it immediately. It should be a priority."

"I know what I want. What is your suggestion?"

"I just want the schedule to be one where there are as few transitions as possible. I also want them to be in one house on school nights. I think it's too hard for kids when they're going back and forth during the school week." The visceral tension in the room increased with each word I said.

Charles smiled tightly. "You think it's all going to be your way? You don't know me very well."

"Charles, I don't want to fight. You make your proposal, and I will make mine. We can discuss our ideas with our attorneys and with the mediator." The scripted phrase resounding in my head was *act with dignity*. That was what Dr. Putman had helped me with in my efforts not to respond to Charles with the internal rage I felt. I was much better at not acting on my rage. Internally, I still felt eaten alive. More and more, I saw the malignancy that was both my illness and my marriage.

## Chapter Thirty-Four

"Mom, can we go to the mall today?" Elli's question startled me, and I dropped the stack of e-mails I had been reading. I quickly picked them up, put them back into the drawer, and locked it. "What's that, Mom?" Elli asked, as she watched me.

"Oh, you just surprised me, that's all. I didn't know you were even awake yet," I got up from my desk and gave her a hug. Then I offered to start breakfast.

Sammy was already in the family room when we came downstairs, watching his regular Saturday morning shows.

"Did you ask Mom about the mall?" Sam pulled Elli over, whispering in a not-very-quiet voice.

"What's at the mall today?" My eyes scanned the two faces in front of me.

"Oh, nothing." Sam quickly added, "We just want to go to that new game store that opened."

"Yeah, I wanted to go there, too." Elli rolled her eyes at Sam, and then smiled back at me.

"Okay, as long as we go early, because I have a lot of things to get done today." The words were hardly out of my mouth when they both ran upstairs to get dressed.

After breakfast, we headed out, the pink and purple azaleas glowing brilliantly in the late-April sunshine. The soft, invigorating breeze was a good antidote for my earlier feelings of despair. The mall was still pretty quiet when we arrived, and Elli and Sammy's laughter echoed through the hollow space. It didn't take them long to find the store, and they immediately started their exploration. I walked around with them for a bit and then told them that I would be sitting on the bench in front of the store.

About twenty minutes later, they appeared. "Mom, Sammy wants to go to the video store. I don't mind taking him. You can just sit here and relax, okay?" Elli said, in an unusually mature tone that was hard to ignore.

"Yeah, Momma, let Elli take me. You stay right here and relax." Sam was already pulling his sister by her arm.

"If I didn't know better, I'd think you wanted to get rid of me. Is there something I should know?"

"No, Momma. I just want to go with Elli. We're not babies." Sam pulled on Elli even harder.

"Okay." I sighed. "I'll be right here, but I want you to go only to the video store and then come right back."

"Great, we will," they said in chorus, as they started to run off. "If you're not back in twenty minutes, I'll come to the video store."

"Thanks, Mom. I promise I'll keep him next to me," Elli called back to me.

It was hard to let them go off by themselves, even though I remembered all the things I had done on my own when I was their age.

Times were different now, but . . . I continued to watch them until they turned down the corridor toward the video store. The filigree hands on the ornate gilded clock that hung from the apex of the vaulted ceiling moved very slowly. Perhaps if I only stared harder, the minutes would move more quickly. I took some breaths and tried to will myself to relax. It was no use.

Just as I was about to get up and walk to meet them, I saw their two curly heads, smiling, as they bounded toward me. It was hard to miss the shopping bag with the Kay Jewelers logo in Sam's hand.

"I was just about to come find you. What have you guys been up to?" I asked, looking at the bag.

"We got a surprise!" Sam blurted out.

Elli, rolling her eyes at him, intervened. "We just had something we had to get."

It was the end of April. The mall was adorned with signs about Mother's Day, so it didn't take long for me to figure out what was going on. As we walked to the car, there were lots of whispers and giggles between the two of them. Just as we got to the car, Elli said, "Mom, we have a surprise for you."

"Yes, it's for Mother's Day," Sam added. "Would you like to open it early?" he asked, clearly hoping I would say yes.

"It's hard to keep a surprise." I laughed. "You know I'm not too good at keeping them."

"Momma, please open it. It's so special," Sam continued.

"Wow, this is a hard decision. I'm so excited, but are you sure you wouldn't rather wait until Mother's Day?"

"No." Sammy was emphatic, and Elli laughed.

I was able to convince them that we should at least wait until we got home, because that would make it even more special.

As we drove the short distance home, I wondered how I had managed to have these two, most magnificent children.

Charles was not there when we arrived home, and the kids pushed me toward the sofa, telling me to sit down.

"Here, Momma. This is from both of us because we love you." Sam looked at his sister and smiled. I did try to hold the tears back, but it didn't work.

"Mom, really it's from Sammy; I just helped him put it all together." Elli smiled at her younger brother.

Inside the shopping bag was a white gift box tied with purple ribbons.

"Wow, this beautiful. It's almost too pretty to open," I said. Their faces were glowing.

Sammy quickly responded, "You have to open it, Momma. The best part is inside."

Wanting to savor every moment, I carefully unwrapped the gift. The purple tissue paper inside crinkled as I pulled it open. Out of the box, I took a soft, fluffy white bear. He had a purple ribbon around his neck and held a small purple-and-silver gift box in his hands.

"Oh, this is so lovely. I am so happy to be your mother. I love him. He is so beautiful. Thank you." I got up and moved to grab them close to me.

"Mom, you didn't open the present yet." Elli looked slightly exasperated. "The box he's holding is the present, Mom," she said, emphasizing the word, *Mom*.

"Oh, really? I didn't know. I thought the box was just a decoration." We all laughed at my foolishness. I then opened the small box.

There lay on a cushion of black velvet, a golden ring. As I lifted it, I saw that it had two rows of small diamonds on the top. On the edge, the word *Mom* was cut out in the gold. I looked at my two beautiful children, pulling them close, and I cried. "It's so pretty!" I closed my fingers tightly around it. "How were you able to do this? Where did you get the money? This was expensive!" Still with wet eyes, I slipped the ring on. "And it fits. How did you do this?"

"Mom, we took one of your rings with us so we could make sure it would fit." Elli, smiling, moved to her backpack, opened a compartment, and handed me my wedding ring, which I had stopped wearing when Charles had given me that letter.

"Momma, it was my idea," said Sammy. "I put all my birthday and savings money together and bought it. Do you like it? The lady was so nice. She even sold it to us for cheaper than it was s'pose to be. Right, Elli?" Sammy came and sat on my lap as he spoke.

Elli said, "Mom when we walked in, the saleslady asked if we were with a grown-up. I told her no and that we wanted to buy the ring on the sign outside the store—"

Sam interrupted: "She asked if our dad had given us the money to buy something, and I told her that it was my own money, and our dad didn't even know about it." Sam's eyes glowed with pride.

Elli continued, "So the lady asked how much money we had, and I told her we had eighty-seven dollars. She told us to wait a minute. She went and talked to a man, and when she came back, she said that even though the ring was a little more expensive than that, she would sell it to us for eighty-seven dollars! She was so nice, Mom!"

"Then she said she would make a great package for it, and she put in the box the bear was holding. That was so cool!" Sammy added. "And you thought the bear was the present. That was so funny, Momma!" Sam turned his curly-topped head to his sister and gave her a high five.

Maybe what Charles said about my being a bad mother, a poor role model for the children, was not true. It was just so hard not to feel wounded knowing he thought that about me. I heard his rejection in everything he said and did. The move to the new house felt as if it couldn't come fast enough.

Charles had told me that he didn't want much of the furniture and other possessions we had collected over the course of our marriage. That, too, felt like a rejection, until an incident involving Elli pushed me over the edge.

Elli was an artist. At two years old, she could draw a person with differentiated body parts better than some eight-year-olds, probably better than some adults. When she was seven and in first grade, I insisted one day that we go through her bulging backpack. From the bottom of the bag, I salvaged three, slightly scrunched, stapled pieces of orange construction paper.

"Charles, you have to see this," I called from the kitchen in the house on St. John's Lane. I turned to Elli, who had moved from the table to the pantry to find a snack. "Elli, this is a phenomenal drawing."

"It is? I thought I had thrown it out. I guess I just stuck it in my backpack." Elli's mouth was filled with chocolate chip cookies. Charles had walked into the room and stood over me, looking at what I held in my hand.

"Wow, did you do this, Elli? It's fabulous! Do you know this is like a painting by a famous artist?" Charles's eyes were wide with amazement as he looked at the face of a dog: an eye on each of the two top papers, and the snout on the bottom. "I have a book I want to show you, Elli." He walked into the office, and Elli and I followed.

"Mommy, what's so special about this dumb dog's face? I was just playing around!" Another cookie went into her mouth.

"I think I know what Daddy wants to show you. I think you're going to be surprised." Charles was standing at his desk, flipping pages in a thick book of paintings. "Here it is. Look at this painting by Paul Klee, Elli. What does it look like?"

"It looks just like mine, but it's a cat's face. How did he have the same idea that I did? It's pretty cool, though."

"Next time we go to New York, we'll go to the Museum of Modern Art so you can see the real painting," Charles said, still shaking his head in amazement.

"This is something we have to frame and hang so everyone can see it," I added.

"Maybe they'll want to hang mine up, too. So we should take it with us when we go. But it's kind of scrunched up." Elli took a deep breath.

"I think the person at the frame shop will know how to fix that," I assured her, as Charles and I glowed with pride at our daughter's very real talent.

The large, framed picture of the dog adorned the center of the wall of the staircase on St. John's Lane. When we moved to the rental house, I didn't have much interest in decorating. Nevertheless, we hung the dog in a place of honor. And now Elli had made it very clear that she wanted the picture to hang over the fireplace in our new house.

One evening in early May, Charles said he wanted to go through photos so that he could have some for himself. As we began to sort through the first box, Charles looked up and said that one of the few things he wanted was Elli's dog picture.

My stomach tightened, but despite that feeling in my gut, I told him, "Elli has said that she wants the picture. She knows where she wants to hang it."

"You really are something else. You manipulated her. I want the picture," he said.

"It's Elli's picture. She should be able to decide where she wants it," I said.

"Get out of here. I can't stand the sight of you. I don't know what I would do if you were in my presence any longer, so get out." His eyes raged.

I started to leave, going up the stairs from the basement. "It's *Elli's* picture," I said, turning to him. "It has nothing to do with me."

"It has everything to do with you. Everything has everything to do with you. You think only of yourself!"

The fierceness of his tone, the aggression in his voice, put me in a place where I couldn't hold back. "What are you going to do to me? Shoot me like you shot Mr. Buttons?" I couldn't believe I'd said that. Had that been the noose hanging loosely around my neck for years? I ran up the stairs before he had a chance to respond.

## Chapter Thirty-Five

Despite the longer days, the warming sun, and the blooming colors, I still found it hard to get out of bed some mornings, and my first thought was still sometimes, *Help me, Momma.* Then I would think of Elli and Sam and force myself to put one leg on the floor and then the other.

I was determined to see my children grow up, and I knew I would have more of a chance at survival once I was out of this house and away from the toxicity that was here. The move was getting closer.

Meanwhile, I met with my attorney and told him that Charles had said I didn't have to worry about my financial future.

"Diane, that's bullshit. He will try his best to give you nothing." Dan shook his head and smiled sadly.

"He said he'd pay for the movers. So you don't think I should believe him, do you?" I asked.

"If he does, that will be great, but you should have a backup plan, because I wouldn't expect anything from him. He's not a stable man. He's not a nice man."

Nothing could have been truer.

For Mother's Day, the children made me beautiful cards and brought me breakfast in bed. Surprisingly, Charles gave me a gift, too. It was a rock waterfall fountain. It was very beautiful, but why did he do it? I knew he thought this gesture reflected his belief that he had a new, more "spiritual" self, that he existed on some "higher plane," as he often implied in his journal entries, but I also knew better than to believe such premeditated bullshit. Although I had no way of knowing what would come next, I knew there would be something. One thing I had learned over these past months was that there was always, always an ulterior motive when Charles did something nice.

That same night, I got an e-mail from Katja, the German au pair who had lived with us for a year when Sammy was two and Elli was five. She had been eighteen and like a teenage daughter to me. She had been close with Charles, too, but her bond with me had been extra special.

*Diane, I am so sad. I received a letter from Charles, and he tells me you are separating. That makes my heart break for all of you, especially Sammy and Elli. But, Diane, I am also angry and want to send a letter to Charles and tell him how angry I am for what he wrote. But I am writing you instead. In his letter he said that when I was with you, "Katja, you were really the mother; you did everything." How could he say that? It wasn't true. I helped you when you were working, but I still needed a mother. I was homesick and you took care of Sammy, Elli, and me. I helped with the kids, but only you were the mother. It makes me so mad . . .*

Then I read his journal, and, as I expected, his words about me as a mother were scathing:

*She is incompetent as a mother. She has no control over the children. They don't respect her. She had trouble even becoming a biological mother . . .*

I was going to give him the fountain back to let him know what I thought of his gift. Instead, I just put it in the trash without saying anything. Saying anything was pointless.

The days passed, and the renovations on the new house were under way. The kids and I went over there several more times, and I sat with the neighbors on the porch while Elli and Sammy played Capture the Flag in the courtyard with their new friends. Within the fourteen townhouses in the court, there were eight single mothers. There would be a lot of support and camaraderie.

It was a Tuesday evening, and we had been over at the new house for a couple of hours. Moments after we arrived home, Charles walked in. "My parents are going to visit this weekend," he said, as he opened the refrigerator to get a drink.

"This weekend? We're in the middle of packing. Is this really a good time for a visit?" I asked, sensing that he was setting me up for something.

"Well, they want to see the kids before the upheaval of the move," he continued, as if there were nothing at all strange about this.

I thought back to when I was ill and my father would come over to the house to see me, and Charles would get angry, saying that it was an intrusion to have Dad there. He said the same thing when my niece, Lisa, visited from Denver during my illness. In those instances, my relatives helped me. This was an intrusion. This was inappropriate. I bit my tongue and said nothing. I knew we were going to have to go over the child custody agreement before the move, so I figured it was better to save my energy for that battle.

His parents arrived, and as was always the case when Charles was around them, his tension was high. This time, though, he didn't have me to entertain them. For the most part, everyone but my children ignored me.

An enlightening conversation with Albert, Charles's father, took place that Saturday afternoon. I was working in the kitchen, and Charles and his mother had taken the children to the pool.

Albert had fallen asleep on the oversized chair in the family room. When he awoke, he walked into the kitchen and sat down on the pine, ladder-back chair. As he placed his hands flat on the table, the darkened spots on his skin spread like brown puddles of ink across the wood.

"Would you like something to eat or drink?" I asked.

"No, thanks, Di. I'm fine." He sat quietly for several minutes; the silence was heavy.

"This is hard for all of us." I paused. "I don't know what Charles has told you, but I hope that we can continue to have a relationship." I was being polite more than genuine, although I did want the children to maintain a bond with their grandparents.

"I don't know. You've done some terrible things." His jaw tightened, and when I looked closely enough, I could also see the muscle in his left eyelid twitching ever so slightly.

*What?* I thought. But I said, "I'm sure we've both done things in our relationship that have brought us to this point. But, you know, when someone's partner is very ill, I think that loyalty and support should be paramount. I have been very ill. Charles has been nonexistent in my life and pretty much the same toward the kids."

"I won't believe that Charles did anything unless he tells me that he did something," he added. "You poisoned him against his mother."

I was incredulous. From the day I had met Charles, he had spoken of hating his mother, and now I was being accused of turning him against her? I said to his father, "Albert, I really don't know what you're talking about, I've done no such thing. What evidence do you have?"

"At your mother's funeral, Charles got up and spoke and said that your mother was like a mother to him. He *has* a mother!" His usual passivity was now markedly aggressive.

It took effort to stay calm, but I did. "You know, Albert, I can understand that hearing Charles say that must have been hurtful to both Marcy and to you. But those words came from him, not me." If only Albert knew the things Charles had said about his parents to everyone. If only he knew how Charles wished for them to die in a "fiery crash on 95" so he could inherit their money. Those desires had nothing to do with me, but I didn't tell Albert any of this.

I was finding myself short of breath, and I knew I needed to get away from this conversation.

"I'm really sorry that you feel so angry at me, but this is very difficult to listen to. It really is not at all based on what's happened, and I am physically having a hard time listening to this." I didn't move, but my fingers clenched the cup in my hand so tightly that my knuckles cracked.

"You have not treated us nicely for years when we have visited," Albert continued, completely ignoring my shallow breathing and increasing distress.

"Albert, I'm the only one who's been around when you and Marcy have visited. Charles is the one who totally ignores you when you're here. How can you blame me for something that's his fault?"

"Don't you have a mind of your own?" he countered.

"When you visit, I plan things for us to do; I cook meals for us. It would be nice if your son participated, don't you think?" I stopped talking. This was as distorted and crazy-making as what Charles did to me. I couldn't win. I also couldn't breathe.

I stood up and poured the remainder of my tea into the sink. As I watched the golden liquid splash against the stainless steel, I imagined spitting out the venomous sputum that was caught in the back of my throat. "This is too disturbing and crazy; I can't—and I won't—listen to it," I said, avoiding Albert's gaze. "I have to leave. I'm going to help my dad pack for the move."

With those words, I placed the cup in the dishwasher, picked up my pocketbook, and walked out. I could hear Albert still talking as I closed the front door behind me. I got in the car, and as I started the engine, I burst into tears.

I started driving. I turned left out of the gatehouse, my head in what had become a familiar state of dazed confusion. I then made a right and headed north. The canopy of branches enveloped me as I drove, and I felt sheltered. I drove without any clear sense of where I was going. I found myself continuing north on Falls Road. By the time I reached Mt. Carmel Road, the landscape was rural.

The landmarks I passed all held memories of the twenty years I had spent with Charles. I passed the supermarket we shopped in when we first dated and lived together; My Favorite Things, a small shop that sold dollhouse miniatures, where Elli and I had spent hours; the Wagon Wheel, a local eatery that served the best breakfast anywhere; and the spot where one snowy night I had gotten stuck on Big Falls Road and Charles had come to shovel me out of a snowdrift and get me up the hill so I could go home.

There were so many memories. There was nothing in Baltimore that didn't in some way connect me to Charles. As I found myself driving past all of these places that comprised our life together, I was still trying hard to understand. Had we ever really had a relationship? This would be a question I would struggle with for a very long time. My tears flowed, but my body felt eerily numb.

Next, I drove the winding back roads toward the small cottage where we lived when the children were born. I smiled as I approached what the kids had come to call the Whee Hill, because I would speed up a bit as I went up the hill and then take my foot off the gas as we went down, squealing, "Whee!" with delight. After we moved, the kids would sometimes want to return for a ride down the hill, and we would do that. As I approached the hill now, I smiled and accelerated, then cruised down, enjoying the exhilaration and the memory.

I then drove off the road into the development that Charles hated so much. I parked at the top of a hill and spent a while looking down at our old property. It was very quiet. I could see the rolling hills, the narrow creek that wound its way toward the Gunpowder River, the fenced horse pasture that stood empty now, one lone board missing on the loafing shed that was still in good condition. The chicken coop had been taken down, and it looked like an addition was being built onto the house. Life wasn't perfect back then, either, but, looking down from the hill, I saw paradise. I closed my eyes and breathed in the cool, colorful spring air, feeling weightless and ethereal.

I walked back to my car and slowly drove off the hill. This time, I got on the highway and arrived at Dad's apartment. He was on the phone when I walked in; he hung up when he saw me.

"I just tried to call you at the house. I was beginning to get worried. Where have you been?" As he spoke, my feelings gushed out and I told him about the conversation with Albert.

"I don't understand those people; there's something wrong with them. I called them a few months ago, and they never returned my call. We've known each other for years. We're like family. You'd think they'd want to talk to me. The apple sure doesn't fall far from the tree." He looked tired and sad more than he looked angry. He hugged me tightly and said, "It'll all work out, Di. I know it will."

His tone was far less convincing than his words.

"The movers will be coming at nine on Monday. I'd like it if we carried over some of your mother's delicate things. I've put them all together in my bedroom."

"Do you have some more boxes and paper, or should I run down to the car and bring up what I have in there? I think we should wrap things even if we're carrying them ourselves." I started toward the bedroom, thinking of the beautiful things my mother had collected over the years, overwhelmed with the thought of the unpacking that lay ahead. I saw a stack of boxes in the corner of the bedroom and a pile of packing paper in the corner before my dad had a chance to say anything.

"Oh, I see you have everything we need. I should have known you would." I smiled at him, and he smiled back.

"Come on. Let's get started so we can get these things over to the house. Then maybe we can go have some dinner—a good meal will make us both feel better." He winked at me and handed me a piece of packing paper, and I began to wrap two antique bisque vases, one with two delicately sculpted little boys climbing up the sides, the other with the same two boys climbing down. When I was a child, those vases sat on top of two bookcases in my parents' living room. I would sit on the couch across from them and make up stories about these boys: what adventures they were having, the camaraderie between them, their challenges, and their successes.

After packing about five boxes, we carried them down to my car and put them in the backseat. The rest of Dad's apartment was already packed. He had decided to stay at Lydia's until the renovations were completed. He wasn't comfortable staying with us. He didn't want to be around Charles.

By the time I got back home later that evening, the house was quiet. Marcy and Albert had clearly gone back to their hotel, the kids were asleep, and Charles was down in the basement. I went into my bedroom, and, although I didn't usually lock my door, this particular night I did. If the kids wanted me, they could knock. I didn't want anyone, meaning Charles, walking in.

## Chapter Thirty-Six

I sat on the floor in the new house, surrounded by boxes and Dad's furniture. The lights inside were off. The porch light filtered prism-like patterns through the glass onto the face of the grandfather clock that stood tall in the corner. It was midnight, and sticky, hot, and humid, not unusual for an early-June night in Baltimore. The children and I had not yet moved; it would be another week before we did. The predictable chimes of the clock brought some sense of order to the disarray of the room. Even without air-conditioning, in the midst of the renovations and all of the accompanying disorder, with the scent of freshly sawed wood permeating the air, I could finally breathe for the first time in two years.

I was waiting for Jeff, one of my new neighbors, a plumber, who had said he would come over to check the air-conditioning because it didn't seem to be working.

When he arrived, he spent quite some time in the back, knocking and tapping and checking things, while I sat on the steps, just waiting.

When he reappeared, he looked up to where I was sitting on the stairs and said, "Hmm. I'm not sure exactly what it is. Just give me a few more minutes. I'll figure this out." With that, his eyes stopped, and he moved his flashlight to a red switch on the wall over my head. He walked over and flipped the switch up. Immediately, the sound of the air conditioner came on. "I think the problem is solved." Jeff touched my shoulder and smiled. "Your luck is turning!"

"I guess it is," I said; then we both laughed and hugged. I thanked him for his help, and after he left, I again sat in the dark, smiling and breathing.

It was after two in the morning when I got back home. I saw that Charles was sitting on the couch in the family room. He was on his cell phone, clearly speaking with Victoria, because she was the only person he spoke with at all hours of the night. He averted his eyes as I glanced in his direction. I was well practiced in remaining stone-faced and continued up the stairs. Elli's tape player was still on, and I turned it off and pulled the covers over her, kissing her forehead gently. When I looked in Sam's room, I found his bed empty and saw that his patchwork blankie was not there, either. I walked out onto the landing of the loft looking down over my bedroom. There he was, his curly brown mop spread out across a pillow, arms and legs twisted and tangled between blankets and sheets. The long, ragged, faded-red satin piece of his blankie was tucked under his right cheek, clutched between his thumb and his index finger. I walked down the carpeted steps and placed the throw blankets over him, kissing the curls on his head. Then I went upstairs and fell asleep on his bed.

The next morning, Sam wrapped his arms around my neck and asked, "Momma, where were you last night? I waited here for you, but you didn't come!"

"I thought I told you that I would be at the new house, waiting for Mr. Jeff to come and take a look at the air conditioner to see if he could fix it. Guess what was wrong with it?"

"What?" Elli asked, as she walked down the stairs from the loft above my bedroom.

"Well, after Mr. Jeff checked everything and was beginning to get frustrated because he couldn't figure out what was wrong, he flashed his flashlight up toward the ceiling. Guess what he saw?"

"A spider?" Sammy blurted out.

"I bet it was the power switch." Elli rolled her eyes. "What else could it be?"

"She's right—it was the main switch. Somehow it had gotten flipped off while the guys were working down in the basement and never got flipped back on."

"Some people are so dumb," Elli added.

"Elli, those things happen to everybody. It doesn't make them dumb." Elli was becoming increasingly more critical of others. It wasn't something I liked to see in my usually sweet and empathic child. I hoped it wasn't a reflection of the tension she was experiencing, because that was beyond her control.

"Come on. Sam, you go upstairs and get washed and dressed for school, and then come back down for breakfast. Elli, why don't you come into the kitchen and set the table so we can catch up while I start breakfast?"

I watched as Sam raced up the stairs, taking two steps at a time. His resilience seemed much greater than his sister's did at this point. I sighed.

"How about some French toast?" I asked, as Elli and I walked into the kitchen. She plopped herself onto one of the white wooden chairs, sunlight streaming in and casting a halo around her yellow curls.

"Nah, I'll just have a bagel and cream cheese." She scowled as she got up, got out the orange juice, and poured herself a glass. "Okay, but I'm going to make French toast for Sam, and there will be enough if you want some. Can you set the table, please, and take out the butter and syrup from the fridge?" I asked, as I began dipping pieces of bread into the egg-and-cinnamon mixture I had just made.

"Mom, can I tell you something?" Elli was walking to the table with a stack of dishes and cutlery in her hands as she spoke.

"Sure, you can tell me anything." My stomach clenched tightly.

"I know you hate Dad, but I feel really sad that he's going to be all alone. Especially since he'll still be in this house for a few weeks after we move out."

I'm not sure how long it was before I said anything, but when I spoke, I took Elli's face in my hands and looked her in her sad aqua eyes. Thoughts of feeling like a failure as a wife and as a mother flooded my head. My guilt that I had not been able to keep the promise I felt I had made to Joni, Elli's birth mother, to give Elli a stable and loving family for life was overwhelming.

"Elli, I don't hate your father. I am very angry at him, and I am very hurt, and I am also very sad. I know this is very hard for you, and you don't know how much I wish it could be different. I promise you, though, we will get through this. We all will." Tears ran down my cheeks as I spoke, and as I hugged her, the saltiness of my tears mixed with the saltiness of hers. I prayed that my words would be true.

## Chapter Thirty-Seven

The knife rhythmically hit the wooden cutting board as I diced the blood-red beets. The pinkish juices slowly seeped into the lone crack that ran down the center of the board. I had been prepping myself all afternoon. I had my lines practiced so that I didn't go off script. It was still the only way I could deal with Charles's verbal dexterity. The way he used words was really verbal masturbation—he got off on it. I, on the other hand, was merely a prop. My words were just self-stimulatory tools for him.

The movers would be coming on Wednesday morning. Charles had said that he would take the kids to camp, and I had arranged for my dad to pick them up. He had told me that he would give me the $2,500 for the movers. He had not yet told me how much he was going to give me each month for the children. Nor had he signed our custody agreement. Damn, it was hard to get into court. Short of having a butcher knife impaled through one's chest, blood dripping on the courthouse steps, nothing was an emergency. I was getting out because of a legal term, *constructive abandonment*. But I still wanted him to sign the agreement! It was going to be a battle, and it all had to do with money. He wanted to make sure he'd pay as little as possible in child support.

Baltimore was such a small community; I didn't even have to read this in his journal. I heard that Charles had said to someone, "I've supported them all these years. Now it's her turn!" Listening to him, one might have thought I had been out playing tennis for the past decade, rather than juggling a part-time practice, running a household, and actively taking care of two children—not to mention going through infertility treatments and, after that, a diagnosis and treatment for cancer. Heaven forbid I might have felt the need to slow down and have some time to recover and get my strength back. Charles would have said that was selfish, though. He would have said that I was in victim mode. Maybe that was true. I needed to find my equilibrium, to stay focused and on script.

The front door opened and then closed. It was only four thirty. I looked up, and Charles was standing in the archway that separated the kitchen from the family room. My hands were over the sink, beet juice dripping down my fingertips. I let the hot water from the tap wash the red color from my hands and run down the drain.

"Oh, I'm glad you got home early. The kids are over at the new place with my dad. He'll have them back in about an hour for dinner. It would be great if we talked about the custody agreement."

"What do you want to say about it? I've been very clear about what I want. I want custody split down the middle. Everything fifty-fifty." He began going through the mail that lay piled on the table.

"Charles, the children and I are moving the day after tomorrow. I would like the agreement signed before we move. I've agreed to joint legal custody, but I want physical custody. The kids should have as few transitions as possible during the school year; we can always be more flexible during summer and vacations. We can make sure that you get the number of overnights you want. I just want the schedule to involve as few transitions as possible." I was trying to be direct and not confrontational, but it was impossible to know how I really sounded, and inside I shook with fright.

"You are not going to tell me what to do. Do you understand that?" Even when Charles didn't yell, there was more venom in his words than there had ever been when I had raged my loudest. To me, my screams seemed more like shouts of frustration; his words felt deadly. But did he experience his words the way I had experienced mine?

"I am not telling you what to do. You don't want to talk with me about anything, and you don't want to negotiate anything. You say you want joint custody. I'm afraid, Charles, that seems to be an oxymoron. If you can't or won't communicate with me, joint custody will not be very successful. You bought the kids beepers so that we can have as little direct contact as possible. What in the world do a nine-year-old and an eleven-year-old need with beepers? Within two days, the kids will have lost them. If that's what you want to do, that's fine, but don't expect me to be involved with them. I think they're ridiculous, and they do not allow for any real communication."

"You don't like the idea because you think it came from Victoria." Each of his words was clipped.

"I don't like the idea because I don't think it's appropriate, and I think that we need to be communicating directly. And until we have a signed agreement, I'm not sure I can agree to overnight visits." The water was still running, so I turned to the sink, pushed the stainless-steel lever down, and walked out of the kitchen. Then I turned back to Charles and said, "I'm willing to talk about this further, but I want the agreement signed before the move."

I walked through the living room, feeling unbalanced, then walked into the bedroom, taking deep breaths, trying to make the shaking stop, wishing desperately that it would. I took a deep breath, called my dad, and asked him to take the children to dinner and bring them home at eight thirty. I knew the conversation with Charles was not over, and I knew it was better if the kids were gone.

"You'd better not try to keep me from seeing the children." There was Charles in the doorway. "You don't know me at all if you think I'd let you get away with that!" He stared at me, his dark eyes narrowed and piercing.

"Charles, I would rather that we handled this in a reasonable way. All I want is to have a signed agreement before the move. I don't know why you're making it so difficult. You have an equal legal say in all of the decisions about the children. It isn't good for kids to move between houses on school nights; that's all I want to avoid." I wanted to say that he was more interested in money than he was in his children. Suddenly, he wanted all this time with them when he'd never had time for them before. I didn't say that. In any event, I already knew that once he got his way, he wasn't going to have any time for them. Nevertheless, I needed to stand firm.

"I'm done supporting you," he said. "That's it! I'm not going to sign the agreement. I'm not paying for the movers—get some other stooge to do that. And just so you know what you will get, I will be giving you ten dollars per child per week for child support." He glared at me, and I could see that nearly imperceptible twitch in the corner of his mouth.

"You're pathetic!" I shouted. I slammed the bedroom door and turned the lock, gritting my teeth as volcanic rage roared inside me. *He got me, damn it!* I had lost it—again.

I didn't have the money to pay the movers. I couldn't and wouldn't ask my dad for the $2,500. He had already put a huge down payment on the house, had paid for all of the renovations and his move, and had bought me my minivan, and for months he had been giving me extra money for groceries and expenses for the kids. I couldn't ask him for anything else.

No, I would not allow that to happen. I rubbed the palms of my hands over my thighs slowly, pressing down hard with all of the strength in my upper body. I squeezed the muscles in my arms and legs tightly. Slowly I breathed in, feeling the rise in my chest. Then, as I released my breath, I allowed my muscles to relax. In two days, we were moving. I would find a way. I had survived many things. I would find a way to get the $2,500. That seemed like nothing in comparison with everything else.

I began to do a mental inventory of all the things I could sell but realized quickly that that should come after the move, so the kids and I had money on which to live. Twenty dollars a week in child support wasn't going to do much, and I didn't even have a court date yet.

I called my friend Peg, and she said that she would lend me the money. I didn't let Dad know that Charles hadn't given it to me. It would be a number of months before I would be able to pay Peg back. In fact, without asking, I began receiving a lot of checks in the mail, unsolicited, all given as gifts. I kept a close tally of how I would repay it all, as I didn't want gifts, but it was not lost on me that friends and family were rallying around me in all sorts of ways.

My experience was funny in that dark sort of way that allows one to feel pain, humiliation, and embarrassment that would otherwise be too excruciating to acknowledge. I had felt it first when I was going through treatment for my cancer. At that time, I thought about how I had lost all sense of physical pride. I was aware that I had no sense of shame or humiliation. I could bare my body to anyone—it was just a vessel—or at least I was great at dissociating myself from the sense of degrading mortification or an inkling of embarrassment. Now, with no money and the need to support myself and my children, I would be juggling air and borrowing from Peter to pay Paul. I would be writing checks, smiling sweetly, hoping the checks I deposited in the bank would clear before the one I was writing at the cash register reached the bank.

I needed desperately to get a real job with benefits. Private practice, especially when I was in such profound physical and emotional despair, would not be enough to sustain us.

Next, I called Dan, my attorney, and told him about what Charles had said.

"Can he legally give me twenty dollars a week in child support?" I asked incredulously, always feeling that Charles must know something I didn't know.

"Of course he can't do that legally. It's way below the guidelines based upon the number of kids you have and his income. But until we get to court, he can do anything he wants to do. You already know he will do anything to get out of taking any sort of responsibility, but in the end, he'll have to give you the back money."

"But now is when I need it, Dan. My practice isn't taking off. I just can't get it together. As soon as we move, I'm going to start looking for a job." I knew I sounded desperate and whiny, but that was exactly how I felt. I wanted someone to take care of me. As much as I longed for that, I knew I could and would take care of my children and myself.

"I'll send a note to his attorney, Diane, but I'm not sure it will make a difference, because your husband doesn't listen to his attorney. I'm trying to get us a court date as quickly as I can. Focus on the move and getting settled. Then find a friend who lives somewhere nice and take the kids on a road trip for a visit. It'll be a good break after the move, and it won't cost too much."

---

MOVING day arrived.

"Momma, I don't want to go to camp today. I want to help with the move," Sam said.

Elli rolled her eyes, as always. "We have to go to camp today. Mom is going to be busy with the move, and she doesn't need to have you underfoot, making a mess of everything."

"Nah-nah-nah-nah-nah . . . You're not the boss of me, Elli! Momma, I want to stay home with you and help move. You go to camp if you want to—I don't!" Sam stuck his tongue out and slapped his hand under his armpit, making a farting sound.

"You are so immature," Elli sighed, sauntering up the stairs.

"Listen, you're both going to camp today. I'm going to be busy with the move, and it won't be any fun to be with me. At camp, you'll have a great day with your friends, and when you get to the new house, you'll have your bunk beds all set up. Won't that be cool?"

"I don't want to go to camp!" Sam yelled, as he yanked on my arm.

"Sam, that hurt; I've told you I don't like it when you pull on my arm that way. You're going to camp today. It is not an option. Now, go upstairs and get dressed while I make breakfast."

Charles passed by Sam as he stomped off. "I guess your mom is in one of her bossy moods this morning, isn't she?" Charles said to him. Sam didn't respond.

Charles never supported my being firm with the kids, even when things were good between us. Of course, he always forgot that he became a tyrant when he got angry at them.

*Just a few more hours*, I thought.

As much as I had been walking around with terror about this move, as much as I had felt a constant tightening of my chest and racing of my heart, as much as I knew Charles would still undermine everything I said and did, I was sure that my life was about to become much easier emotionally. This was finally the day when easier would begin.

After breakfast, I told the kids that Poppy would pick them up from camp and I'd see them at the new house. "I know you'd rather be part of the move, but I think it will be more fun at camp, and it'll be easier for me to get things set up if I don't have to be concerned about what you're doing." I knelt down as I spoke and hugged both kids. "I'll see you after camp. Have fun. I love you."

Charles was silent. He opened the door. The kids called goodbye and followed him out to the car. I was shaky, but I kept repeating to myself, over and over again, *This, too, will pass.*

I knew in my head that there had been a time when I had loved coming home, knowing that Charles would be there, but that had been so long ago. These past two years had been unspeakably horrific. I also now knew what I hadn't been able to admit before: that my emotional and physical chains had been strangling me for many years before that. I just hadn't been able to acknowledge what I saw or what I felt was happening. I hadn't been able to accept that my very early misgivings had become the horrors of my existence. But I was not going to go there. I was out and finally in my own space. The healing could finally begin.

## Chapter Thirty-Eight

The heat that summer was deadly. My dad looked more and more tired and increasingly sad. Still, he played an early round of golf with his buddies a few times a week.

"Poppy, can I go with you and ride in the golf cart?" Sammy often asked.

That was one of the things that always made my dad smile.

"Sure, sure! You'll be my caddie for the day!" They would laugh, and off they would go into the humidity of Baltimore's greens. They loved it.

But when Charles came to pick the kids up, if my dad was sitting at the kitchen table when Charles walked in, my dad would nod his head, without meeting Charles's eyes, and leave the room.

It wasn't long before one of Charles's interminably rambling e-mails arrived.

*Di,*

*Knowing that you will soon enough receive a response from the universe to the thoughts about me that you indulge in and plant in the minds of others, and aware of how precious is the time we are given, I have been uninterested in commenting on all that you express that I disagree with. And then it seems there comes a point.*

*The way your father treats me when I come to pick the children up is clearly the result of the poisonous thoughts that you have implanted in his mind. I have been only good and kind to your father, and for him to treat me with such disrespect when I come to get the children is highly insulting and inappropriate.*

*You never had much of an idea of whom you were dealing with, and you still don't. Educational opportunities in this area await you. If you don't want to receive preliminary installments such as this one, make*

> sure your father understands that I do not like the way he is treating me, especially in front of the children. And stop indulging yourself in your poisonous delusions.
>
> Charles

The e-mails started immediately after we moved. The language sounded crazier than ever; it was undigested word salad. Unlike Charles, I never communicated with him by e-mail. I responded angrily to him with spoken words, but I never put anything in writing. As brilliant as he thought he was, he didn't seem to be concerned that he was putting all of his craziness on paper, giving me a record of it all.

Nevertheless, the e-mails, particularly this one, were disturbing. I was still so easily triggered into thinking I was at fault, that maybe he was right. Now, though, I could feel myself clawing out of the hazy confusion when I felt myself ensconced in it, and my escape from the fog was quicker, my disorientation shorter. He was still trying to dictate and control how I did things, but now he did so through these e-mails, as condescending as ever:

> About bread . . . I am not in any way telling you what you should do in your house, but I've been frustrated not to be able to get Elli and Sam to eat anything other than white bread, challah [white bread with egg yolks], and bagels. Naturally, if that is the only thing they get the majority of the week, when they are with you, that's what they will insist on here and in the lunches I make. I certainly hope we can coordinate an effort to help them appreciate the taste and texture of bread that has fiber and nutrients in it and that would promote greater health . . .

If I hadn't been saving these daily e-mails and letters for my legal case, as well as for the book I might someday write, I would have just thrown them out. As it was, I still did read them, even though that was not a smart thing to do. It would take quite some time before I was really able to disengage enough to stop caring about what Charles thought of me. For now, the situation still felt very crazy; I felt crazy.

Despite the e-mails, despite my not knowing what was and wasn't real, and despite my lack of money, so many things in life were so much better—namely, my kids were happy again.

---

"I'M going out to play Capture the Flag," Sam called one evening, as the door slammed behind him.

Elli followed him. "Mom, I'm going next door to Carol's, okay?" "Sure, have fun," I said, but the door closed before she even heard me.

We had just finished eating dinner, and as had become the custom, the dishes were barely off the table before both of them were gone.

"You know, Di," my father said, "I think this is a great place for them. It's a real neighborhood. They just walk outside and have loads of kids to play with. I think it's great. They seem so happy here." My father smiled. Anything that had to do with his grandchildren being happy gave him so much pleasure.

"Dad, speaking of the kids, I got an e-mail today from Charles. He doesn't like it that you ignore him when he comes over to pick them up. He feels insulted."

There was a long pause, and then Dad said, "*He* feels insulted? What a joke! I'm afraid he's just going to have to deal with it. I've already told him what I think of the way he's conducting himself. I'm not pretending I think he's a great guy. If he wants to have more of a conversation, let him ask me himself."

"It's fine, Dad. It's just an uncomfortable situation. I agree with you, but he doesn't want to look bad in front of the kids."

"He doesn't want to look bad in front of his kids?" He stood up and started pacing. A moment later, with a reddened face and enraged constraint, he continued, "For the past two years, his kids have seen their father treat their dying mother with horrible contempt and disrespect. They have watched him treat her in ways someone shouldn't treat a stranger, never mind his wife or the mother of his children. He doesn't want to look bad because I ignore him. Well, that's just too bad! As we used to say in Brooklyn, he can bite my biff!" Dad's face had now lost all of its color, and he was breathing hard. I was afraid he was having a heart attack. I didn't know if I'd ever seen my mild-mannered, softspoken father this angry.

"Daddy, sit and calm down. I'm sorry I brought it up. I understand. Believe me, I agree with you completely, and I appreciate how much you've been here for me and the kids." My eyes were welling up with tears.

"Di, you don't need to be upset. Please don't read his e-mails; they're not good for you. They're poison."

I closed my eyes and took some deep breaths. "I know, I know. I'm trying, and I'm getting better. I really am. I'll be okay, Dad." I went and poured a glass of iced tea for each of us and suggested we go outside and sit on the deck.

The cool sweetness of the tea, the softening light at the end of a summer day, and the peals of laughter from children playing all seemed to lighten the heaviness that both my father and I carried in our chests. We sat quietly for a few minutes and settled into our own rhythms.

After a few minutes, I spoke. "Dad, I'm taking the kids to the beach for the day tomorrow; we're leaving at about six. Do you want to come with us? It'll be a fun day."

"No, thanks. I have an eight o'clock tee time. But it's a long drive. Why don't you stay over?" He looked puzzled.

"The kids will enjoy it just as much if we just go for the day, and that's all I can afford. Even a day is a stretch, but it'll be fine. I'll pack our bikes, food, and drinks, and the ocean is free."

"I'll give you the money to stay over. It's no big deal," he continued.

"It's just not necessary. It's the middle of the week, so we won't hit traffic, and it will just be a nice break for all of us. We'll go on the boardwalk and the beach and then drive back. You know, you always tell me I have a lead foot when I drive, so it won't take so long." I smiled and hugged him.

When I told the kids that we were going to go to the beach the next day, they were thrilled. Charles never wanted to go to the beach, especially not during the summer season, the time when kids enjoy it most. They were so excited that they had no trouble getting up early. I had the van packed, and we were on our way by six thirty. Needless to say, my father slipped each kid fifty dollars to give to me.

I checked my e-mail before we left the house, and, sure enough, there was something from Charles. I hesitated to open it, not wanting his negativity to color the day in any way, but, despite my better judgment, I started reading.

> Di,
> 
> I just got off the phone with Elli, and she told me that you're planning to drive to the beach for the day tomorrow. Is this really the best use of your time and resources right now? It seems to me that with the financial difficulties we face, having a day at the beach is an unnecessary extravagance. Then again, that has never been something that has been at the forefront of your mind, has it?
> 
> Charles

Although my chest tightened and my usual feeling of *I am doing something bad* crossed my mind, I quickly replaced that thought with *this is none of his goddamn business* and, contrary to my typical habit of saving all of his written communications, impulsively hit the DELETE button and erased the message from both my inbox and the trash, not wanting him questioning any of my decisions on this day.

The drive to the beach was easy. I had packed breakfast, and we ate as we drove and listened to music and stories on tape. The whole way there, the kids made a list of all the things they wanted to do: ride the waves, go to Joe's Comic Store, drive bumper cars, play putt-putt golf. It went on and on.

We arrived at nine thirty. "How about we park the van and ride our bikes around first to see where all the things we want to do are?" I suggested, as we made our way down the main thoroughfare.

"Great idea, Mom," Elli shouted out.

"Yes. It'll be so cool to ride on the boardwalk," Sam added.

It was a long and fun-filled day. I was amazed at how many things we packed in. We swam and went on rides and laughed a lot. It was about seven thirty when we climbed into the van to make our way home. As we drove down the main thoroughfare, we passed a water park and, without skipping a beat, both kids yelled out, "Mom, can we just stop here and just go down that huge waterslide one time, pleeeaase?"

"Really?" I laughed. "Aren't you exhausted?"

"No," two separate voices chimed in. We were on a roll, and so I made a U-turn and pulled in to the water park.

"Remember, guys, just one time. We do have to get home, and it's a long drive." I was realizing that I no longer had the energy I had before I was sick. It wasn't only that I was getting older; I hadn't totally recovered yet.

"Momma, you come, too." Sammy started to grab my arm but then realized that he shouldn't do that, and just hugged me and pleaded, "Pleeeaase, Momma."

It did look like fun.

"Yeah, Mom, come on," Elli urged.

And so I did, and it was exhilarating. We went down the slide two more times, then dried off, got back in the van, and started the drive home.

We had been driving for only about fifteen minutes when Sammy said, "Momma?"

"Yes, Sam?"

"Thank you. This was the best day ever."

"He's right, Mom. Thanks," Elli added.

"I love you, Momma," Sam added.

"Well, I love you guys, too! More than you'll ever know. I wanted you to have a great day. I had a great time, too!"

There was silence in the car, and then I realized both of the kids had fallen asleep.

It was a day well worth the drive.

## Chapter Thirty-Nine

I think I was pretty good at hiding my tears and panic from the children. Dr. Putman and my friends were not so lucky. My worst times were when they were with their father.

Those times, I felt as if I were cloaked in a dark, heavy pall.

Money still wasn't coming in; summer was always slow for private practice, and I really had not had the energy to reestablish myself. I'd been selling everything I could think of; I'd taken a load of stuff to Great Finds and Designs, a high-end consignment shop that sold household furnishings, antiques, and paintings. And Charles continued to do what he did best, play head games with me. He loved head games about money. He was cutting back on how much he worked. He had "been through so much." He needed to "rest and heal."

He called one day to tell me that he wanted to make some changes to our health insurance so that it would be entirely in his name. I told him that I would have to discuss that with my attorney. He was incredulous and went on to say, "I really don't want to do anything fraudulent."

It was a good thing he couldn't see me snickering through the phone, as I thought, *Mr. Upstanding Citizen, who's sleeping with one of his patients, doesn't want to be fraudulent?*

By the next day, he called again to say that he had thought further about it and had decided there was no real advantage to making any changes. As always, when I really stood up to him, he backed down.

A couple of days later, he started in about not having money for the bankruptcy payments and began to blame me, but as soon as I said I would call the bankruptcy trustee, his problem seemed to be resolved. It was always the same.

I retained my own bankruptcy attorney, who was going to separate my bankruptcy case from Charles's so that I could diminish any further financial tricks that he might try to pull. Charles kept saying to me, "You don't know who you're dealing with," but I guess he didn't really know who he was dealing with, either.

Charles had planned on taking the kids on a camping vacation for a couple of weeks, which would give me time to get the house together and put some real legwork into job hunting. About a week before they were to go, he sent an e-mail:

> Di,
> 
> *I'm not going to be able to take the kids on vacation next week. It would mean the loss of $6,000–$7,000 weekly pretax income. We really can't afford the loss of income right now. I may take a few days to go camping by myself, but I won't be taking the children on vacation this year. It would be a financially irresponsible thing to do.*
> 
> Charles

Unbelievable—even what he was bringing in weekly was more than double what I had for the entire month. I was learning quickly what I should have seen for years: he was great with words, but action was not his strong suit.

Elli was not at all disappointed about not going camping. As for Sam, when he said, "I'm glad we're not going. I hate camping," I could see the disappointment behind his long brown lashes.

"Daddy never wants to do anything fun with us anyway," he added. "I'd rather be here with Momma and Poppy."

Going to Charles's new house was becoming an issue for the kids. Sometimes it was Sam who didn't want to go. Sometimes it was Elli. Charles was not handling it well at all. One day, when I wasn't home, my neighbor saw Charles pulling Sammy out of the house by his arm, and he was screaming. She was going to call the police, but Sam calmed down and she didn't.

I'm sure there were lots of reasons the kids didn't want to go. They complained about his anger, and they complained about the big gong that they had to ring when they entered and left his house, as a greeting and farewell to the gods. They complained that their dad insisted on swinging a crystal pendulum to make even the smallest decision. I think it was scary for them to see their father this way. I also think that they didn't like the underlying message they got from him that their mother was not doing a good job raising them, and that he had to undo everything and teach them how to live properly. Whether it was about eating the right foods or handling money, their mother had done a lousy job, and he was going to "fix" them. So, they had lots of rules, which translated into lots of things he expected me to do at my house as well. He set them up with account books to keep track of all of their incoming and outgoing money. They were to carry these books back and forth between houses. I, of course, was to be monitoring them and making sure they did all of the recording. Never was there a discussion about whether I thought his system was developmentally appropriate. I totally ignored the whole thing. He gave up on the account books when he realized that I had no intention of honoring his wishes.

It was all so strange because we had two great, normal kids. They did well in school, they had friends, they had interests, and they never got in trouble. They were kind and polite and generous. Their teachers and their friends' parents loved them. I couldn't understand what he wanted from them.

Yes, I did. I knew it really wasn't about them at all. Again, I needed to be seen as a bad mother. The only way I could be a bad mother was if my kids needed to be fixed. For a long time, my greatest worry was that he would be able to convince them that in fact I was not a "good mother"—that I was Marcy.

# Chapter Forty

Dad continued to have his regular golf games a couple of times a week, but he wasn't looking well. He fell asleep a lot and suddenly seemed very old.

My college roommate, Susan, whom I hadn't seen in years, lived in upstate New York. Her house was right on Lake Ontario, close to Niagara Falls. She invited us to come visit, along with my dad and Knaidl.

Only Knaidl came.

"You go and have a great time," Dad said, casually adding that he had made a couple of doctor's appointments for the two weeks when we would be gone.

"Well, we don't have to go; maybe it would be better if I was here when you went to the doctor. I could go with you," I suggested.

"Don't be ridiculous. I'm fine. You and the kids should go. They'll love seeing Niagara Falls and swimming in Lake Ontario. Doesn't Larry have a sailboat?" he asked.

"How do you remember that? You haven't seen them in years." I laughed.

"You think I'm old? I'm a young dude. I don't forget anything—just remember that, young lady."

So, prepared with twenty hours of *Harry Potter and the Goblet of Fire* on audiotape, Knaidl in the backseat, and bags of snacks, the kids and I set off on our trip.

When we started out, I was keeping a tight lid on a kettle of my own shakiness, trying not to jostle the deep crack I felt in the core of my equilibrium. It was early evening when we reached western New York. The sun was hanging low in the sky as we drove along the shoreline of Lake Ontario. The pinks and purples on the horizon looked like watercolors splashed behind the white sailboats that bobbed in the harbor. By the time we arrived at Susan and Larry's house, I didn't know if I felt less broken or if I just felt more whole being in the presence of old friends who had known me in another lifetime.

On our sixth day in New York, we spent the afternoon flying up the Niagara River basin in a jet boat. We sped up the river, plunged headlong into some big waves, and got drenched. Then we headed back to Susan and Larry's house to help them get ready to have people over for dinner that night. The kids and dogs went out back and threw Frisbees, and I was helping Susan in the kitchen, when I stopped short. "Damn, I forgot. Today is the day my dad was going to see the cardiologist. I'll be right back. I want to go give him a call and see how it went," I told her.

Dad picked up on the first ring. He sounded tired.

"Hi. I thought you were going to call after you saw the doctor this morning."

"Oh, I was going to call later." I could tell he was being overly casual and not wanting to say what had happened. "Dad, what did the doctor say? Tell me."

"Well, he did a bunch of tests and said I have a blockage. I have to go in for a procedure on Monday."

"Dad, please just tell me what's going on."

"Okay. I just don't want you to worry. I have to go in to the hospital on Monday for quadruple bypass surgery. The doctor said that if I wasn't generally as healthy and active as I am, he wouldn't even consider doing it at my age, but he thought that I could handle it." He was silent.

"Well, that's a real compliment, but do you think you should get a second opinion?" I asked.

"No. He's an excellent doctor. If I don't do the surgery, my heart will give out. If I do the surgery and it works, that's great. If not, I've had a full life." He sounded so sure of what he was saying. "I don't want to cut your vacation short. I want you and the kids to stay and enjoy yourselves." He paused.

"Dad, we will be coming home tomorrow. You are not going to be having major surgery with us off on a vacation. I will take you to the hospital on Monday morning."

We had had a wonderful time. Although Susan and I hadn't spent this kind of intense time together for many years, there were some things that hadn't changed. I had arrived for the visit with a profound sense that my memory of the past was wrong, especially as it related to Charles. If that was true, then perhaps it was true about all of my memories. And if my memory of the past was wrong, then I had truly lost my footing in the world. If my memory was wrong, then I had lost the meaning that had been the underpinning of my life as I had known it. But our recent talks, late into the night, on the dark shores of the lake, had not been so different than those we'd had as two frightened college freshmen sitting in the dorm, sharing our deepest secrets. We still laughed the same way.

The next morning, feeling somewhat less broken by having had this time away here with a dear old friend, we packed up the van, said long good-byes, loaded the next audiotape of *Harry Potter and the Goblet of Fire*, and pulled out of the driveway. We got home just as the story ended.

"That's amazing, Mom. What timing!" Elli shook her head in astonishment.

## Chapter Forty-One

"Poppy's home, Momma," Sammy called to me as he ran into the house, Elli following.

My dad and Lydia were sitting at the kitchen table, eating bagels, cream cheese, and lox. We were all hungry, so we sat down and joined them.

"Poppy, are you sick?" Sammy leaned over and whispered to his grandfather. The whole table became silent.

"Is that what you heard?" My father put his arm around his shoulder. "You know, I'm getting older. Like an old car, sometimes you need a tune-up. The doctor says my heart needs a tune-up, and so on Monday I'm going in to the hospital and getting it done!"

"What hospital, Poppy?" Elli wanted to know.

"Sinai. It's a good hospital, Elli." He was looking closely at her, clearly seeing she was upset.

"I hate that hospital!" she said.

"Why? They have good doctors there. That's where Grandma was. They took good care of her."

Dad tried to continue, but Elli cut him off. "And she died there! I hate that place! I don't want you to go there!" Her eyes were welling up with tears, and her face was getting the red blotches she got when she became upset.

My dad looked over to me, wanting help. I stepped in. "Elli, Grandma was very sick. They really tried to help her and make her comfortable, but by the time she came to live with us and then went to Sinai, she was already very, very sick and we knew she was going to die. We didn't want her to suffer anymore. It really wasn't the hospital's fault. I know you don't like hospitals. A lot of scary stuff has happened there. But it wasn't Sinai's fault. And Poppy has a very good doctor."

"Well, Poppy, it scares me to go to hospitals. Can I talk to you on the phone while you're there? 'Cause I don't think I can come visit. It scares me too much. It makes me think about my mom being in the hospital, too." Elli looked pleadingly at her grandfather.

"Of course, sweetie! None of you should come visit. I'm not even going to be there that long. We can talk on the phone, and I'll be home in a few days."

She looked relieved. Somewhere in the dark recesses of my mind, my own worries about my dad's health were lurking, but I couldn't bear to allow the weight of those troubles to surface on top of everything else.

Dad had to be at the hospital at five o'clock Monday morning. I would drop him off, and then I would have to work out my schedule and childcare for the rest of the week. I realized that I would have to let Charles know what was going on. He would be picking up the kids on Wednesday evening and would have them through the next weekend. I decided I would send him an e-mail after I got the kids off to their playdates later in the morning.

It was still dark when Dad and I started out the front door.

"Poppy?" We both turned. There stood Sam in his camouflage pajamas, in the hallway, a few feet behind us.

"What are you doin' up, champ?" My father walked over and put his arms around him.

"I wanted to give you this to take with you." Sam held out a pale blue rock with the word *believe* etched onto its smooth surface. It was scotch-taped to a photo of Dad, Sam, and Elli. "This is so you know we're thinking of you, and you can think of us."

"I will keep these with me every minute, champ!" They hugged, and then I walked Sam back up to his bedroom and Dad and I drove to the hospital.

The doctor was right: Dad came through the surgery well. By the second day, he was sitting up, had good color, and was eating. Wednesday, he continued to make gains. So when the children went to Charles's house Wednesday night, they went knowing that Poppy was okay.

Then things changed very quickly. Dad was doing well, and then, suddenly, he wasn't. He was rushed back to the cardiac intensive care unit.

On Saturday evening, the lights in the waiting room were low and I was alone. The medical fellow was working hard to do everything he could for my father; this young, Orthodox Jewish doctor had been with him continuously for twenty-four hours. Every half hour, I went in to see Dad for five minutes. The photo that Sammy had given him was taped to the IV pole next to the bed. In his hand, Dad held the rock Sam had given him.

Finally, I said, "Daddy, I'm so sorry that I've taken out so much of my frustration over all of this stuff with Charles on you. I've been a horrible daughter." I held his hand, tears falling.

He laughed softly and shook his head.

"Don't be silly. Call Uncle Leon if you need anything. I love you. You're the best."

The medical fellow came in and said it was time for me to go out to the waiting room. I hugged Dad and walked back into the hollow darkness.

I don't know how long it was before the medical fellow appeared.

His eyes were sad and tired.

"I'm sorry. I really tried. Your father was such a good man. I really liked him."

The deep wail that came from within me was a mournful cry for all of the pain and all of the losses—a cry of anguish, terror, and guilt. The young medical fellow put his arm around my shoulder and walked me to a separate waiting area, where he helped me sit, took my hands, and listened for a long time. After a while, we sat in silence.

Then he said, "I've enjoyed talking with your father these last couple of days, and I wish I could have done more. But he was ready; his journey was done. Despite everything, he knew you and your children would have the strength and resilience to face the future. He told me that he had come to his destination."

I looked at this wise young man and realized that he was a messenger. Dad had been preparing and was ready. I had to do the same.

I went back in to see him one last time. The doctor stood with me for a moment, touched my father's hand, touched my shoulder, and walked out. Dad looked very peaceful. I hugged him and could feel the warmth leaving his body. The rock had slipped from his hand and lay on the side of the bed. I picked it up, and my fingers moved over the etched word *believe*. I untaped the photo from the IV pole and stood in the dimness, before walking back into the darkened waiting area.

I did whatever needed to be done at the hospital, and then my friend Penny drove me, through the blackened streets, back to my house. Some calls would have to wait until dawn to make; others I needed to make immediately. I called the funeral home for the release of the body. I called Lydia. I called my nieces, my sister-in-law, and my aunts and uncles and cousins. I called all of the people who I knew would want to come immediately.

Then I called Charles.

As soon as he answered, I started speaking. "Charles, my father died."

There was a brief but audible horror-stricken gasp. Just as quickly, he composed himself and offered no words of comfort or condolence. With that, I knew both that my father's death had had an impact on him, and that Charles would not be there for me. I said, "I'd like the children to come back in the morning, Charles, and I would like to tell them myself."

"Okay. Sure. What time would you like them to be at your house?"

"I don't even know. There's so much to take care of," I said.

"Well, they get up pretty early, so whenever you're ready for me to bring them over, call and I will."

"Thanks," I said, and he hung up, quickly fleeing from any real connection with me—as was the case with all of our interactions.

When I called in the morning to make plans for the children to come home, his response was strange. "My parents think they would like to come and visit with the children. Would that be, okay?"

I hesitated for only a moment. "No, that won't be okay. If they want to come and pay their respects to my father by coming to his funeral, of course they are more than welcome to do that, but this is not the time to come for a visit with the children." I surprised myself at how clear I was with Charles. I wondered if his parents really had made that offer or if this was just more evidence of how unable Charles was to demonstrate any genuine emotion.

Charles and his parents did come to the funeral. His parents seemed genuinely upset by my father's death. They visited at the house several times in the days that followed. Despite his presence at the funeral, Charles never said anything to me about my father's death. He sat behind the children during the service, wearing a Buddha-like smile, and appeared to have put himself into a trance-like state. I know he told the children, "Poppy was a good man," but to me, he said nothing.

What stays with me to this day about my father's death has little to do with Charles, though. The evening after the funeral, the house filled with family and friends. I saw a face I had not expected. The young medical fellow who had been so kind to my father, and to me, appeared.

He approached me, smiled warmly, and his dark eyes unwavering, spoke softly. "I wanted to come to see you and pay my respects to your father. I wanted to extend my condolences to you and to your children. You know, in the short time I knew him, I liked your father very much. He was a good and wise man."

My voice cracked as I said, "Thank you."

He smiled. "In Judaism, we're taught that once the formal grieving period is over, it's time to stand up and it's time to come out from the darkness of the Shiva house. You don't have to do anything in particular; you don't have to accept anything; you don't even have to move on. You just stand up and come out into the light, make space for brightness to come to you and to your children. Please—" he paused, "do that." He smiled again. "Do that in your father's memory and do that for yourself and for your children. I needed to come and say that to you, and I'm glad I came. Please take care of yourself, and I pray that you will stay well." He squeezed my hands and turned, and I watched silently as he left.

I realized that I didn't even know his name, but as he walked away, I felt as if an old, wise friend had visited me. The notion of "making space for the lightness" resonated deep within me.

---

THAT night, I had the dream again. It was a little different this time.

I was alone in a darkened theater. On the large screen, the credits began to roll, and then my grandfather's image appeared. Ever the dapper English gentleman, he stood in his topcoat and hat and smiled at me. I watched as he turned his head and looked over his shoulder. My father and mother were walking toward him. When they reached him, Dad put his arm around Grandpa's shoulder. They all turned toward me. Both Dad and Grandpa nodded in my direction, and Mom smiled with her beautiful, warm, laughing eyes. As they all looked at me, the warm gleam in their eyes spoke volumes.

This time when the screen went blank, I was no longer in the theater but in a sun-drenched meadow of wildflowers.

## Chapter Forty-Two

"Momma, you didn't say hello to Poppy and Grandma." Sammy was waving his arms out the window as we drove down St. John's Lane and passed the cemetery where my parents were buried.

"I did say 'Hi;' I just said it in my head. I'm sure they heard me." I laughed. "It's such a beautiful day—do you think they're out playing golf?"

"For sure. Can we drive around the road so we can find some rocks to put on their headstone? We haven't done that in a while." It really wasn't a question. Sam's voice was insistent.

"Sure, but we can't stay long, because we have to pick up Elli from Jenna's house." I made a U-turn and pulled off onto the quiet, parklike ring road that wound its way in graceful curves around the perimeter of the small cemetery. There were no other cars in sight, and as soon as I stopped and turned off the engine, Sam leaped from the backseat and began his search.

"Momma, look at this one. It's *so* white, but it has little bits of silver in it. How cool." Sam tossed the small, jagged stone into my hand, and I began inspecting it closely.

"It's really neat, Sammy. I think Poppy and Grandma will like it a lot."

"I just found this plain old gray rock from Elli. Do you think it's okay, Momma?"

"It's like I always tell you: it's what's in your heart that counts, not what something looks like." I found a couple of small stones, and I walked over to the gravesite and placed them on top of the headstone, where there already were other stones from previous visits. Some were little pebbles, and some were rocks the children had painted and decorated; some were personal treasures that they had found in a stream or in a field and thought Poppy or Grandma would like. All of them were a way of saying, *We were here.*

"Momma, I always worry that this one will get lost, but it's still here." Sammy picked up the smooth blue stone with the word *believe* etched into it. "This is my favorite, and I want it to stay here forever, so when Poppy looks down, he can see it."

"I'm sure he'll always know it's here, just like he will always be here," I said, pointing to Sammy's heart and then his head with my finger.

"I think it's so weird when you do that." Sammy shook his head. "Why weird?" I wanted to know.

"I don't know—it just is." He was already wandering over to a nearby stone bench, covered with intricate engravings.

I walked over and sat on the bench. "Remember when we saw *E.T.*?" Sam nodded, and I continued. "Do you remember at the end, when E.T. is going home and Elliott is really sad that he's leaving? What he does is touch Elliott's head and say, 'I will always be here.'"

"Oh, so he's telling Elliott that the memory in his head is a connection forever, even if they're not together."

I hugged Sammy. "Exactly."

I knew memories could ground both Sam and Elli when the earth beneath their feet was shaky. I turned toward the van and said, "Come on, Sam, we've got to pick up your sister. Let's get in the car."

The realization that Dad was now gone was so enmeshed with all of the other losses that I couldn't yet differentiate the overwhelming feelings from one another. Nevertheless, the children and I moved forward. Countless muddy patches and ruts in the road were still ahead of us, but we kept walking on. It was important for me to believe we weren't lost, that we just had to keep walking until we got there.

# Epilogue

*In the depth of winter,*
*I finally learned that within me lay an invincible summer.*
— *Albert Camus*

It's hard to believe how many seasons have passed and how many flocks of birds have flown south for the winter, returning for spring. I've measured the years with the coming of Yom Kippur every fall, the day I was diagnosed with cancer. In the Jewish religion, it is the Day of Atonement; for me, it has become the Day of Gratitude.

When I was diagnosed, my prognosis was not good. Although no one ever told me what it was in terms of time, and I, uncharacteristically, didn't ask, I knew that my doctors, and Charles, did not expect that I would see my children through their grade-school years. I proved them, and myself, wrong. It is twenty-one years since I divorced Charles, and it has been twenty-five years that I have been cancer-free. Elli and Sam have now finished school and are living on their own. Elli is thirty-five, a talented artist who works in marketing and lives in Maryland. Sam is thirty-two and is an attorney in New York. As I expected, the road was not always easy.

I make my way to the café to meet them. Sam is coming from New York for the weekend; Elli is meeting him at the train station. I drive along the familiar streets that I remember so well, knowing I'll pass my old painted lady, the house I lived in when Charles and I first met. Although the towering trees along the road are still tall and majestic, and the grandeur of the old Victorian sprawl remains, as I approach, I see that my lovely lady has taken on the tired and worn-out look of an old burlesque queen who has seen better days. The gnarled and knotty tree trunks are entangled with brush, and the lawn in front is covered in torturously matted weeds and nettles. The flagstone walkway is broken up into jagged rocks and gravel, and a weathered FOR SALE sign stands posted at the end of the drive. Beneath, nailed to the post, is an AUCTION SALE sign with next week's date.

I stop the car, lower the window, and breathe in the fresh autumn air. As I look up at the house, my lip quivers, and beneath the soft silk of my shirt, I can feel the tremor of my heart. The glass French doors leading to the porch have been covered with wooden planks. A veil of sadness falls over me. I loved how those glass doors allowed me to move freely between the inner and outer worlds. In those early years with Charles, I was enveloped in open hopefulness. Now, the desolate bleakness of the house stirs old familiar feelings of forsaken love. Bittersweet sorrow rises within me as fleeting images of a younger me dancing on the needle-covered lawn with a young Charles and a romping Winnie float through my mind. Even with these ethereal images, the hollowness in my chest remains and reminds me that there is always a shadow that falls between what is a dream and what is reality.

It is this shadow that holds the truth, and it is this truth that I must never forget. It's true that there were good times. There were the unrestrained belly laughs, which back then I interpreted to mean that Charles and I were viscerally connected. Then I believed that we didn't need words to understand each other. It was only much later that I came to realize those beliefs were likely colored as much by wishes and dreams as by reality. It was only with time that I came to understand that Charles's laughter was not a genuine connection to me, but rather just a mirroring of my own laughter, attitudes, behaviors, and coping styles. Whether it was conscious or unconscious, it was his way of drawing me in. It was part of "the catch," along with the flowers that came for so many years—until they stopped. I was charmed by Charles's intelligence, air of confidence and sensitivity; and the signs I did see of how fragile his own sense of self was, I ignored. I was blindly in love and so I willingly made a relationship contract with a narcissist—someone to whom I had to lose myself in order to be both mirror and echo for him. My adoration of him served as a reflection of the adored image of himself that he so desperately needed to see. For the narcissist, seeing the adored reflection of oneself is the only way he knows he truly exists. What I was unaware of then was that the contract meant that I would be losing my voice and myself in the process.

For a long time, the positives seemed to outweigh the negatives, even when I saw how controlling and critical Charles was—some of my needs were met. I enjoyed being with him; he was fun, smart, and interesting, and I got the children and family I so desperately wanted. Of course, wearing rose-colored glasses did make it easier to minimize the red flags which I did see from the beginning. But I now know that the greatest mistakes I made were the times when I saw or experienced things happening that didn't feel quite right, when I felt inside that things were going in the wrong direction, but nevertheless I turned a blind eye. I ignored what I felt, what I saw, what I knew. I didn't question, I didn't protest. I didn't use my voice. I didn't say what I needed to say when I needed to say it. It is this that I regret most.

My reverie ends when a young couple walking with an Old English Sheepdog pass by and smile. I smile back and start the car, momentarily looking back at my painted lady, pulled toward the memories; but now I know that although it is more comfortable to remember things the way I wish they had been, I only have control over my choices for the future by seeing the reality of the past as it was, without having it diluted by dreams.

I drive off, wondering what other memories that old house holds within its walls. Unlike the way the house looks, I realize that I feel remarkably well. Although one never knows what tomorrow may bring, my health has been stable for a number of years.

Elli and Sam aren't at the café when I arrive, so I get a table outside, order a cup of ginseng orange tea, and take out my laptop to work on the edits for the second edition of my book about the journey that I've been on.

Those first years after the separation were a quagmire filled with strangling, choking vines. At the beginning, in the ubiquitous confusion that overwhelmed me, all I wanted was clarity. Back then, it was all about Charles. I believed that the pain would cease only if I could understand him, understand if what I had thought was a relationship had ever existed. Trying to validate my own perceptions of what was real was a big part of why I was addicted to reading Charles's journal and e-mails despite how toxic that was for me. I needed the continual validation of my own perceptions, of which I had become so uncertain. At that point I wasn't thinking in "diagnostic terms." I wasn't thinking in terms of "narcissism" or "gaslighting;" I was a victim of it. I no longer was certain of my own reality and all I was desperate for was validation that I was not crazy.

When Charles and I first separated, even apart, I could not disengage from his internal presence. I was lost. My sense of self had been nibbled away at for years and eventually devoured. Charles had become so much a part of my identity that I clung desperately to the tattered remnants of what had been. I couldn't remember myself from times before him. There were no thoughts or words, no shift in weather, no road I drove on, that did not bring me back to my life with him. It took enormous mental and physical energy to stay present in my daily life. My insides were a constant, aching, and echoing void. I would call my therapist in the throes of panic attacks between sessions with my own patients. In the grocery store, I would stand before a case of beans, removing and replacing the same can, unable to decide whether to purchase it. My first thought each day when I awoke, struggling to get out of bed, was, *Mama, help me.*

Was it a mere coincidence that I chose a partner whom I believed I always needed whenever he disappeared emotionally? Something he had always done. Probably not. At that time, it was hard to really understand that what happened with Charles and myself was not a solo act—it was part of our dance. Charles may have taken the lead in the dance, but I needed to understand how my own responses/steps fueled the momentum of the dance. Relationships start with dreams—some are conscious, some are shared, and some lie within the soul of our inner child. It would take time before I understood fully my own part in the dance, but at some level I did know that if I didn't gain an understanding of what I brought to the relationship, I would likely make the same mistakes over and over again. I needed to understand my own vulnerabilities and where they came from, how they served me—how at one time perhaps they had even protected me. It would only be then that I would be able to move on.

My mother became ill with rheumatic fever when I was an infant and was hospitalized and then in a convalescent facility for almost a year, a very long time for an infant. That early loss likely was significant in setting the stage for my vulnerabilities. Despite having a loving father and grandparents who cared for me, I am sure that early psychological vulnerability to loss and abandonment made me more susceptible to what followed. Much more significant, I am also certain, was the unpredictability of living with a mentally ill and abusive older brother, who not only terrorized me but terrorized the entire family and left me with an ever-present anxiety about my own safety and the safety of those I loved. Despite my parents' efforts to protect me, my brother's abusive behaviors were not only frightening, but created intense shame and humiliation, and of course, caused unexpressed—and unacceptable—rage.

As is often the case in families with one dysfunctional child, I became the Good and High-Functioning Child. I learned to be an observer, an interpreter of the psychological pain enveloping me and others. I wore these characteristics as a shield to protect myself from my own pain. With this Psychologist Shield, I also developed the belief that I could handle anything, handle anyone's pain or trouble. I became a psychologist. This was the part of me that was resourceful, competent, and successful, and those very same characteristics protected me from feeling my own pain, early vulnerabilities of loss, neediness, and powerlessness.

At the same time, I believe that these early experiences set the stage for my acceptance of the later cycle of expectation and hope each time Charles gave me a smile or some compliment, and when he didn't, I could excuse it because, "I could understand." My own unconscious and protective and grandiose belief that I "could handle anything" led me to keep trying with Charles, and that was predetermined long before he appeared on the scene. If only I had been able to pay attention to what I saw.

Not that I think I caused the abuse, I absolutely do not. I do believe though, that my own early needs and vulnerabilities reinforced my ability to ignore what I saw, to not use my voice, to be too compliant, to care for his needs more than my own and more than my own well-being and safety. Believing I could handle anything prevented me from leaving when I could have, when I should have.

We all have an internal world of assumptions and beliefs that develop from the beginning of our own being. It consists of everything we have experienced, everything we know and think we know. It's our expectations, wishes, conscious and unconscious, memories, beliefs from the past, and dreams for the future. We carry with us our familial and cultural ancestry, even when it is out of awareness. This internal understanding of the world grounds us and gives us stability. These views orient us in how we understand our relationship with others in our lives.

Cancer made it necessary to come face to face with my own mortality and the excruciatingly painful possibility that my young children would be left without a mother. My treatment for cancer destroyed the invasive cells and left me with residual seizures and congestive heart failure. Yet, at least in retrospect, that felt manageable compared with the muddied mind and then the volcanic, searing pain I experienced in my marriage. In so many ways the emotional abuse, although subtle for many years, was far more crushing psychologically than was the cancer. I was unaware that throughout my marriage so many of my core beliefs about caring, trust, and relationships were slowly, and imperceptibly, being gnawed at and, in the end, torn apart. It was the subtlety of it, spreading hidden tentacles that trapped and strangled how I viewed the way I understood relationships, that was the most destabilizing and traumatic. Despite my training, my clinical understanding of human behavior, my own therapy, I ignored things I should have questioned at the beginning of the relationship. I ignored things not only about Charles, but about myself as well. I ignored things that I saw that were important. I did not give enough credence to my own intuition. I did not use my voice. When I stood in the doorway when Charles and I were newly married and thought, *I know if I ever get really sick, he will not be able to be there for me,* I remembered it but did not use the information to protect myself. When Charles would not come to the hospital when my lung was punctured and I needed an angiogram, I was terrified, and I remembered it, but I ignored what I saw and discounted what I knew. And on our very first date, when I recoiled as Charles so contemptuously spoke of his mother and her voice, I heard it, I registered it, and years later when I was his wife, dying of cancer, those exact words were written in his journal: "I can't tolerate being around her, I can't stand the sound of her voice . . ."

Although there had been multiple events in my relationship with Charles that had been an assault and shattering of my basic core beliefs about relationships, nothing compared with the assault and trauma I experienced by his killing of Mr. Buttons six years before my cancer diagnosis. My response to this horrific event was like the response of many to traumatic events: I "forgot" about it. I have come to realize, cognitively and viscerally, that it was fear—actually, terror; and that is what is so interesting about those terrifying moments in our lives. They are so easy to bury, not quite forget, but bury as if one puts the memory of that terror beneath a pile of old clothing, both clean and dirty, in a closet. If you never open the door and sort through the pile, it is possible that you may never remember that exact terrifying moment again, at least not consciously. That was the way it was for me after Mr. Buttons was killed. I had two young children to care for, I did all the things I had to do. I just became depressed. I withdrew from Charles, was no longer so accommodating, no longer the adoring, need-fulfilling wife. I was less tolerant of his controlling behaviors and his constant and insidious criticalness. I began to object, yell, sometimes scream at him. His needs for total need-fulfilling adoration was no longer there. Thus, his sadism and gaslighting gradually increased until it crescendoed at the time of my diagnosis and during my cancer treatment. It was then, at the height of his sadism, sitting in Dr. Putman's office and seeing her gray tabby cat, that the closet door opened and there was the pile of clothes that could no longer be hidden from my consciousness. The terror was no longer hidden, and with its exposure the armor I had so carefully erected to protect myself was in real danger of crumbling.

But I had to survive, I had to survive to protect my children first, and so I could not think of doing anything until I finished my treatment. My blinders, though, were off. For the first time, I was talking in therapy about what was happening in my marriage. For the first time, I was using my voice.

I think that for each of us, there are always certain issues that we continually bump up against. And whatever those issues are that we start out with, we just keep finding them, disguised in different costumes. It's as if there is a master plan set out for each of us and we get to keep trying until we get it right. The ante just keeps on getting raised, until we finally get it—or, as in my case, perhaps die. I think that's what happened to me.

After we separated, Charles continued to play both money and mind games with me. He stuck to his decision to give me $10 per child per week until we finally got to court, two years later. Financially, I struggled; I was perpetually juggling air. I was enveloped in a clinging, gauzy blackness that took hold of me. I managed as best as I could to hide it from my children while Dr. Putman and my closest friends shared the brunt of it. My basic beliefs and internal life narrative about a caring marriage and relationships, and trust, had been shattered. Although I did it, it was hard enough to get out of bed each day. I did not have the wherewithal to re-establish my private practice. I needed the structure of a job, with a regular salary and benefits. Re-starting my private practice as my main source of income would have to wait.

I started to look for work and soon learned that there were several school psychologist vacancies open in the county school system. I immediately called the Director of Psychological Services and luck was finally in my corner: I was able to speak directly to her. She asked me to fax her my résumé. Within two hours, I had an interview arranged for the next morning. That afternoon I was offered a position. I was still depressed, often not wanting to get out of bed, yet at some point I realized that each day there were also moments of laughter.

Charles and Victoria continued their sporadic relationship for several years. I am not sure if it was her doing or if someone else intervened on her behalf, but ultimately, having a relationship with the man who had been her psychiatrist seemed to become too much for her. She sued Charles, and he lost his medical license. This, of course, was another reason for him to not have any money. Because of my job, when this happened, I was not beholden to him. When he agreed with things I thought the children needed, he contributed, but when he didn't, I found a way to pay for those things myself, even if it was a struggle.

I continued to see Dr. Putman for a while, but scheduling became difficult, and she then moved to New York. Over the next year and a half, although doing better in some ways, I remained very depressed and was more than ever in touch with the long-term emotional abuse that had existed in my marriage. I had never thought about it in those terms until I was ill and it was no longer subtle, and then I could see clearly that my marriage had been an abusive one for years and that I was still experiencing the effects of the traumas of that relationship. I did still need help to sort through all of that. After Dr. Putman, I saw a couple of different therapists briefly, but neither was the right fit.

"Do you know Sarah Weinstein?" my friend Peg asked when we were talking about experienced therapists I might see.

I laughed. Of course, I knew Sarah. She was one of the first psychologists I had met when I arrived in Baltimore to do my postdoc. She had been a few years ahead of me in the program and was one of my supervisors during my postdoc year. Now she was an internationally renowned trauma specialist. "I never thought of calling Sarah. We're not really friends, but I've known her forever. I refer people to her all the time." The more I thought about it, the more I thought it would be a good idea to give her a call.

Sarah evidently knew that I had been ill; in fact, she was surprised and relieved that I was still alive. Evidently, there had been rumors that I had not survived.

"Sarah, I don't know if this would be appropriate or not, but Charles and I just finalized our divorce and although on the surface I'm doing okay, I'm really a mess and need to find a therapist. I was wondering if you would be able to see me?"

There was a pause, and then she said, "Wow, I'm really flattered that you would ask me." Those few words startled me; there was a distant memory that I could almost touch when I heard them. *She's flattered that I called her. That must mean she thinks I have value.* I hadn't realized how long it had been since I'd felt valued.

I did begin to work with Sarah, whose office was still on the hospital grounds where I had worked years earlier. There was something both therapeutic and comforting about coming back to a place where my successes had been all mine, where my memories were entirely separate from Charles. I felt a connection to a part of myself with which I had lost touch, from which I had been isolated for many years while in my relationship with Charles. I began to realize even more clearly how in my marriage I had become isolated from so many people in my life; I had allowed myself to lose essential parts of who I had been.

Working with Sarah, I began to see the reflection of myself in her eyes. In my relationship with Charles, I saw the reflection of what he wanted me to be. Now I was seeing the reflection of who I was, of who I had been and who I had become. Gradually, Charles became less a part of the internal landscape of my life. Although I still didn't have all of the answers about why things happened as they did, I realized that I probably never would. What changed was that I no longer felt compelled to know the "whys" of what Charles did. The focus began to shift from Charles to myself. With that shift, I was able to begin to let go of the need to have answers to unanswerable questions—accepting that there were things that were, that are, and that will always be beyond my control. This allowed me the freedom to move on, to accept what had been, and to find myself once again.

I also developed a much deeper understanding of what it meant to be in a relationship with a narcissist, with someone for whom I could have been anyone, as long as I met his needs. I was truly interchangeable with anyone else. Even after twenty years and the two children we struggled so hard to have, once I wasn't useful, I no longer existed. For me, it was a relationship; for him, I was a need-gratifying object, a mirror, an echo.

There were times when something happened with one of our children when I would have liked to be able to talk with Charles, as friends. But it wasn't possible and so now they are adults, and we have as little contact with each other as possible. Am I still angry at him?

No. My life is full. Now I take care of myself. There is such a thing as healthy narcissism, a state of being where one values oneself. That is a life lesson I have finally learned.

When I started writing my memoir, the title which was most meaningful to me was *Scheherazade's Cancer*. I have always been a storyteller as was Scheherazade. According to the ancient *One Thousand and One Tales of the Arabian Nights*, of which Scheherazade is the narrator, Shahryar, the king of ancient Persia, upon discovering that his wife was unfaithful to him, had her beheaded and then resolved to marry a new virgin every day and to have her beheaded the next morning before she could dishonor him. Eventually, the king's minister could find no more virgins of noble blood, and against her father's wishes, Scheherazade volunteered to marry the king.

Scheherazade was beautiful, well-read, and intelligent, and she was a talented storyteller, able to weave together stories for her listeners. She married the king, and on their wedding night, she told him a tale late into the night, but it was so late she couldn't finish it, so the king put off the beheading so she could finish the story the following night. Scheherazade continued to weave fascinating and adventure-filled stories night after night, leaving the king on tenterhooks until he eventually fell in love with her and allowed her to live.

Scheherazade had a voice . . . but it was her wiles that kept her alive. For me, the first title of my memoir, *Scheherazade's Cancer*, was meant to be my statement that, *I must tell my story or else I will die* . . . from either cancer or at my husband's hand.

But as I wrote, and as I processed that I was in an emotionally abusive relationship with a narcissist, I realized I had lost my voice within the relationship—likely having come into the relationship with an already weakened voice. I was more like the nymph Echo in Ovid's Greek myth, "Narcissus and Echo" . . . I was truly *Lost in the Reflecting Pool*.

Something that is often asked of women who are in abusive relationships is, "Why don't you just leave?" Or, once you have left, people say, "Get over it." The reality is—it is not so simple. By the time Charles and I separated, I was in a state of post-traumatic stress. My disentanglement and disengagement from Charles was a process. It involved not only taking off the blinders and seeing what was happening in the relationship but also looking at and absorbing what I saw. It involved looking at myself as well. Sometimes it was painful. It took time, a long time, which I needed to allow myself. I found that I needed to be kind to myself, which is not easy when you are encased in an abyss of darkness and internal turbulence and people around you want to see you "get over it." I worked hard to view each step as practice so that when there were setbacks in my responses to Charles's behavior, I would not plummet into self-loathing and recrimination. I also needed a solid support system. It took time for me to see how much of myself I had lost and to understand what was happening in the relationship. My diagnosis of cancer both complicated and clarified the picture. I did not have the emotional, physical, or financial resources to "just leave."

But do I forgive Charles? A year after finishing my treatment for cancer, the children and I moved out. For a long time, the road forward was muddy and rough. In the months before we moved out, and then afterward, on many occasions, I would ask Charles if we could sit down and talk—if we could try and process what had happened to our relationship, to us. His response was always the same:

"I'm willing to tell you my point of view. But I have no interest in hearing what you have to say; I'm not interested in your truth. You just want to be a victim."

Forgiveness. More and more, I wondered about the meaning of forgiveness. Some would tout the idea that only by granting forgiveness could someone move on. *Don't forgive me, and you will forever be a victim,* Charles implied. Of course, he wasn't interested in even hearing about what he had done that had caused me such pain. What would I forgive if Charles didn't care to hear about why I felt as I did? While I believed then and believe now that the capacity to forgive is important and hope that I have demonstrated that to my children, I questioned then and believe more fervently now, that while forgiveness is a personal choice in how it serves an individual, it was not, for me, a prerequisite for healing.

Forgiveness can be defined in many ways. I felt that genuine forgiveness could only be given if Charles cared enough to listen to how he had hurt me, and if he had been truly interested in taking responsibility for the pain he had caused to our children, and to me—if he had shown some remorse. Instead, one of his responses when I tried to have a discussion with him was, "You expect me to be Jesus Christ?" He was not remorseful at all, or his shame prevented him from expressing it. As I pondered the concept of genuine forgiveness, I realized that in all of the years Charles and I were together, he had never apologized for anything. He was so good with words; it was one of the things I had ignored for years until the end when his narcissistic behaviors were on full display. To forgive, or not to forgive, someone is a personal choice, but I do not believe it is a necessary choice in order to heal. From this perspective, just as falling in love involves more than one person, so does forgiveness. And it is a journey that evolves. Charles was not willing to take the journey that for me was necessary for me to forgive him.

For me, writing my memoir was an integral part of how I processed my own traumatic experiences. There were many others involved in my being able to heal and to whom I feel tremendous gratitude, but Charles was not involved in the healing process. At first, my writing was cathartic; it was the raw expression of the pain and anguish that was my life. My writing then became more focused and became a way not only to tell my story but to give it meaning, and as a way to find my voice which I had lost in my marriage.

Through writing and reflecting on what I wrote, I was able to view my pain with more distance, gradually developing more detachment from it and viewing my life with a more nuanced perspective. It was then easier to find solutions to problems that it had been more difficult to see earlier. Processing my experiences, understanding my own vulnerabilities and my own steps in the relationship dance helped me to move on. The anger at Charles lessened. Forgiveness, though, is not a word I would use to speak of how I moved through this life-altering experience. It was through Understanding and Acceptance. My memoir, *Lost in the Reflecting Pool,* is a story of transformation. The pain was something I processed and accepted; forgiveness was not involved.

Through the writing of my memoir, through sharing my story, I found my voice and was able to re-write my life narrative.

Writing continues to be an integral part of how I process my life experiences. Putting the words on paper, objectifying the experience, has allowed me to distance the pain enough that I can see the pictures of my life with greater clarity. Occasional waves of sadness wash over me, but then, just as quickly, the tide changes and a new day comes. Understanding, not just theoretically, that feelings shift, and change, has helped me to know that even on the darkest of days, the sun will always shine again.

Now I use writing not only for myself, but as a tool for healing within my practice.

Suddenly, I'm startled out of my reverie by a familiar voice and a hand on my shoulder.

"Hi, Momma. Sorry, the train was late. Let me give you a hug." Sam throws his arms around me and embraces me tightly. He's always been such a great hugger. Elli pecks me on the cheek and sits down, laughing affectionately at her brother.

"Are you going to always call Mom "Momma?"

"Yes, I am, because my momma loves it—she told me so!"

"I'm afraid he's right, sweetie. I do love the way it sounds. Just like I love when you call me "Mom." We all laugh.

"So, what's happening with the book, Momma?" Sam glances over at his sister, smiling. She gives a familiar eye roll and nose crinkle and then hugs him.

"Almost done, I'm hoping that by putting on my psychologist hat and adding the afterword, the book will be more useful for readers. Did I ever tell you about the time someone asked me, "Why are you writing this story?" and then said, "Your story really isn't so special or unique."

"I don't remember if you did but it sure doesn't sound very nice. What did you say to him?"

"I actually surprised myself. I told him that was the very reason for writing the book, because other than some specific details of my story, it touches on universal themes: relationships, love, loss, life, death, parenting, commitment, ethical and moral behavior, family, friendship—all the things that make up a life. I told him that I wrote it because I wanted the reader to know that when our basic life assumptions and beliefs are shattered, life can lose meaning. I am hoping with the afterword the book will be more than inspirational, but also useful in helping people re-find their footing and voice if they have lost it."

"I like it, Mom. I think it will work." The sunlight catches the blonde of Elli's hair as she squeezes my hand and smiles—my sunflower.

"Momma, I love you and I'm proud that you're my Momma." Sam smiles his crooked smile, and his eyes shine.

I grab them both and we all hug tightly.

"Okay," Sam says. "I'm hungry. The last time we went to the Corner Stable, the ribs weren't as good as I remembered; where should we go?"

"I'll surprise you. I'll drive," Elli says and picks up her car keys.

"Okay." I pay my bill and follow behind them; it's funny to remember Elli towering over her little brother when they walked together as kids.

I get into the backseat of Elli's car. The two of them are catching up and it's comforting to hear the familiar rhythm of their voices. There was a chance I might not have had the opportunity to watch them grow to adulthood. I feel blessed. There is no escaping pain and disappointment. There are no guarantees. There is only life—and it is miraculous.

# AFTERWORD

## How to Recognize an Emotionally Abusive Relationship
## and
## What to Do About It

I hope *Lost in the Reflecting Pool* provided something meaningful to you. There were several reasons I wrote my story. As a psychologist, I wanted to share the experience of dealing with an emotionally abusive relationship and, by doing so, provide others with an understanding of the painful process of moving through the muck and still being able to emerge with clarity and a renewed sense of power. What better learning experience for others than to invite them into my clinical consulting room, simultaneously being both clinician and client, to observe my journey through the ups and downs of this type of relationship: the honeymoon phase—the stage of initial charm—with love-bombing and mirroring, wearing rose-colored glasses, using denial and wearing blinders, the difficulties in recognizing the relationship for what it was, taking off the blinders, identifying my vulnerabilities and how they played into keeping things going as they did, and then, finally, doing what I needed to do for myself and my children, and the pain in the process of extricating myself from the relationship.

In my case, my partner was a narcissist. However, it's essential to keep in mind that not all abusers are narcissists, and all narcissists are not abusers. Narcissism, like many other personality traits, exists on a spectrum and is not inherently good or bad. Individuals can show tendencies towards more or less narcissism under different circumstances. Thus, understanding narcissism as a spectrum helps us think about it in a nuanced way, recognizing its potential benefits and its drawbacks.

At one end of the spectrum is *healthy narcissism, which involves a balanced and adaptive sense of self that allows individuals to navigate the world with confidence, empathy, and resilience while also fostering positive relationships.* I want to stress in this discussion how vital developing healthy narcissism is for someone who is a victim of an abusive relationship. It is essential to have a state of being where one has enough good self-esteem to establish boundaries to protect oneself while still being a caring and empathic individual. I hope that by presenting what follows, I will help readers tap into their healthy narcissism and use these resources to protect themselves from and within toxic relationships.

So, let's begin.

Are you in a relationship that often leaves you feeling drained, confused, and emotionally barraged or battered? Perhaps you brush it off as everyday conflict, but what if deeper, more insidious forces are at play? What if it is emotional abuse, not everyday conflict? It can be challenging to tell the difference between the two, but it is possible. One way to distinguish the two is to examine the intention behind the action. In everyday conflicts, both people usually want resolution and understanding. In abusive relationships, both emotional and physical, the abuse is driven by something else. Whether it is conscious or unconscious, manipulation is at the heart of the abuser's behavior, with the aim being power and control. Abusers often engage in tactics such as guilt-tripping, shaming, and blaming their partners for their own shortcomings. They may also use tactics like withholding affection, silent treatment, or threats to maintain control over their partner. Unlike physical abuse, the wounds inflicted by emotional abuse may not be visible. Still, they are every bit as deep and do leave long-lasting scars on the victim's emotional and mental well-being

Let's take a moment to reflect on the descriptions below to see if any of them resonate with your feelings about your relationship with your partner or perhaps remind you of a relationship with a couple you know:

- **Walking on Eggshells:** You feel cautious and sensitive with what you say and do, as if any wrong move could lead to a negative outcome. You're always trying to guess what the result will be.

- **Dr. Jekyll/Mr. Hyde:** You feel that you see very extreme sides of good and evil in how your partner treats you and perhaps others, making you uneasy. Putting these two parts of their behavior together is hard.
- **"I'm Sorry":** You feel that you constantly say, "I'm sorry," and take the blame/responsibility for things in the relationship even when they are not your fault. Your partner never actually says they are sorry for anything.
- **Never Good Enough/Constant Criticism:** You never seem able to please your partner. No matter how hard you try, it is never good enough. There is constant criticism, sometimes "constructive advice," occasionally subtle, sometimes joking—but criticism that makes you feel worthless and inadequate.
- **Blame-Shifting:** your partner often shifts the blame onto you, making you feel responsible for their behaviors and problems.
- **Self-Doubt:** You are constantly second-guessing and doubting yourself.
- **Isolation - Giving Up Interests/ Friends/Other Relationships:** You have withdrawn from people, activities, and interests that were significant to you because of your partner's influence.
- **Emotional Rollercoaster:** Your partner's hot and cold behavior has you on an emotional roller coaster.
- **Gaslighting:** Interactions with your partner sometimes make you question your reality or sanity—the interactions feel "crazymaking." Does your partner subtly manipulate you into doubting your perceptions, memories, and even your sense of yourself? They may twist the truth, deny events or statements, or rewrite history altogether. The goal is to erode your confidence, leaving you confused, powerless, and dependent on the abuser for validation and guidance.
- **Projecting Their Flaws:** Your partner projects their negative traits/behaviors onto you, accusing you of things they are guilty of themselves.
- **Disregarded:** Your partner constantly disregards your boundaries, decisions, and personal space, and you often feel like you have no control over your life.

- **Inconsistent Emotional Support:** Your partner may provide intermittent emotional support and validation, making you dependent on their approval and creating a cycle of love-bombing (excessive flattery and attention) and devaluation. Your partner needs constant emotional validation but doesn't genuinely empathize with your feelings.

Do any of these descriptions characterize your relationship or hit too close to home? If so, it's important to "trust your gut" and use your voice to set boundaries within your relationship. This is the time to make sure you have help and support in your life. Recognizing emotional abuse is the first step towards breaking free from its toxic grip. By understanding the signs and patterns, you can gain the knowledge and tools to recognize the red flags and take appropriate action.

Emotional abuse typically follows predictable patterns and manipulative behaviors. While the specific sequence may vary, a common pattern begins with the initial Honeymoon/Charm stage of "blind love."

In the intricate dance of emotional abuse, the initial charm stage sets the foundation for the toxic cycle to unfold. This is the phase where the abuser wraps themselves in a facade of love, adoration, and compassion, leaving you feeling captivated and utterly charmed. Love-bombing and Mirroring are the deceptive tactics employed during this stage, designed to lure you into their tangled web.

Love-bombing is like being showered with affection and adoration. It's as if the abuser has unlocked the secret to your heart and effortlessly showers you with love and compliments, making you feel like the most special person in the world. It's easy to fall blindly in love with this intense care and attention.

Mirroring is another device used as part of the seductive arsenal in the initial charm phase of the relationship. Here, your partner subtly observes your preferences, interests, values, and behaviors. They pay close attention to how you react and what you like, and then they begin to mirror these characteristics. They might use similar language, express interest in the same things you do, and even mirror your body language. By appearing to be just like you, they create a sense of familiarity and comfort, a shared identity, and you, in turn, develop trust in this person who seems to be such a *kindred spirit*. They reinforce the perception of a strong bond: *"I feel as if I've known you forever."* Whether conscious or not on the abusive partner's part, beneath the surface of this enchanting charm lies a darker truth. Love-bombing and mirroring are not genuine acts of love but are means to gain power and control. The abuser is laying the groundwork for establishing an intense emotional bond rooted in dependency. They ensure you become emotionally invested and deeply attached by presenting themselves as the perfect partner.

Thus, recognizing and being cautious in the initial charm stage can be the first step toward not getting caught in the toxic cycle of emotional abuse. By understanding that this excessive attention and flattery may not be genuine, you can start to question the motives behind the abuser's actions. Trust your instincts and pay attention to discrepancies between their words and behaviors. True love involves mutual respect and equality, not an overpowering one-sided obsession. In the throes of "blind love," the next tactic flows easily in an abusive relationship, so it is necessary to be cautious and go slowly.

By creating a sense of dependency, the abuser often employs Isolation and cutting you off from your support systems. When this happens, the abuser gains a greater level of control over your emotions, thoughts, and actions. Having a social support system is necessary for everyone's emotional well-being, and it is important to maintain this at all points in any relationship. Attempts at isolation can take many forms, both subtle and overt. It may begin with the abuser discouraging you from spending time with friends and family, claiming that they are a negative influence, or that they don't truly understand your relationship. They may insist on being the only source of emotional support and gradually isolate you from anyone who might challenge their control over you. It may take the form of discounting or discouraging hobbies or activities you enjoy because they make you less available "to the relationship." It can extend to social, emotional, and even financial realms. The abuser may manipulate situations to ensure you become increasingly reliant on them, making it harder for you to escape their grasp.

BEWARE: Attempts at Isolation are a major red flag in any relationship. When a partner wants/demands that it is "you and me against the world—no one else matters or is needed," it is a real problem!

Criticizing is another powerful weapon used in abusive relationships. Whether it's nitpicking at your appearance, belittling your accomplishments, or constantly finding fault in your actions, your partner may be using criticism as a means to undermine your sense of self. They chip away at your self-confidence through relentless criticism, leaving you doubting your abilities and worthiness. This makes it easier for the abuser to maintain their power and control over you as you begin to rely on their judgment and seek their approval.

When your partner avoids taking responsibility for their actions and, instead of acknowledging their faults or mistakes, continuously shifts the blame onto you, it is called Blame-shifting. They twist the narrative, making it seem as if you are the one to blame for their abusive behavior. By doing so, they not only avoid accountability but also further undermine your self-esteem. You're left questioning your judgment and sanity, trapped in a cycle of self-doubt and guilt.

Likewise, Gaslighting is another manipulative tactic that is utilized to distort your perception of reality and make you doubt your judgment, actions, perceptions, or memory—"*You sound delusional, that never happened,*" but you remember it happened, don't you?

The emotional abuser intensifies efforts to erode your self-esteem and self-confidence. This Devaluing systematically undermines your worth and belittles your achievements, making you doubt your abilities and question your value. Their words and actions are aimed at making you feel insignificant, irrelevant, and undeserving of love and respect. This can be the most painful and confusing, as the abuser withdraws affection, attention, and validation. They may become distant, cold, and indifferent, leaving you desperate for any sign of their previous affection and approval. The goal of the abuser is to make you feel disposable, unimportant, and utterly alone. The emotional abuser may actively seek opportunities to reject you, whether through silent treatment, withholding affection, or even physically leaving without warning.

Recognizing and acknowledging these manipulative tactics is essential in breaking free from the cycle of a toxic relationship. By understanding that it is not appropriate, acceptable, or normal to be treated this way in a relationship and that it is not a reflection of your worth or actions, you can begin to reclaim your power. Breaking free from the abuser's control starts with recognizing the manipulative tools used by him and refusing to internalize the false narratives about you. It may be challenging to accept this reality, especially if you have been conditioned to believe that the abuse is your fault or that you deserve it. However, by educating yourself about emotional abuse and recognizing the patterns of manipulation and control, you can regain a sense of agency and begin to rebuild your self-esteem.

It may be hard to always remember your abuser's motives, which are control and power, and if you do forget, you may find yourself using some of these INEFFECTIVE *ways* of responding:

- **Appeasement:** If you placate to avoid conflict and anger, it empowers the abuser, who sees it as a weakness and an opportunity to exert more control.
- **Pleading:** Another sign of weakness is that abusers are uncomfortable with themselves and others. They may react dismissively with contempt or disgust.
- **Withdrawal:** This is an excellent tactic to collect your thoughts and emotions, but it is not an effective strategy for dealing with abuse because when you withdraw only, you are not dealing directly with the abusive behavior itself.
- **Arguing and Fighting:** Arguing over the facts is meaningless. Most abusers are more concerned with justifying their point of view and being right than hearing facts. Verbal arguments can quickly escalate to fights that drain and damage you. Nothing is gained because you wind up feeling hopeless and once more like a victim.
- **Explaining and Defending:** Deny a false accusation. When you try to explain yourself or defend something, you've said or done, you give your partner permission to be your judge, to approve or disapprove and you do not owe anyone that right. Your response

sends the message: "You have power over my self-esteem. You have the right to approve or disapprove of me."
- **Seeking Understanding:** When the NEED to be understood drives your behavior, it can be self-defeating. When you desperately need to be understood, it's based on the false hope that the abuser wants to understand you, while in actuality, he is only interested in winning a conflict and having the superior position.
- **Criticizing and Complaining:** Although they may act tough, because abusers are insecure, inside, they're fragile. They can dish it out, but they can't take it. Complaining or criticizing an abuser can provoke rage and vindictiveness. You wind up on the short end. Set boundaries of what is and is not acceptable rather than criticize and complain. Use "I" messages:
- **Denial:** Don't fall into the trap of denial by excusing, minimizing, or rationalizing abuse. Don't fantasize about it going away or improving in the future. The longer it goes on, the more it grows, and the weaker you can become.
- **Self–blame:** Don't blame yourself for an abuser's actions and try harder to be perfect. This is unrealistic thinking. You haven't caused anyone to abuse you. You're only responsible for your behavior. Nothing you do will be good enough for an abuser to stop their behavior, which stems from their psychological issues, not from you. You don't have to, nor can you, "save" anyone but yourself.

To deal with emotional abuse EFFECTIVELY, you must keep these things in mind:

- It is essential to Confront Abuse: Allowing someone to treat you with abusive behavior is damaging to your self-esteem, and therefore, it is essential to address it directly. You don't have to yell and scream. You need to use your voice to speak up for yourself calmly and directly, demonstrating that you have boundaries to protect your mind, emotions, and body.
- You Have Personal Rights: You are entitled to be treated with respect and you have specific rights, such as the right to your

feelings and thoughts, the right not to have sex if you decline, a right to privacy, a right not to be yelled at, touched, or disrespected. If you have a history of abuse, you may not trust this to be accurate, but YOU DO HAVE THESE RIGHTS, even though your self-esteem has likely been weakened along with your basic trust. Seek therapy and get support.
- Be Assertive: It takes practice to use your voice effectively. It takes practice to avoid being passive or aggressive. Try these short-term responses to dealing with verbal put-downs:
  o "I'll think about it."
  o "I don't like it when you tell me I'm crazy. Please stop it." (Then walk away)
  o "That's your opinion. That's okay. I just don't see it that way."
  o "It's okay if we see things differently." (Then walk away)
  o "I'm not going to discuss these things in front of the children. Let's talk about it when they go to bed."

It often helps to develop a script for difficult recurrent situations so that you have an automatic response that you can practice on your own so you can say it automatically and calmly, without intense emotion, when the actual provocative situation arises.

One of the key aspects of healing from emotional abuse is rebuilding one's sense of self-worth and reclaiming personal power. This involves recognizing and re-writing the negative scripts and self-doubts you have come to believe about yourself. Surrounding oneself with a strong support system of friends and loved ones who provide genuine validation and understanding can also be instrumental in healing.

Reconnecting with one's own interests, passions, and personal goals can help rebuild a sense of identity that may have been eroded during the abuse. Therapy can also aid the healing journey.

When it comes to relationships, it's important to remember that they are a dance between partners, with each step influencing the other. This is especially true when it comes to intimate relationships affected by emotional abuse. While it's essential to hold the abuser accountable for their actions, it's also crucial to recognize the role we play in shaping the dynamic. This is not to say that we are responsible for the abuser's behavior, but rather that our patterns and behaviors may unknowingly contribute to the unhealthy dance. By embarking on a journey of self-reflection and growth, we empower ourselves to recognize the warning signs of an unhealthy relationship. This self-awareness allows us to identify how we may unintentionally enable or tolerate emotional abuse. It also equips us with the necessary skills and resilience to establish healthier, more fulfilling connections. Ultimately, gaining insight into ourselves is crucial to the healing journey. By examining our patterns and behaviors, we can break free from the cycle of abuse and build healthier relationships that bring us true joy and fulfillment. Psychotherapy, counselling, support groups, and journaling can all be helpful resources in this regard.

Individuals can reclaim their autonomy and pave the way for healing and recovery by seeking support and taking action. It's important to remember that breaking free from emotional abuse is not an overnight process. It takes time, patience, and, importantly, self-compassion. However, by prioritizing your emotional well-being, you can begin to rebuild your life and create a future free from the shackles of abuse. Remember, you can use your pain and regrets as fuel for recovery and empowerment.

# With Gratitude

In the years since publishing the first edition of *Lost in the Reflecting Pool*, many travelers have influenced my wanderings and the reality of this book. My deepest gratitude and love to all who have touched my life during these years; you are a part of this story, and I thank you.

Despite *Lost in the Reflecting Pool*'s focus on the difficult times in my life, it may surprise others when I say that my life has been fulfilling, and the positives have outweighed the negatives. I feel fortunate that in my life, there have been so many people I have loved and who have provided me with love, care, and the tools I've needed to weather whatever storms I have faced.

The British pediatrician and psychoanalyst Donald Winnicott coined the expression "The Good Enough Mother" in 1953. He did not discuss the "perfect mother" or "perfect parent." He saw that babies and children benefit when their parents "fail" them in manageable ways. (I'm not talking about major failures, such as child abuse and neglect, of course). With this in mind, I would like to thank my parents, for having been loving, caring, available, and human. They provided me not with perfection but the resources that allowed me to become a *resilient woman*.

For this, and for so much more, I am lovingly and eternally grateful. You are with me every day.

If it had not been for my extraordinary medical treatment, I would not be here to tell this story. Dr. Katherine Tkaczuk, Dr. Sherry Slezak, Dr. Lauren Schnaper, and all of the medical and ancillary personnel at the University of Maryland's Marlene and Stewart Greenebaum Cancer Center, words alone cannot express my gratitude to you. My thanks is not only for what you have given me personally, but for your daily dedication to providing compassionate, respectful, and genuinely caring treatment for all who come to you.

I feel lucky to find myself surrounded by others who possess such great talent. To Patti Fors and all of those at Muse Literary involved with the publication of this second edition, I thank you sincerely.

Every aspect of working with graphic designer Claudine Mansour to create a new cover for this book has been a wonderful and productive experience. I am so grateful for your powerful and insightful work and appreciate your generosity.

To Jane Ubell-Meyer, Rebecca Smith Galli, Elyse Garlick, Ruthellen Josselson, Holly Maddox, Emily Samuelson, Gail Wenger, Jane Aviv, and Sally Winston who read, edited, and commented on the revisions for this edition: your input made the final product possible, and you have my sincere gratitude.

And to my children—you have always been and continue to be, "the wind beneath my wings." I love you and I thank you!

# About the Author

For more than forty years, Dr. Diane Pomerantz has been a practicing psychologist, teacher, supervisor, and speaker in the Baltimore-Washington metropolitan area. Dr. Pomerantz has done research in the areas of child abuse and early child-parent attachment. Dr. Pomerantz has published professional articles on topics of childhood trauma and personality development. She has also been published in online literary magazines.

This is the second edition of her award-winning and best-selling memoir, *Lost in the Reflecting Pool*. In this edition, she dons her psychologist hat to provide readers with more direct information about identifying abusive characteristics within their own relationships and how these issues can best be addressed.

Dr. Pomerantz has two grown children and lives in Maryland with her Sheepadoodle puppy, Tink.

Printed in the USA
CPSIA information can be obtained
at www.ICGtesting.com
JSHW020246261124
74269JS00005B/21